Evolutionary Computation

Evolutionary Computation
A Unified Approach

Kenneth A. De Jong

A Bradford Book

The MIT Press
Cambridge, Massachusetts
London, England

MIT Press books may be purchased at special quantity discounts for business or sales promotional use. For information, please email special_sales@mitpress.mit.edu or write to Special Sales Department, The MIT Press, 55 Hayward Street, Cambridge, MA 02142.

This book printed and bound in the United States of America.

Library of Congress Cataloging-in-Publication Data

De Jong, Kenneth A.
Evolutionary computation : a unified approach / Kenneth A. De Jong.
    p. cm.
    "A Bradford book"
Includes bibliographical references and indexes.
ISBN 0-262-04194-4 (hc. : alk. paper)
1. Evolutionary programming (Computer science). 2. Evolutionary computation. I. Title. II. Series.
QA76.618 .D45 2006
005.1–dc22

                                                        00-048674

10 9 8 7 6 5 4 3 2 1

Contents

Chapter 1

Introduction

The field of evolutionary computation is itself an evolving community of people, ideas, and applications. Although one can trace its genealogical roots as far back as the 1930s, it was the emergence of relatively inexpensive digital computing technology in the 1960s that served as an important catalyst for the field. The availability of this technology made it possible to use computer simulation as a tool for analyzing systems much more complex than those analyzable mathematically.

Among the more prominent groups of scientists and engineers who saw this emerging capability as a means to better understand complex evolutionary systems were evolutionary biologists interested in developing and testing better models of natural evolutionary systems, and computer scientists and engineers wanting to harness the power of evolution to build useful new artifacts. More recently there has been considerable interest in evolutionary systems among a third group: artificial-life researchers wanting to design and experiment with new and interesting artificial evolutionary worlds.

Although these groups share a common interest in understanding evolutionary processes better, the particular choices of what to model, what to measure, and how to evaluate the systems built varies widely as a function of their ultimate goals. It is beyond the scope of this book to provide a comprehensive and cohesive view of all such activities. Rather, as the title suggests, the organization, selection, and focus of the material of this book is intended to provide a clear picture of the state of the art of evolutionary computation: the use of evolutionary systems as computational processes for solving complex problems.

Even this less ambitious task is still quite formidable for several reasons, not the least of which is the explosive growth in activity in the field of evolutionary computation during the past decade. Any attempt to summarize the field requires fairly difficult choices in selecting the areas to be covered, and is likely be out of date to some degree by the time it is published!

A second source of difficulty is that a comprehensive and integrated view of the field of evolutionary computation has not been attempted before. There are a variety of excellent books and survey papers describing particular subspecies of the field such as genetic algorithms, evolution strategies, and evolutionary programming. However, only in the past few years have people begun to think about such systems as specific instances of a more general class of evolutionary algorithms. In this sense the book will not be just a summary of existing activity but will require breaking new ground in order to present a more cohesive view of the field.

A final source of difficulty is that, although the goals of other closely related areas (such as evolutionary biology and artificial life are quite different, each community has benefitted significantly from a cross-fertilization of ideas. Hence, it is important to understand to some extent the continuing developments in these closely related fields. Time and space constraints prohibit any serious attempt to do so in this book. Rather, I have adopted the strategy of scattering throughout the book short discussions of related activities in these other fields with pointers into the literature that the interested reader can follow.

For that strategy to be effective, however, we need to spend some time up front considering which ideas about evolution these fields share in common as well as their points of divergence. These issues are the focus of the remainder of this chapter.

1.1   Basic Evolutionary Processes

A good place to start the discussion is to ask what are the basic components of an evolutionary system. The first thing to note is that there are at least two possible interpretations of the term *evolutionary system*. It is frequently used in a very general sense to describe a system that changes incrementally over time, such as the software requirements for a payroll accounting system. The second sense, and the one used throughout this book, is the narrower use of the term in biology, namely, to mean a Darwinian evolutionary system.

In order to proceed, then, we need to be more precise about what constitutes such a system. One way of answering this question is to identify a set of core components such that, if any one of these components were missing, we would be reluctant to describe it as a Darwinian evolutionary system. Although there is by no means a consensus on this issue, there is fairly general agreement that Darwinian evolutionary systems embody:

- one or more populations of individuals competing for limited resources,

- the notion of dynamically changing populations due to the birth and death of individuals,

- a concept of fitness which reflects the ability of an individual to survive and reproduce, and

- a concept of variational inheritance: offspring closely resemble their parents, but are not identical.

Such a characterization leads naturally to the view of an evolutionary system as a process that, given particular initial conditions, follows a trajectory over time through a complex evolutionary state space. One can then study various aspects of these processes such as their convergence properties, their sensitivity to initial conditions, their transient behavior, and so on.

Depending on one's goals and interests, various components of such a system may be fixed or themselves subject to evolutionary pressures. The simplest evolutionary models focus on the evolution over time of a single fixed-size population of individuals in a fixed environment with fixed mechanisms for reproduction and inheritance. One might be tempted to dismiss such systems as too simple to be of much interest. However, even these simple systems can produce a surprisingly wide range of evolutionary behavior as a result of complex nonlinear interactions between the initial conditions, the particular choices made for the mechanisms of reproduction and inheritance, and the properties of the environmentally induced notion of fitness.

1.2   EV: A Simple Evolutionary System

To make these notions more concrete, it is worth spending a little time describing a simple evolutionary system in enough detail that we can actually simulate it and observe its behavior over time. In order to do so we will be forced to make some rather explicit implementation decisions, the effects of which we will study in more detail in later chapters. For the most part these initial implementations decisions will not be motivated by the properties of a particular natural evolutionary system. Rather, they will be motivated by the rule "Keep it simple, stupid!" which turns out to be a surprisingly useful heuristic for building evolutionary systems that we have some hope of understanding!

The first issue to be faced is how to represent the individuals (organisms) that make up an evolving population. A fairly general technique is to describe an individual as a fixed length vector of L features that are chosen presumably because of their (potential) relevance to estimating an individual's fitness. So, for example, individuals might be characterized by:

< hair color, eye color, skin color, height, weight >

We could loosely think of this vector as specifying the genetic makeup of an individual, i.e., its genotype specified as a chromosome with five genes whose values result in an individual with a particular set of traits. Alternatively, we could consider such vectors as descriptions of the observable physical traits of individuals, i.e., their phenotype. In either case, by additionally specifying the range of values (alleles) such features might take on, one defines a five-dimensional space of all possible genotypes (or phenotypes) that individuals might have in this artificial world.

In addition to specifying the "geno/phenospace", we need to define the "laws of motion" for an evolutionary system. As our first attempt, consider the following pseudo-code:

```
EV:

    Generate an initial population of M individuals.

    Do Forever:

        Select a member of the current population to be a parent.
```

```
        Use the selected parent to produce an offspring that is
        similar to but generally not a precise copy of the parent.

        Select a member of the population to die.

        End Do
```

Although we still need to be more precise about some implementation details, notice
what enormous simplifications we already have made relative to biological evolutionary
systems. We have blurred the distinction between the genotype and the phenotype of
an individual. There is no concept of maturation to adulthood via an environmentally
conditioned development process. We have ignored the distinction between male and female
and have only asexual reproduction. What we have specified so far is just a simple procedural
description of the interacting roles of birth, death, reproduction, inheritance, variation, and
selection.

The fact that the population in EV never grows or shrinks in size may seem at first
glance to be rather artificial and too restrictive. We will revisit this issue later. For now, we
keep things simple and note that such a restriction could be plausibly justified as a simple
abstraction of the size limitations imposed on natural populations by competition for limited
environmental resources (such as the number of scientists funded by NSF!).

In any case, undaunted, we proceed with the remaining details necessary to implement
and run a simulation. More precisely, we elaborate EV as follows:

```
    EV:

        Randomly generate the initial population of M individuals
        (using a uniform probability distribution over the entire
        geno/phenospace) and compute the fitness of each individual.

        Do Forever:

          Choose a parent as follows:

            - select a parent randomly using a uniform probability
              distribution over the current population.

          Use the selected parent to produce a single offspring by:

            - making an identical copy of the parent, and then
              probabilistically mutating it to produce the offspring.

          Compute the fitness of the offspring.

          Select a member of the population to die by:
```

```
     - randomly selecting a candidate for deletion from the
       current population using a uniform probability
       distribution; and keeping either the candidate or the
       offspring depending on which one has higher fitness.

   End Do
```

There are several things to note about this elaboration of EV. The first is the decision to make the system stochastic by specifying that the choice of various actions is a function of particular probability distributions. This means that the behavior of EV can (and generally will) change from one simulation run to the next simply by changing the values used to initialize the underlying pseudo-random number generators. This can be both a blessing and a curse. It allows us to easily test the robustness and the range of behaviors of the system under a wide variety of conditions. However, it also means that we must take considerable care not to leap to conclusions about the behavior of the system based on one or two simulation runs.

The second thing to note is that we have used the term "fitness" here in a somewhat different way than the traditional biological notion of fitness which is an *ex post facto* measure based on an individual's ability to both survive and produce viable offspring. To be more precise, in EV we are assuming the existence of a mechanism for measuring the "quality" of an individual at birth, and that "quality" is used in EV to influence an individual's *ex post facto* fitness.

A standard approach to defining such measures of quality is to provide a function that defines a "fitness landscape" over the given geno/phenospace. This is sometimes referred to as *objective fitness* since this measurement is based solely on an individual's geno/phenotype and is not affected by other factors such as the current makeup of the population. This confusion in terminology is so deeply ingrained in the literature that it is difficult to avoid. Since the evolutionary computation community is primarily interested in how evolutionary systems generate improvements in the quality of individuals (and not interested so much in *ex post facto* fitness), the compromise that I have adopted for this book is to use the term *fitness* to refer by default to the assessment of quality. Whenever this form of fitness is based on an objective measure of quality, I generally emphasize this fact by using the term *objective fitness*. As we will see in later chapters, the terminology can become even more confusing in situations in which no such objective measure exists.

Finally, note that we still must be a bit more precise about how mutation is to be implemented. In particular, we assume for now that each gene of an individual is equally likely to be mutated, and that on the average only one gene is mutated when producing an offspring. That is, if there are L genes, each gene has an independent probability of $1/L$ of being selected to undergo a mutation.

If we assume for convenience that the values a feature can take on are real numbers, then a natural way to implement mutation is as a small perturbation of an inherited feature value. Although a normally distributed perturbation with a mean of zero and an appropriately scaled variance is fairly standard in practice, we will keep things simple for now by just using

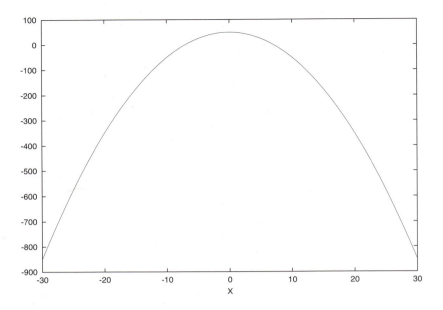

Figure 1.1: L1, a simple 1-D objective fitness landscape.

a fixed size delta to be added or subtracted with equal probability to the value inherited from a parent.

1.3   EV on a Simple Fitness Landscape

We will examine additional EV implementation issues in more detail later in this chapter and, for the interested reader, the source code for EV is described in appendix A.1. For our purposes here we will ignore these details and focus on the behavior of EV under a variety of different situations. We begin by considering a simple one-dimensional geno/phenospace L1 in which individuals consist of a single "trait" expressed as a real number, and their objective fitness is computed via a simple time-invariant function of that real-valued trait. More specifically, an individual is given by $< x >$ and the fitness of individual $< x >$ is defined by the objective fitness function $f(x) = 50 - x^2$, a simple inverted parabola as depicted graphically in figure 1.1.

Running EV on L1 with a mutation delta of 1.0 and a population of size 10, we observe the following initial output:

```
Simulation time limit (# births): 1000
Random number seed (positive integer): 12345
Using an inverted parabolic landscape defined on 1 parameter(s) with
   offset 50.0,  with parameter initialization bounds of:
      1: -100.0  100.0
```

```
and with hard parameter bounds of:
    1: -Infinity  Infinity
Using a genome with 1 real-valued gene(s).
Using delta mutation with step size 1.0
Population size: 10

Population data after 10 births (generation 1):
  Global fitness:  max = 43.02033, ave = -4599.12864, min = -8586.50977
  Local fitness:   max = 43.02033, ave = -4599.12793, min = -8586.50977
  Indiv  birthdate    fitness        gene values
    1       1        -713.93585      -27.63939
    2       2          43.02033        2.64191
    3       3       -7449.33398       86.59869
    4       4       -6909.38477       83.42293
    5       5       -4387.99414       66.61827
    6       6       -8499.85352      -92.46542
    7       7       -1154.42651      -34.70485
    8       8       -5584.96094      -75.06638
    9       9       -2747.90723      -52.89525
   10      10       -8586.50977      -92.93282
```

At this point in the simulation, an initial population of 10 individuals has been randomly generated from the interval [-100.0,100.0] and their objective fitnesses have been computed. Notice that exactly 1 new individual is produced at each simulated clock tick. Hence each individual has a unique "birth date".

Since EV maintains a constant size population M, we introduce the notion of a "generation" as equivalent to having produced M new individuals, and we print out various things of interest on generational boundaries. Thus, after 10 more births (clock ticks) we see:

```
Population data after 20 births (generation 2):
  Global fitness:  max = 43.02033, ave = -5350.27546, min = -8586.50977
  Local  fitness:  max = 43.02033, ave = -3689.70459, min = -8499.85352
  Indiv  birthdate    fitness        gene values
    1       1        -713.93585      -27.63939
    2       2          43.02033        2.64191
    3      18        -659.65704      -26.63939
    4       4       -6909.38477       83.42293
    5       5       -4387.99414       66.61827
    6       6       -8499.85352      -92.46542
    7       7       -1154.42651      -34.70485
    8       8       -5584.96094      -75.06638
    9      20        -713.93585      -27.63939
   10      15       -8315.92188      -91.46542
```

By looking at the birth dates of the individuals in generation 2 we can see that only 3 of the 10 new individuals produced (birth dates 11–20) were "fit enough" to survive along with 7 members of the previous generation. Global objective fitness statistics have been updated to reflect the characteristics of all individuals produced during an entire simulation run regardless of whether they survived or not. Local objective fitness statistics have been updated to reflect the individuals making up the current population.

Note that, because survival in EV involves having higher objective fitness than one's competitor, the average objective fitness of the population is monotonically nondecreasing over time. If we now let the simulation run for several more generations, we begin to see more clearly the effects of competitive survival:

```
Population data after 60 births (generation 6):
  Global fitness:   max = 49.58796, ave = -2510.92094, min = -8586.50977
  Local fitness:    max = 49.58796, ave =    41.44871, min =    28.45270
  Indiv  birthdate    fitness        gene values
     1       52        47.30414        1.64191
     2       37        49.58796        0.64191
     3       48        36.73652        3.64191
     4       53        36.73652        3.64191
     5       35        43.02033        2.64191
     6       59        47.30414        1.64191
     7       32        47.30414        1.64191
     8       46        49.58796        0.64191
     9       55        28.45270        4.64191
    10       56        28.45270        4.64191
```

Notice that the gene values of all 10 members of the population are now quite similar, but still some distance from a value of 0.0 which achieves a maximum objective fitness of 50.0 on this landscape. Continuing on, we see further movement of the population toward the region of highest fitness:

```
Population data after 120 births (generation 12):
  Global fitness:   max = 49.87177, ave = -1231.82122, min = -8586.50977
  Local fitness:    max = 49.87177, ave =    49.84339, min =    49.58796
  Indiv  birthdate    fitness        gene values
     1       62        49.87177       -0.35809
     2       89        49.87177       -0.35809
     3       91        49.58796        0.64191
     4       65        49.87177       -0.35809
     5      109        49.87177       -0.35809
     6       72        49.87177       -0.35809
     7       96        49.87177       -0.35809
     8      108        49.87177       -0.35809
     9       77        49.87177       -0.35809
    10      100        49.87177       -0.35809
```

By generation 25, the population has become completely homogeneous:

```
Population data after 250 births (generation 25):
  Global fitness:  max = 49.87177, ave = -565.91903, min = -8586.50977
  Local fitness:   max = 49.87177, ave =   49.87177, min =    49.87177
  Indiv  birthdate    fitness       gene values
    1       62        49.87177       -0.35809
    2       89        49.87177       -0.35809
    3      248        49.87177       -0.35809
    4       65        49.87177       -0.35809
    5      109        49.87177       -0.35809
    6       72        49.87177       -0.35809
    7       96        49.87177       -0.35809
    8      108        49.87177       -0.35809
    9       77        49.87177       -0.35809
   10      100        49.87177       -0.35809
```

And, if we let the system run indefinitely from here, we see that EV has, in fact, converged to a stable fixed point:

```
Population data after 1000 births (generation 100):
  Global fitness:  max = 49.87177, ave = -104.82450, min = -8586.50977
  Local fitness:   max = 49.87177, ave =   49.87177, min =    49.87177
  Indiv  birthdate    fitness       gene values
    1       62        49.87177       -0.35809
    2       89        49.87177       -0.35809
    3      248        49.87177       -0.35809
    4       65        49.87177       -0.35809
    5      109        49.87177       -0.35809
    6       72        49.87177       -0.35809
    7       96        49.87177       -0.35809
    8      108        49.87177       -0.35809
    9       77        49.87177       -0.35809
   10      100        49.87177       -0.35809
```

An immediate question that comes to mind is whether EV will converge this way in general. To see that this is the case for simple static fitness landscapes, recall that EV has no upper limit on the lifetime of an individual. Individuals only die when challenged by new individuals with higher objective fitness, and the only way to increase objective fitness is via the mutation operator which introduces small fixed-size perturbations of existing individuals. In the example above we see that from generation 25 on there has been no change in the population. This is because, at this point, every mutation results in a gene value farther away from 0.0 and thus lower in objective fitness.

This raises an important issue that we will revisit many times: the importance of distinguishing between:

- the conceptual geno/phenospace one has in mind to be explored,

- the actual geno/phenospace that is represented and searched by an evolutionary algorithm, and

- the subset of the represented space that is actually reachable via a particular evolutionary algorithm.

In the example above, the conceptual space is the infinite set of all real numbers, the actual space is the finite set of all real numbers representable using the computer's 32-bit floating point representation, and the set of reachable points are those which are can be produced by repeated applications of the mutation operator on members of the randomly generated initial population. In this particular case, each of the 10 members of the initial population can be mutated only by using a mutation delta of 1.0, implying that only a relatively small number of points are reachable during a particular simulation!

To illustrate these ideas, we run EV again changing only the initial random number seed, which results in a different initial population and a different stable fixed point:

```
Simulation time limit (# births): 1000
Random number seed (positive integer): 1234567
Using an inverted parabolic landscape defined on 1 parameter(s) with
   offset 50.0, with parameter initialization bounds of:
      1: -100.0   100.0
   and with hard parameter bounds of:
      1: -Infinity   Infinity
Using a genome with 1 real-valued gene(s).
Using delta mutation with step size 1.0
Population size: 10

Population data after 10 births (generation 1):
 Global fitness:   max = -59.71169, ave = -2588.03008, min = -8167.49316
 Local fitness:    max = -59.71169, ave = -2588.02979, min = -8167.49316
 Indiv .birthdate    fitness       gene values
      1        1     -2595.38550     -51.43331
      2        2      -669.55261      26.82448
      3        3     -2490.53003      50.40367
      4        4       -59.71169     -10.47433
      5        5      -118.75333     -12.99051
      6        6     -1659.58362     -41.34711
      7        7     -1162.48181      34.82071
      8        8     -7870.33447      88.99626
      9        9     -8167.49316      90.65039
     10       10     -1086.47461     -33.71164
```

```
Population data after 100 births (generation 10):
  Global fitness:  max = 43.87767, ave =  -659.01723, min = -8349.79395
  Local fitness:   max = 43.87767, ave =    34.34953, min =    20.03166
  Indiv  birthdate    fitness      gene values
    1       57        20.03166      -5.47433
    2       96        37.92900      -3.47433
    3       93        37.92900      -3.47433
    4       66        29.98033      -4.47433
    5       65        29.98033      -4.47433
    6       84        37.92900      -3.47433
    7       77        37.92900      -3.47433
    8       94        29.98033      -4.47433
    9       78        37.92900      -3.47433
   10      100        43.87767      -2.47433

Population data after 500 births (generation 50):
  Global fitness:  max = 49.77501, ave =   -93.92220, min = -8349.79395
  Local fitness:   max = 49.77501, ave =    49.77500, min =    49.77501
  Indiv  birthdate    fitness      gene values
    1      154        49.77501      -0.47433
    2      158        49.77501      -0.47433
    3      323        49.77501      -0.47433
    4      251        49.77501      -0.47433
    5      306        49.77501      -0.47433
    6      155        49.77501      -0.47433
    7      188        49.77501      -0.47433
    8      151        49.77501      -0.47433
    9      145        49.77501      -0.47433
   10      144        49.77501      -0.47433
```

Note that on this run convergence occurred slightly farther away from 0.0 than on the previous run. Looking at the initial population and recalling that mutation only can change gene values by adding or subtracting 1.0, it is easy to see that this convergence point is the result of a sequence of successful mutations of individual 4. It is also interesting to note that a sequence of successful mutations of individual 6 would have gotten even closer to the boundary. However, for that to happen during the run, each of the individual mutations in the sequence would have to occur and also to survive long enough for the next mutation in the sequence to also occur. Hence we see that there are, in general, reachable points that may have higher fitness than the one to which EV converges, because the probability of putting together the required sequence of mutations in this stochastic competitive environment is too low.

A reasonable question at this point is whether much of what we have seen so far is just an artifact of a mutation operator that is too simple. Certainly this is true to some extent.

Since the genes in EV are real numbers, a more interesting (and frequently used) mutation operator is one that changes a gene value by a small amount that is determined by sampling a Gaussian (normal) distribution $G(0, \sigma)$ with a mean of zero and a standard deviation of σ. In this case the average step size s (i.e., the absolute value of $G(0, \sigma)$) is given by $\sqrt{2/\pi} * \sigma$ (see the exercises at the end of this chapter), allowing for a simple implementation of the Gaussian mutation operator $GM(s) = G(0, s/\sqrt{2/\pi})$.

To see the effects of this, we rerun EV with a Gaussian mutation operator $GM(s)$ using a step size $s = 1.0$, and compare it to the earlier results obtained using a fixed mutation delta of 1.0:

```
Simulation time limit (# births): 1000
Random number seed (positive integer): 12345
Using an inverted parabolic landscape defined on 1 parameter(s) with
    offset 50.0, with parameter initialization bounds of:
        1: -100.0   100.0
    and with hard parameter bounds of:
        1: -Infinity  Infinity
Using a genome with 1 real-valued gene(s).
Using Gaussian mutation with step size 1.0
Population size: 10

Population data after 10 births (generation 1):
 Global fitness:  max = 43.02033, ave = -4599.12864, min = -8586.50977
 Local fitness:   max = 43.02033, ave = -4599.12793, min = -8586.50977
 Indiv  birthdate    fitness       gene values
    1       1       -713.93585      -27.63939
    2       2         43.02033        2.64191
    3       3      -7449.33398       86.59869
    4       4      -6909.38477       83.42293
    5       5      -4387.99414       66.61827
    6       6      -8499.85352      -92.46542
    7       7      -1154.42651      -34.70485
    8       8      -5584.96094      -75.06638
    9       9      -2747.90723      -52.89525
   10      10      -8586.50977      -92.93282

Population data after 100 births (generation 10):
 Global fitness:  max = 49.98715, ave = -1078.09662, min = -8586.50977
 Local fitness:   max = 49.98715, ave =    49.80241, min =    49.50393
 Indiv  birthdate    fitness       gene values
    1      89         49.84153       -0.39809
    2      70         49.85837        0.37634
    3      90         49.50393       -0.70433
    4      75         49.66306       -0.58047
    5      96         49.79710       -0.45044
```

6	74	49.89342	0.32647
7	22	49.85916	0.37529
8	48	49.98715	0.11336
9	83	49.98008	0.14113
10	76	49.64036	-0.59970

```
Population data after 500 births (generation 50):
  Global fitness:  max = 49.99962, ave =  -176.97845, min = -8586.50977
  Local fitness:   max = 49.99962, ave =    49.99478, min =    49.98476
```

Indiv	birthdate	fitness	gene values
1	202	49.99303	-0.08348
2	208	49.99561	0.06628
3	167	49.99860	0.03741
4	415	49.99311	-0.08297
5	455	49.98476	0.12345
6	275	49.98920	0.10392
7	398	49.99706	-0.05423
8	159	49.99914	-0.02935
9	131	49.99767	-0.04832
10	427	49.99962	-0.01945

Notice how much more diverse the population is at generation 10 than before, and how much closer the population members are to 0.0 in generation 50. Has EV converged to a fixed point as before? Not in this case, since there is always a small chance that mutations still can be generated that will produce individuals closer to 0.0. It is just a question of how long we are willing to wait! So, for example, allowing EV to run for an additional 500 births results in:

```
Population data after 1000 births (generation 100):
  Global fitness:  max = 49.99999, ave =  -64.39950, min = -8586.50977
  Local fitness:   max = 49.99999, ave =   49.99944, min =    49.99843
```

Indiv	birthdate	fitness	gene values
1	794	49.99901	0.03148
2	775	49.99989	-0.01055
3	788	49.99967	0.01822
4	766	49.99949	0.02270
5	955	49.99927	0.02703
6	660	49.99991	0.00952
7	762	49.99999	0.00275
8	159	49.99914	-0.02935
9	569	49.99843	0.03962
10	427	49.99962	-0.01945

Another obvious question concerns the effect of the mutation step size on EV. Would increasing the probability of taking larger steps speed up the rate of convergence to regions of

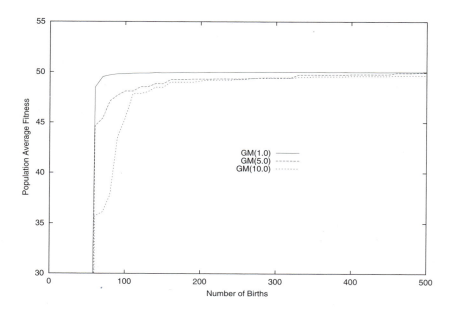

Figure 1.2: Average population fitness in EV using different Gaussian mutation step sizes.

high fitness? One way to answer this question is to focus our attention on more macroscopic properties of evolutionary systems, such as how the average fitness of the population changes over time. EV provides that information for us by printing the "average local fitness" of the population at regular intervals during an evolutionary run. Figure 1.2 plots this information for three runs of EV: one with mutation set to $GM(1.0)$, one with $GM(5.0)$, and one with $GM(10.0)$.

What we observe is somewhat surprising at first: increasing the mutation step size actually slowed the rate of convergence slightly! This is our first hint that even simple evolutionary systems like EV can exhibit surprisingly complex behavior because of the nonlinear interactions between their subcomponents. In EV the average fitness of the population can increase only when existing population members are replaced by new offspring with higher fitness. Hence, one particular event of interest is when a mutation operator produces an offspring whose fitness is greater than its parent.

If we define such an event in EV as a "successful mutation", it should be clear that, for landscapes like L1, the "success rate" of mutation operators with larger step sizes decreases more rapidly than those with smaller step sizes as EV begins to converge to the optimum, resulting in the slower *rates* of convergence that we observe in figure 1.2.

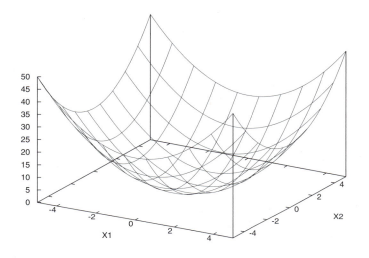

Figure 1.3: L2, a 2-D objective fitness landscape with multiple peaks.

1.4   EV on a More Complex Fitness Landscape

So far we have been studying the behavior of EV on the simple one-dimensional, single-peak fitness landscape L1. In this section, the complexity of the landscape is increased a small amount in order to illustrate more interesting and (possibly) unexpected EV behavior.

Consider a two-dimensional geno/phenospace in which individuals are represented by a feature vector $< x1, x2 >$ in which each feature is a real number in the interval $[-5.0, 5.0]$, and $f2(x1, x2) = x1^2 + x2^2$ is the objective fitness function. That is, this fitness landscape L2 takes the form of a two-dimensional parabola with four peaks of equal height at the four corners of the geno/phenospace as shown in figure 1.3.

What predictions might one make regarding the behavior of EV on this landscape? Here are some possibilities:

1. EV will converge to a homogeneous fixed point as before. However, there are now four peaks of attraction. Which one it converges near will depend on the randomly generated initial conditions.

2. EV will converge to a stable fixed point in which the population is made up of sub-populations (species), each clustered around one of the peaks.

3. EV will not converge as before, but will oscillate indefinitely among the peaks.

4. The symmetry of the fitness landscape induces equal but opposing pressures to increment and decrement both feature values. This results in a dynamic equilibrium in

which the average fitness of the population changes very little from its initial value.

As we will see repeatedly throughout this book, there are enough subtle interactions among the components of even simple evolutionary systems that one's intuition is frequently wrong. In addition, these nonlinear interactions make it quite difficult to analyze evolutionary systems formally and develop strong predictive models. Consequently, much of our understanding is derived from experimentally observing the (stochastic) behavior of an evolutionary system. In the case of EV on this 2-D landscape L2, we observe:

```
EV:
    Simulation time limit (# births): 1000
    Random number seed (positive integer): 12345
    Using a parabolic landscape defined on 2 parameter(s)
    with parameter initialization bounds of:
        1: -5.0   5.0
        2: -5.0   5.0
    and with hard parameter bounds of:
        1: -5.0   5.0
        2: -5.0   5.0
    Using a genome with 2 real-valued gene(s).
    Using gaussian mutation with step size 0.1
    Population size: 10
```

```
Population data after 100 births (generation 10):
  Global fitness:  max = 45.09322, ave = 34.38162, min =  1.49947
  Local fitness:   max = 45.09322, ave = 42.91819, min = 38.90914
  Indiv  birthdate   fitness      gene values
     1     100       44.09085     4.77827      4.61074
     2      98       43.89545     4.70851      4.66105
     3      99       45.09322     4.73010      4.76648
     4      61       40.24258     4.36996      4.59848
     5      82       43.03299     4.66963      4.60734
     6      73       43.03299     4.66963      4.60734
     7      89       43.65926     4.66963      4.67481
     8      93       42.74424     4.58463      4.66105
     9      38       38.90914     4.29451      4.52397
    10      95       44.48112     4.82220      4.60734
```

```
Population data after 500 births (generation 50):
  Global fitness:  max = 49.93839, ave = 32.42865, min =  1.49947
  Local fitness:   max = 49.93839, ave = 49.92647, min = 49.91454
  Indiv  birthdate   fitness      gene values
     1     457       49.91454     4.99898      4.99246
     2     349       49.91454     4.99898      4.99246
     3     373       49.93839     4.99898      4.99485
     4     201       49.91454     4.99898      4.99246
```

5	472	49.93839	4.99898	4.99485
6	322	49.91454	4.99898	4.99246
7	398	49.93839	4.99898	4.99485
8	478	49.93839	4.99898	4.99485
9	356	49.91454	4.99898	4.99246
10	460	49.93839	4.99898	4.99485

```
Population data after 1000 births (generation 100):
 Global fitness:  max = 49.96095, ave = 30.10984, min =  1.49947
 Local fitness:   max = 49.96095, ave = 49.96095, min = 49.96095
 Indiv  birthdate  fitness     gene values
    1     806     49.96095     4.99898     4.99711
    2     737     49.96095     4.99898     4.99711
    3     584     49.96095     4.99898     4.99711
    4     558     49.96095     4.99898     4.99711
    5     601     49.96095     4.99898     4.99711
    6     642     49.96095     4.99898     4.99711
    7     591     49.96095     4.99898     4.99711
    8     649     49.96095     4.99898     4.99711
    9     632     49.96095     4.99898     4.99711
   10     566     49.96095     4.99898     4.99711
```

On this particular run we see the same behavior pattern as we observed on the simpler 1-D landscape L1: fairly rapid movement of the entire population into a region of high objective fitness. In this particular simulation run, the population ends up near the peak at $< 5.0, 5.0 >$. If we make additional runs using different random number seeds, we see similar convergence behavior to any one of the four peaks with equal likelihood:

```
EV:
   Simulation time limit (# births): 1000
   Random number seed (positive integer): 1234567
   Using a parabolic landscape defined on 2 parameter(s)
    with parameter initialization bounds of:
      1: -5.0   5.0
      2: -5.0   5.0
    and with hard parameter bounds of:
      1: -5.0   5.0
      2: -5.0   5.0
   Using a genome with 2 real-valued gene(s).
   Using gaussian mutation with step size 0.1
   Population size: 10

Population data after 500 births (generation 50):
 Global fitness:  max = 49.80204, ave = 33.45935, min =  4.69584
 Local fitness:   max = 49.80204, ave = 49.50858, min = 48.44830
```

Indiv	birthdate	fitness	gene values	
1	494	49.76775	-4.99155	-4.98520
2	486	49.30639	-4.99155	-4.93871
3	446	49.35423	-4.99155	-4.94355
4	437	49.55191	-4.99155	-4.96350
5	491	49.55191	-4.99155	-4.96350
6	469	49.76775	-4.99155	-4.98520
7	445	49.76775	-4.99155	-4.98520
8	410	48.44830	-4.99155	-4.85105
9	497	49.76775	-4.99155	-4.98520
10	471	49.80204	-4.99155	-4.98863

```
Population data after 1000 births (generation 100):
  Global fitness:  max = 49.91475, ave = 31.25352, min =  4.69584
  Local fitness:   max = 49.91475, ave = 49.91109, min = 49.90952
```

Indiv	birthdate	fitness	gene values	
1	663	49.90952	-4.99155	-4.99940
2	617	49.90952	-4.99155	-4.99940
3	719	49.90952	-4.99155	-4.99940
4	648	49.90952	-4.99155	-4.99940
5	810	49.90952	-4.99155	-4.99940
6	940	49.91475	-4.99155	-4.99992
7	903	49.90952	-4.99155	-4.99940
8	895	49.91475	-4.99155	-4.99992
9	970	49.91475	-4.99155	-4.99992
10	806	49.90952	-4.99155	-4.99940

So, these simulations strongly support scenario 1 above. What about the other scenarios? Is it possible for stable subpopulations to emerge? In EV a new individual replaces an existing one *only* if it has higher fitness. Hence, the emergence of stable subpopulations will happen only if they both involve identical 32-bit fitness values. Even small differences in fitness will guarantee that the group with higher fitness will take over the entire population. As a consequence, scenario 2 is possible but highly unlikely in EV.

Scenario 3, oscillation between peaks, can happen in the beginning to a limited extent as one peak temporarily attracts more members, and then loses them to more competitive members of the other peak. However, as the subpopulations get closer to these peaks, scenario 1 takes over.

Finally, scenario 4 (dynamic mediocrity) never occurs in EV, since mutations which take members away from a peak make them less fit and not likely to survive into the next generation. So, we see strong pressure to move away from the center of L2 and toward the boundaries, resulting in significant improvement in average fitness.

It should be clear by now how one can continue to explore the behavior of EV by presenting it with even more complex, multi-dimensional, multi-peaked landscapes. Alternatively, one can study the effects on behavior caused by changing various properties of EV, such as the population size, the form and rates of mutation, alternative forms of selection and reproduction, and so on. Some of these variations can be explored easily with EV as suggested in the exercises at the end of the chapter. Others require additional design and implementation decisions, and will be explored in subsequent chapters.

1.5 Evolutionary Systems as Problem Solvers

EV is not a particularly plausible evolutionary system from a biological point of view, and there are many ways to change EV that would make it a more realistic model of natural evolutionary systems. Similarly, from an artificial-life viewpoint, the emergent behavior of EV would be much more complex and interesting if the creatures were something other than vectors of real numbers, and if the landscapes were dynamic rather than static. However, the focus of this book is on exploring evolution as a computational tool. So, the question of interest here is: what computation (if any) is EV performing?

From an engineering perspective, systems are designed with goals in mind, functions to perform, and objectives to be met. Computer scientists design and implement algorithms for sorting, searching, optimizing, and so on. However, asking what the goals and purpose of evolution are immediately raises long-debated issues of philosophy and religion which, though interesting, are also beyond the scope of this book. What is clear, however, is that even a system as simple as EV appears to have considerable potential for use as the basis for designing interesting new algorithms that can search complex spaces, solve hard optimization problems, and are capable of adapting to changing environments.

To illustrate this briefly, consider the following simple change to EV:

```
EV-OPT:

    Generate an initial population of M individuals.

    Do until a stopping criterion is met:

        Select a member of the current population to be a parent.

        Use the selected parent to produce an offspring which is
        similar to but generally not a precise copy of the parent.

        Select a member of the population to die.

        End Do

    Return the individual with the highest global objective fitness.
```

By adding a stopping criterion and returning an "answer", the old EV code sheds its image as a simulation and takes on a new sense of purpose, namely one of searching for highly fit (possibly optimal) individuals. We now can think of EV-OPT in the same terms

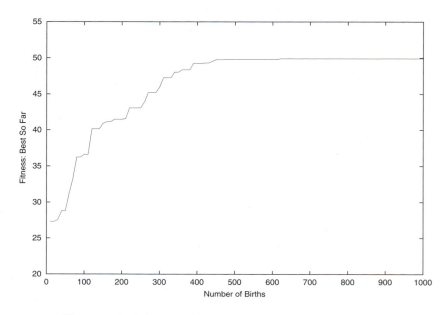

Figure 1.4: A best-so-far curve for EV on landscape L2.

as other algorithms we design. Will it always find an optimum? What kind of convergence properties does it have? Can we improve the rate of convergence?

One standard way of viewing the problem-solving behavior of an evolutionary algorithm is to plot the objective fitness of the best individual encountered as a function of evolutionary time (i.e., the number of births or generations). Figure 1.4 illustrates this for one run of EV on landscape L2. In this particular case, we observe that EV "found" an optimum after sampling about 500 points in the search space.

However, as we make "improvements" to our evolutionary problem solvers, we may make them even less plausible as models of natural evolutionary systems, and less interesting from an artificial-life point of view. Hence, this problem-solving viewpoint is precisely the issue which separates the field of evolutionary computation from its sister disciplines of evolutionary biology and artificial life.

However, focusing on evolutionary computation does not mean that the developments in these related fields are sufficiently irrelevant to be ignored. As we will see repeatedly throughout this book, natural evolutionary systems are a continuing source of inspiration for new ideas for better evolutionary algorithms, and the increasingly sophisticated behavior of artificial-life systems suggests new opportunities for evolutionary problem solvers.

1.6 Exercises

1. Explore the behavior of EV on some other interesting one-dimensional landscapes such as x^3, $sin(x)$, and $x * sin(x)$ that involve multiple peaks.

2. Explore the behavior of EV on multi-dimensional landscapes such as $x1^2 + x2^3$, $x1 * sin(x2)$, $(x1 - 2)(x2 + 5)$ that have interesting asymmetries and interactions among the variables.

3. Explore the behavior of EV when there is some noise in the fitness function such as $f(x) = x^2 + gauss(0, 0.01x^2)$.

4. The average value of the Gaussian (normal) distribution $G(0, \sigma)$ is, of course, zero. Show that the average *absolute* value of $G(0, \sigma)$ is $\sqrt{2/\pi} * \sigma$.

Hint: $Ave(|(G(0, \sigma)|) = \int_{-\infty}^{\infty} prob(x) \, |x| \, dx = 2 \int_0^{\infty} prob(x) \, x \, dx$

where $prob(x) = \frac{1}{\sigma\sqrt{2\pi}} \, e^{-\frac{x^2}{2\sigma^2}}$

Chapter 2

A Historical Perspective

Ideas regarding the design of computational systems that are based on the notion of simulated evolution are not new. The purpose of this chapter is to provide a brief historical perspective. Readers interested in more details are encouraged to consult David Fogel's excellent survey of the field's early work (Fogel, 1998).

2.1 Early Algorithmic Views

Perhaps the place to start is the 1930s, with the influential ideas of Sewell Wright (Wright, 1932). He found it useful to visualize an evolutionary system as exploring a multi-peaked fitness landscape and dynamically forming clusters (demes) around peaks (niches) of high fitness. This perspective leads quite naturally to the notion of an evolutionary system as an optimization process, a somewhat controversial view that still draws both support and criticism. In any case, viewing evolution as optimization brought it in contact with many of the early efforts to develop computer algorithms to automate tedious manual optimization processes (see, for example, Box (1957)). The result is that, even today, optimization problems are the most dominate application area of evolutionary computation.

An alternate perspective is to view an evolutionary system as a complex, adaptive system that changes its makeup and its responses over time as it interacts with a dynamically changing landscape. This viewpoint leads quite naturally to the notion of evolution as a feedback-control mechanism responsible for maintaining some sort of system stasis in the face of change. Viewing evolution as an adaptive controller brought it in contact with many of the early efforts to develop computer algorithms to automate feedback-control processes. One of the earliest examples of this can be seen in Friedman (1956), in which basic evolutionary mechanisms are proposed as means of evolving control circuits for robots.

The tediousness of writing computer programs has inspired many attempts to automate this process, not the least of which were based on evolutionary processes. An early example of this can be seen in Friedberg (1959), which describes the design and implementation of a "Learning Machine" that evolved sets of machine language instructions over time. This theme has continued to capture people's imagination and interest, and has resulted in a number of aptly named subareas of evolutionary computation such as "evolutionary programming" and "genetic programming".

2.2   The Catalytic 1960s

Although the basic idea of viewing evolution as a computational process had been conceived in various forms during the first half of the twentieth century, these ideas really took root and began to grow in the 1960s. The catalyst for this was the increasing availability of inexpensive digital computers for use as a modeling and simulation tool by the scientific community. Several groups became captivated by the idea that even simple evolutionary models could be expressed in computational forms that could be used for complex computer-based problem solving. Of these, there were three groups in particular whose activities during the 1960s served to define and shape this emerging field.

At the Technical University in Berlin, Rechenberg and Schwefel began formulating ideas about how evolutionary processes could be used to solve difficult real-valued parameter optimization problems (Rechenberg, 1965). From these early ideas emerged a family of algorithms called "evolution strategies" which today represent some of the most powerful evolutionary algorithms for function optimization.

At UCLA, during the same time period, Fogel saw the potential of achieving the goals of artificial intelligence via evolutionary techniques (Fogel et al., 1966). These ideas were explored initially in a context in which intelligent agents were represented as finite state machines, and an evolutionary framework called "evolutionary programming" was developed which was quite effective in evolving better finite state machines (agents) over time. This framework continues to be refined and expanded today and has been applied to a wide variety of problems well beyond the evolution of finite state machines.

At the University of Michigan, Holland saw evolutionary processes as a key element in the design and implementation of robust adaptive systems that were capable of dealing with an uncertain and changing environment (Holland, 1962, 1967). His view emphasized the need for systems which self-adapt over time as a function of feedback obtained from interacting with the environment in which they operate. This led to an initial family of "reproductive plans" which formed the basis for what we call "simple genetic algorithms" today.

In each case, these evolutionary algorithms represented highly ideal models of evolutionary processes embedded in the larger context of a problem-solving paradigm. The spirit was one of drawing inspiration from nature, rather than faithful (or even plausible) modeling of biological processes. The key issue was identifying and capturing computationally useful aspects of evolutionary processes. As a consequence, even today most evolutionary algorithms utilize what appear to be rather simplistic assumptions such as fixed-size populations of unisex individuals, random mating, offspring which are instantaneously adult, static fitness landscapes, and so on.

However, a formal analysis of the behavior of even these simple EAs was surprisingly difficult. In many cases, in order to make such analyses mathematically tractable, additional simplifying assumptions were necessary, such as assuming an infinite population model and studying its behavior on simple classes of fitness landscapes. Unfortunately, the behavior of realizable algorithms involving finite populations observed for finite periods of time on complex fitness landscapes could (and did) deviate considerably from theoretical predictions. As a consequence, the field moved into the 1970s with a tantalizing, but fuzzy, picture of the potential of these algorithms as problem solvers.

2.3 The Explorative 1970s

The initial specification and analysis of these simple evolutionary algorithms (EAs) in the 1960s left two major issues unresolved: 1) characterizing the behavior of implementable systems, and 2) understanding better how they might be used to solve problems. To implement these simple EAs, very specific design decisions needed to be made concerning population management issues and the mechanisms for selecting parents and producing offspring. It was clear very early that such choices could significantly alter observed EA behavior and its performance as a problem solver. As a consequence, much of the EA research in the 1970s was an attempt to gain additional insight into these issues via empirical studies and extensions to existing theory. Most of this activity occurred within the three groups mentioned earlier and resulted in the emergence of three distinct species of EAs: evolutionary programming, evolution strategies, and genetic algorithms.

2.3.1 Evolutionary Programming

The evolutionary programming (EP) paradigm concentrated on models involving a fixed-size population of N parents, each of which produced a single offspring. The next generation of N parents was determined by combining both parents and children into a single population of size 2N, rank ordering them by fitness and allowing only the top N to survive. Initial work (Fogel et al., 1966) had proposed both asexual reproduction (single parent with a mutation operator) and sexual reproduction (two parents combining to form offspring via a recombination operator). Since the individuals being evolved were finite state machines (FSMs), mutation took the form of adding/deleting states/arcs, and recombination required combining pieces of two FSMs into a new FSM.

Empirical studies focused on a variety of issues, including appropriate initialization strategies (initial population of FSMs), appropriate frequencies for the various forms of mutation (arcs, states), and an appropriate recombination operator. Extensive simulation studies noted the difficulty of defining an effective recombination operator in this context, but reported impressive results in evolving useful FSMs with only asexual reproduction and mutation. The size of the population and the intensity of mutation varied from application to application.

2.3.2 Evolution Strategies

The focus of the evolution strategy (ES) paradigm was on real-valued function optimization. Hence, individuals were naturally represented as vectors of real numbers. Initial work involved $(1 + \lambda)$-ES models in which 1 parent produced λ offspring and the fittest of the $1 + \lambda$ individuals was selected to be the *single* parent for the next generation of offspring. In this context asexual reproduction took the form of mutating one or more of the parent's gene values (real numbers) via a normally distributed perturbation $G(0, \sigma)$ with zero mean and a standard deviation of σ.

Empirical studies indicated that the performance of these ESs on particular functions to be optimized was highly sensitive to the choice of $G(0, \sigma)$. This resulted in a very early commitment to the design of an adaptive mutation operator. The form this took extended the representation of individuals from a vector of size N (N parameter values) to a vector of size 2N, in which the additional N genes represented the variance σ_i to be used to mutate parameter i using a normally distributed perturbation $G(0, \sigma_i)$. As a consequence, rather than being predetermined, mutation operators coevolved over time in response to the characteristics of the function being optimized.

What remained was to specify which (meta-) operators would be used to mutate the σ_i. This resulted in the now-famous 1:5 rule which is derived from a more formal analysis of optimal rates of convergence. Informally, this rule states that if more than one of five mutations using $G(0, \sigma_i)$ is successful (in the sense that an offspring has higher fitness than its parent), then mutation is in danger of being too exploitative (too small steps), and σ_i needs to be increased. If the rate of success falls below 20%, mutation is viewed as too explorative (too large steps) and σ_i is decreased.

With this adaptive mutation operator in place and an appropriately chosen λ, impressive results were reported for a wide range of difficult functions when using comparative results from more traditional optimization techniques (see for example, Schwefel (1975)).

2.3.3   Genetic Algorithms

In contrast to the early EP and ES work, the early genetic algorithm (GA) focus was on developing more application-independent algorithms. The approach taken used a genetic-like "universal" string representation for individuals along with string-oriented reproductive operators for producing offspring. The easiest string representations to analyze and visualize were fixed-length binary strings. In this context, mutation took the form of a "bit flip" with a fixed probability, and recombination took the form of a 1-point crossover operator, in which a randomly selected initial sequence of genes from one parent is combined with the remaining sequence of genes from a second parent to produce offspring with features of both parents.

Most of the early studies involved "generational" GAs, in which a fixed-size population of N parents produce a new population of N offspring, which unconditionally replaces the parent population regardless of fitness. However, parents are stochastically selected to produce offspring in proportion to their fitness. Thus, the fitter parents contribute significantly more "genetic material" to the next generation.

In order to apply these GAs to a particular problem, the individuals to be evolved over time needed to be represented as fixed-length binary strings. This was an advantage in the sense that few, if any, changes to the GA were required when attacking a new problem domain. However, it quickly became clear that the effectiveness of a GA depended on the choice of the phenotype-to-genotype mapping (and its inverse).

GAs were studied intensively from both an analytical and empirical point of view. The fixed-length string representation led naturally to a series of "schema theorems" (Holland, 1975) concerning the behavior of simple GAs. Much of the early empirical GA studies involved problems in which the fitness landscape was defined by carefully chosen time-invariant memoryless functions whose surfaces were well understood and involved simple binary string representations (see, for example, De Jong (1975)). Out of these early studies emerged a picture of a GA as a robust adaptive search procedure, which was surprisingly effective as a global search heuristic in spite of its universal properties.

2.4 The Exploitative 1980s

What emerged out of the 1970s was a collection of canonical evolutionary algorithms which had evolved to the point of exhibiting rather impressive performance when applied to a focused set of problems. The next obvious step was to use this core set of algorithms as the basis for scaling up to more complex problems and for developing new EA-based problem solvers for other problem domains. The activities during the 1980s resulted in significant developments on both fronts. A brief summary follows.

2.4.1 Optimization Applications

Perhaps the most natural application of EAs is as an optimizer, and so considerable effort was put into applying EAs to various kinds of optimization problems. The simplest of these are parameter optimization problems in which a fixed set of parameters with fixed sets of permissible parameter values define an N-dimensional space over which a performance function is defined. As existing EAs were applied to a broader range of such problems, the results varied from excellent to poor.

In the case of Evolution Strategies (ESs), there were a number of difficulties in scaling up to high-dimensional problems, handling interactions among parameters, and dealing with highly multimodal surfaces. This led to several important extensions to the $(1 + \lambda)$-ES model. The first was a generalization to a multi-parent $(\mu + \lambda)$ model in which the top μ of the $\mu + \lambda$ individuals were selected as the parent population for the next generation. A second variation involved the use of a "generational" model (μ, λ) in which the top μ individuals from the current set of λ offspring are selected as the parent population for the next generation (and no parents survive). In order to handle parameter interactions more effectively, estimates of the N^2 pairwise correlations could be encoded as well and used to guide pairwise mutations of parameter values.

Similarly, as Genetic Algorithms (GAs) were applied to a broader range of parameter optimization problems, a number of difficulties arose. It was observed that GAs frequently did not exhibit a "killer instinct" in the sense that, although they rapidly locate the region in which a global optimum exists, they did not converge to the optimum with similar speed. This turned out to be a property of the fitness-proportional selection mechanism used in simple GAs. A number of solutions emerged, including dynamically scaling the fitness function in order to maintain sufficient selective pressure, or switching to an alternative selection mechanism such as rank or tournament selection (Goldberg, 1989; Whitley, 1989a).

It was also observed that GAs could be "deceived" into converging to non-optimal points in the search space. This led to theoretical analyses of deceptiveness and also practical insights into how such situations might be detected and/or overcome (Goldberg, 1989).

Additional GA performance improvements were frequently obtained by singling out the best and/or worst individuals in the current population for special treatment (elitist policies) (De Jong, 1975; Whitley, 1989a). The effect is to shift the balance toward more exploitation and less exploration which, for some classes of functions, works quite well. However, if no *a priori* information about the functions to be optimized is available, this can result in suboptimal hill-climbing behavior on multi-peaked functions.

The internal representation used by a GA can also have an effect of optimization performance, in that points which are close in parameter space may not be close when mapped onto the standard internal binary representation. Such observations led to experiments with alternative binary representations, such as Gray codes, in an attempt to avoid these problems. Other researchers abandoned the internal string representation entirely and switched to real-valued vector representations.

Additional performance improvements were obtained by building specialized EAs which took advantage of *a priori* knowledge about a particular problem class. This usually took the form of specialized representations and specialized operators for important subclasses such as continuous real-valued functions, combinatorial optimization problems (e.g., traveling salesperson problems), and constrained optimization problems (job shop scheduling problems, etc.).

2.4.2 Other EA Applications

Although function optimization was a dominant GA application area, there was also considerable effort spent in applying GAs to other difficult problem areas. Classifier systems (Holland, 1986; Booker, 1982) were developed as simple models of cognition with GAs as the key component for adaptation and learning. Attempts were made to evolve more complex objects such as neural networks (Harp et al., 1989; de Garis, 1990), collections of rules for executing tasks (Smith, 1983; Grefenstette, 1989), and Lisp code (Koza, 1989). In each case, there were difficult and challenging issues raised regarding how best to harness the power of these simple GAs for the intended purpose.

One clearly emerging theme was the difficulty of representing complex, nonlinear objects of varying size using the traditional fixed-length string representation. A second theme which emerged was the need to understand better how GAs behave in environments with changing and/or noisy feedback. The increased availability of parallel machines gave rise to a third important theme: how to exploit the inherent parallelism of GAs.

2.4.3 Summary

By the end of the 1980s several important trends were in evidence. First, the focus on effective problem-solving performance resulted in new and more powerful EAs, but this was accomplished in most cases at the expense of decreasing their plausibility as models of biological evolutionary systems. These extensions to the canonical EAs resulted in a new, more complex class of algorithms that were well beyond the initial theoretical analyses, creating a need to revisit and extend the theoretical models.

In addition, the level of activity of the field had increased to the point that it required its own conferences, starting with the GA community (ICGA-85, ICGA-87 and ICGA-89), and with plans underway in the ES community for PPSN-90, plans in the EP community for EP-90, and the theoretical community planning FOGA-90.

2.5 The Unifying 1990s

Up to this point in time, much of the research and development of the primary EA paradigms (EP, ES, and GA) was done independently without much interaction among the various groups. The emergence of various EA conferences in the late 1980s and early 1990s, however, changed all that as representatives from various EA groups met, presented their particular viewpoints, challenged other approaches, and were challenged in return.

The result of these first interactions was a better understanding of the similarities and differences of the various paradigms, a broadening of the perspectives of the various viewpoints, and a feeling that, in order to continue to develop, the field as a whole needed to adopt a unified view of these evolutionary problem solvers. The immediate effect was an agreement on the term "evolutionary computation" (EC) as the name of the field and a commitment to start the field's first journal, *Evolutionary Computation*.

A second effect of these interactions was a noticeable crossbreeding of ideas. The ES community found that sexual reproduction with various forms of recombination improved the performance of their function optimizers (Bäck and Schwefel, 1993). The GA community found that problem-specific representations and operators frequently improved the performance of GA-based problem solvers (Michalewicz, 1994). The EP community extended their domain of application to other areas such as function optimization, incorporating ES-like representations and operators. What emerged from all this was a dizzying array of new EAs such as Genitor, Genetic Programming (GP), messy GAs, Samuel, CHC, Genocoop, etc., none of which fit nicely into the canonical EA paradigms and whose capabilities challenged old tenets. It became increasingly clear that a broader and more fundamental view of the field was required (De Jong and Spears, 1993).

A third effect of these interactions was a general sense of the need to revisit many of the fundamental assumptions and underlying theory in order to strengthen and generalize the basic EA paradigms. The FOGA workshops, started in 1990, have resulted in a rebirth of activity in EA theory with new characterizations and analyses in terms of formae (Radcliffe, 1991), Markov models (Vose, 1992), PAC analysis (Ros, 1992), breeder theory (Mühlenbein and Schlierkamp-Voosen, 1993), order statistics (Bäck, 1994), and so on.

2.6 The Twenty-first Century: Mature Expansion

Although really only forty years old, by the end of the 1990s the field of evolutionary computation had the look and feel of a mature scientific discipline. The community now supported three archival journals:

- *Evolutionary Computation*

- *IEEE Transactions on Evolutionary Computation*

- *Genetic Programming and Evolvable Machines*

The amount of interest in evolutionary computation research and applications was reflected by a wide range of peer-reviewed conferences including:

- GECCO: Genetic and Evolutionary Computation Conference

- CEC: Congress on Evolutionary Computation

- PPSN: Parallel Problem Solving from Nature

- FOGA: Foundations of Genetic Algorithms

In addition, the field was producing a steadily increasing number of excellent books including:

- Goldberg (1989), Davis (1991), Holland (1992), Koza (1992)

- Michalewicz (1994), Kinnear (1994), Koza (1994), Rechenberg (1994)

- Fogel (1995), Schwefel (1995), Bäck (1996)

- Banzhaf et al. (1998), Fogel (1998), Mitchell (1998)

- Bentley (1999), Koza et al. (1999), Vose (1999)

- Spears (2000), Bentley and Corne (2001), Deb (2001)

- Langdon and Poli (2001),Goldberg (2002), Coello et al. (2002)

At the same time there was no sense of complacency among the members of the evolutionary computation community. Although they had a reasonably good understanding of simple evolutionary algorithms and their applications, they were continually being confronted with new and more complex problem areas that tested the limits of their current systems. This has led various groups to focus on a number of fundamental extensions to existing EA models that appear to be necessary in order to improve and extend their problem solving capabilities. Among the issues being explored are:

- pros and cons of phenotype/genotype representations

- the inclusion of Lamarckian properties

- nonrandom mating and speciation

- decentralized, highly parallel models

- self-adapting systems

- coevolutionary systems

- agent-oriented models

2.7 Summary

Though a relatively new field, evolutionary computation's roots are quite rich and varied, and can be seen as far back as the 1930s. This historical perspective provides the context that has shaped the field as we know it today, and provides the basis for the unified view presented in the following chapters.

Chapter 3

Canonical Evolutionary Algorithms

3.1 Introduction

A very simple evolutionary algorithm, EV, was introduced in chapter 1 to illustrate the basic ideas and issues involved in evolutionary computation. In this chapter we revisit EV, discuss its features in more detail, generalize it, and then use it to develop simple versions of the three historically important evolutionary algorithms: evolutionary programming, evolution strategies, and genetic algorithms. This leads naturally to a unified view of evolutionary computation that is discussed in detail in chapter 4.

3.2 EV(m,n)

Recall from chapter 1 that EV maintained a fixed-size population of individuals, each of which was a fixed-length vector (chromosome) of real-valued parameters (genes), and whose objective fitness was determined by calling a "landscape" evaluation function. After randomly generating and evaluating the fitnesses of the members of the initial population, EV simulates population evolution by repeatedly selecting a member of the current population at random (uniformly) as a parent to produce a clone offspring. EV then introduces some variation in the offspring via a simple mutation operator which, on average, picks one gene genome in the genome to modify by randomly adding/subtracting a small value to the current value of the selected gene. The new offspring is forced to compete immediately for survival against an existing member of the population selected at random (uniformly). If the objective fitness of the child is greater than the selected member, the child survives and the old member dies off. Otherwise, the child dies without ever residing in the population.

This form of population management in which offspring are produced one at a time and immediately compete for survival is called an incremental or "steady state" model. An alternate model is one in which a larger number (a batch) of offspring are produced from a fixed pool of parents. Only after the entire batch is produced is there competition for survival into the next generation. Such models are often referred to as batch or generational algorithms.

It is easy to transform incremental EV into a batch system by explicitly maintaining two populations, one for m parents and one for n offspring. The two populations interact as follows:

```
For I=1 to n Do:
  Randomly select an individual from the parent population to
  produce a child as before, and add the child to the offspring
  population.

For I=1 to n Do:
  Force offspring I to compete for space in the parent population
  as before.
```

When described this way, it is easy see that the EV system introduced in chapter 1 is just a special case with $n = 1$. So from this point on it will be convenient to adopt the more general notation of $EV(m, n)$ in order to state explicitly the sizes of the parent and offspring populations. Conceptually, this generalization raises an interesting and difficult question: how large a batch of children should one produce before forcing them to compete for survival? Perhaps you have an idea or an opinion already! A good way to test your intuition right now is to experiment a bit with $EV(m, n)$ on the landscapes L1 and L2 that were introduced in chapter 1.

To set the stage for the rest of the chapter, let's observe the behavior of $EV(m, n)$ for one frequently chosen value of n, namely $n = m$ (i.e., identical sizes for both the parent and offspring populations). As we observed in chapter 1, the effects of such changes are easier to see at a macro-level. Figure 3.1 illustrates this by comparing the average fitness of the population that was evolved using both $EV(10, 1)$ and $EV(10, 10)$ on L2, the same 2-D multi-peaked fitness landscape that was used in chapter 1.

In this particular, case we observe $EV(10, 1)$ converging at a slightly faster rate to a region of high fitness. Is this what you expected? Is this true in general or is it just a property of these particular experiments? We will have a better understanding of this issue by the end of the chapter, but we will have to wait until chapter 4 to be more definitive.

We are now in a position to use $EV(m, n)$ as the basis for a more detailed look at some of the traditional evolutionary algorithms. To keep things simple I will continue to use the real-valued fitness landscapes, L1 and L2, and focus on the differences in the mechanics of evolution.

3.3 Evolutionary Programming

One observation about the design of $EV(m, n)$ is that it appears unnecessarily stochastic. By randomly selecting parents, it is quite possible that some members of the current population never produce any offspring in spite of the fact that they may have high fitness. Similarly, by randomly picking members from the current population to compete with children for

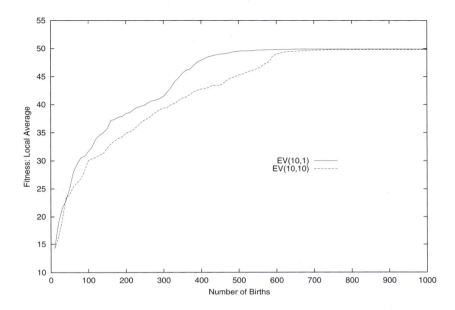

Figure 3.1: Average population fitness with different offspring population sizes on landscape L2.

survival into the next generation, it is quite possible that weak individuals may survive by the luck of the draw and not by merit.

It is easy to make EV more deterministic if we assume, as in the previous section, that both the parent and offspring populations are of equal size $(m = n)$ and modify EV as follows:

```
For I=1 to m Do:
  Use parent I to produce 1 child and add it to the offspring
    population.
End Do
```

```
From the combined pool of 2m parents and children, select only
    the m individuals with highest fitness to survive.
```

This is precisely the form that the early evolutionary programming (EP) algorithms took (Fogel et al., 1966). Unlike $EV(m, m)$ in which parents produce one offspring *on the average* but with high variance due to stochastic effects, parents in $EP(m)$ produce exactly one offspring. Unlike $EV(m, m)$ in which low fitness individuals have some small chance of survival, they have none in $EP(m)$.

What are the effects of these changes on evolutionary behavior? Figure 3.2 shows the effect on average fitness using L2, the 2-D landscape from chapter 1.

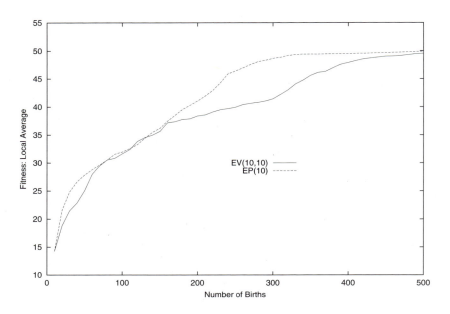

Figure 3.2: EV and EP average fitness on landscape L2.

In this case EP converges somewhat faster than EV to a region of high fitness. The reason for this should be fairly obvious: EP implements a much stronger "elitist" survival scheme in which only the top 50% survive, resulting in an increase in average fitness along with a decrease in diversity. Is this a useful property? It certainly appears to be on this particular 2-D landscape. But, as we will see later, this can also increase the likelihood of converging to a suboptimal peak. In general, achieving a proper balance between the components that increase variation (e.g., mutation) and those that decrease it (e.g., selection) is one of the most important factors in designing evolutionary algorithms.

The interested reader can find additional details about EP in Fogel (1995).

3.4 Evolution Strategies

Another observation about the EV and EP algorithms developed so far is that producing a very small number of offspring from a parent is not a very reliable sample of its potential for producing useful progeny. In nature organisms that produce only a few offspring are the exception rather than the rule. Computationally, it is quite easy to extend the EV and EP paradigms to encompass this idea by just allowing the size of the offspring population n to be greater than m, the size of the parent population. Having done so raises two interesting questions: how many offspring should each parent produce, and given that we are now using parents more efficiently, can we reduce the size of the parent population?

These ideas correspond directly to the early Evolution Strategy (ES) algorithms (Schwe-

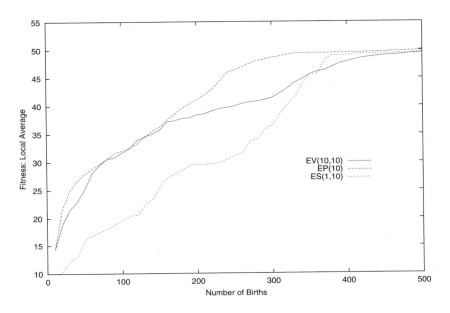

Figure 3.3: EV, EP, and ES behavior on landscape L2.

fel, 1975), which took the form of $(\mu + \lambda)$-ES models in which μ specified the size of the parent population and λ specified the size of the offspring population. Perhaps most striking about this early work was the focus on $(1 + \lambda)$-ES models in which the entire next generation was produced from a single parent! For those who are familiar with Dawkins' work (e.g., Dawkins (1986)), this is also quite similar to the evolutionary model he uses in his examples.

To get a better feeling for the effects of these ideas on evolutionary behavior, we can run a $(1 + 10)$-ES model by simply running $EV(m, n)$, setting $m = 1$ and $n = 10$, and observing the differences between it and the previous EV and EP simulations. Figure 3.3 plots the observed effect on average population fitness.

The results are quite striking. One might expect that, since an $ES(1, 10)$ is even more elitist than $EP(10)$, it would converge even faster. But this example illustrates nicely the critical role that the population plays, namely, providing a natural mechanism for parallel adaptive search. In this particular example, the initial randomly generated parent for the $ES(1, 10)$ model happened to be not particularly close to any of the four peaks. From there, progress toward a peak can be made only via a long series of mutation increments. By contrast, the initial populations of both EV and ES had at least one randomly generated member reasonably close to a peak. After a few generations, selection abandoned the other parallel search threads and sampled almost exclusively in the areas near peaks. By simply increasing the ES parent population size, the behavior more closely approximates EV and EP as illustrated in figure 3.4.

Alternatively, one could view this as a fundamental problem with the mutation operator that we have been using, namely that it is controlled by a time-invariant Gaussian probability

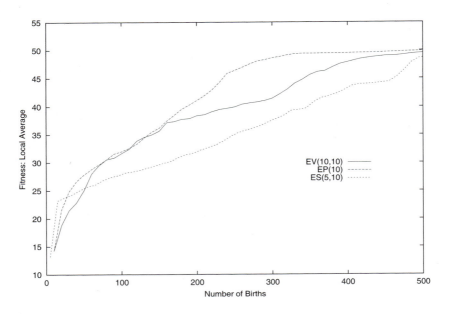

Figure 3.4: EV, EP, and ES average fitness on landscape L2.

distribution $G(0, \sigma)$ that *a priori* sets the average mutation step size. If this step size is small relative to the distances that need to be traveled, a long sequence of "successful" mutations (those that improve fitness) will be required. Conversely, if the average step size is too large, final convergence will be negatively affected by the lack of small step sizes. Figure 3.5 provides a simple illustration of these effects on average population fitness for mutation step sizes of 0.1, 0.5, and 5.0.

Such observations resulted in an early focus in the ES community on self-adapting the step size of the mutation operator (Rechenberg, 1965). Initial theoretical work on optimal rates of convergence (convergence velocity) resulted in an interesting 1:5 self-adaptation rule for mutation which states that if more than 20% of the mutations are successful using a given σ, then the step size is too conservative (exploitative) and σ needs to be increased. Similarly, if fewer than 20% of the mutations are successful, the step size is too explorative and needs to be reduced. More difficult to derive theoretically are "meta" parameters such as how often to adjust σ and by how much (Bäck and Schwefel, 1993; Schwefel, 1995).

To get an initial sense of how this affects the behavior of ES systems, consider the output of a modified version of $EV(m, n)$ that implements a simple version of the 1:5 rule in which σ is adjusted (if necessary) by 10% each generation. The effects of this adaptive step size feature are shown in figure 3.6.

In this example the mutation σ was set initially to 1.0. This value was classified by the 1:5 rule as too conservative and was increased for several generations, and then decreased continuously from there on. The overall effect is to improve both initial and final convergence rates.

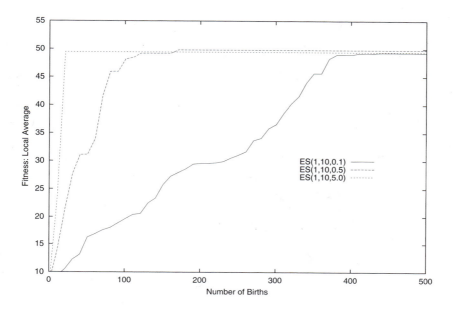

Figure 3.5: The effects of mutation step size on landscape L2.

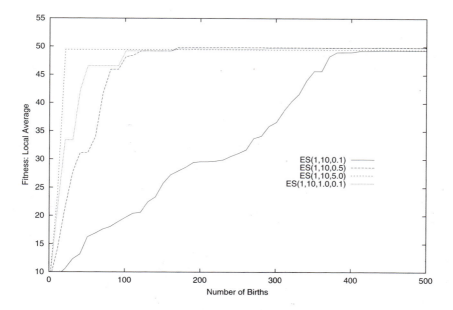

Figure 3.6: The effects of an adaptive mutation step size on landscape L2.

As one might expect, things get more complicated for higher-dimensional problems in which it may be beneficial to maintain a separate step size for each dimension. If there are strong interactions among the parameters of the search space, simultaneous correlated mutations may prove useful. These ideas will be explored in more detail in later chapters.

Self-adaptation can also be viewed as the simultaneous evolution (the coevolution) of both the objects of interest (in this case parameter vectors) and the operators required to evolve them. How one designs and implements coevolutionary systems is a fascinating but difficult topic that will be deferred to a later chapter.

The interested reader can find many additional details about ESs in Rechenberg (1994) and Schwefel (1995).

3.5 Genetic Algorithms

An important observation regarding the evolutionary systems we have studied so far is that individuals die off only when replaced by younger individuals with higher fitness. Evolutionary systems of this type exhibit the convenient property that local population statistics, such as maximum, minimum, and average fitness, are monotonically non-decreasing functions of time, resulting in nice mathematical convergence properties. However, such systems are neither biologically plausible nor computationally desirable in cases in which the fitness landscapes are more complex than the simple ones that have been used so far. Intuitively, allowing individuals to survive and reproduce indefinitely can result in a significant loss of diversity in the population and can increase the likelihood of becoming trapped on a false peak.

There are a number of ways one can address this problem. One approach is to occasionally allow new individuals to replace existing individuals with higher fitness. A more direct method is to use a generational model in which parents survive for exactly one generation and are completely replaced by their offspring. This is the form that standard genetic algorithms (GAs) take (Holland, 1975; De Jong, 1975; Goldberg, 1989), and also the form that the (μ, λ)-ES models take (Bäck and Schwefel, 1993; Schwefel, 1995).

GAs also implement the biological notion of fitness (the ability to survive *and* reproduce) in a somewhat different fashion than we have seen so far. The EV, EP, and ES systems all use objective fitness to determine which offspring survive to adulthood (i.e., which ones make it into the parent population). However, once in the parent pool, there is no additional bias with respect to which individuals get to reproduce – all parents have an equal chance.

Alternatively, one could allow *all* offspring to survive to adulthood and then use objective fitness to select which parents are allowed to reproduce. This is precisely the form that standard GAs take, namely:

```
GA:

Randomly generate a population of m parents.

Repeat:
    Compute and save the fitness u(i) for each individual i
        in the current parent population.
```

```
Define selection probabilities p(i) for each parent i
    so that p(i) is proportional to u(i).

Generate m offspring by probabilistically selecting parents
    to produce offspring.

Select only the offspring to survive.

End Repeat
```

Notice that the pseudo-code actually specifies a particular form of selection, called fitness-proportional selection. It is easy to show that using this selection mechanism, individuals in the current population with average fitness will produce on average one offspring, while above-average individuals produce more than one and below-average individuals less than one (Holland, 1975).

Figure 3.7 illustrates the effect that this has on the average fitness of an evolving population. Notice first that fitness-proportional selection appears to be stronger initially than that of ES, but then weakens considerably. The second, and more striking, outcome to note is that, since all parents die off after one generation, it is possible for the average fitness of the next generation (the offspring) to drop. Is this desirable? For simple landscapes, probably not. But for more complex, multipeaked landscapes this can decrease the likelihood of converging to a local optimum.

3.5.1 Multi-parent Reproduction

Another important difference between GAs and the other models is the way in which offspring are produced. From the beginning, Holland stressed the importance of sexual reproduction as a source of variation in the offspring produced (Holland, 1967). The basic idea is that offspring inherit gene values from more than one parent. This mixing (recombining) of parental gene values, along with an occasional mutation, provides the potential for a much more aggressive exploration of the space. Holland's initial ideas for this took the form of a "1 point crossover" operator in which a randomly chosen initial segment of genes was inherited from one parent and the remaining segment inherited from a second parent. These ideas were later generalized to "2 point crossover" and "n point crossover" operators (De Jong, 1975).

Since all of these crossover operators are equivalent for individuals with exactly two genes, we run a GA with crossover (GA-X) on landscape L2 and plot the effects on average population fitness in figure 3.8.

In this case, crossover provides an additional source of variation involving larger initial steps, improving the initial rate of convergence. Since crossover does not introduce new gene values, its influence diminishes as the population becomes more homogeneous, and the behavior of GA-X becomes nearly identical to a GA with no crossover.

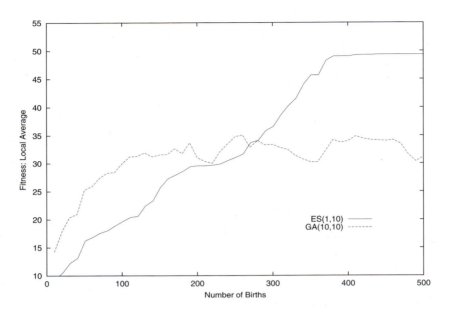

Figure 3.7: Average population fitness of a GA on landscape L2.

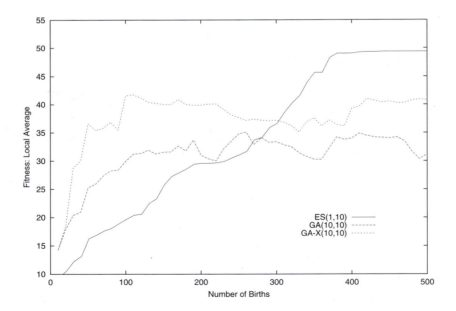

Figure 3.8: Average population fitness of a GA with crossover on landscape L2.

3.5.2   Universal Genetic Codes

Holland also emphasized the importance of a universal string-like "genetic" representation to be used internally by a GA to represent the genome of an individual. By doing so, one can focus on a single problem-independent set of reproduction operators, rather than requiring new ones for each new problem-specific representation. For simplicity, Holland initially suggested a binary string representation in which each bit is viewed internally as a gene, and the mapping to the external phenotype is left unspecified and problem specific. Crossover and mutation operate as before at the gene level, except that they do so at a much finer level of granularity. In the case of a binary representation, mutation simplifies to a "bit flipping" operator.

To make this more concrete, consider how one might map real-valued parameter optimization problems into an internal binary representation. A standard way of accomplishing this is to require parameter resolution information in addition to upper and lower bounds. So, for a 1-D landscape one might specify a resolution of 10^{-4} in addition to parameter bounds of $[0.0, 5.0]$. This permits a calculation of the number of bits required to represent each point of a grid uniformly spaced on the interval $[0.0, 5.0]$ with the grids points 10^{-4} apart. We can then easily compute the corresponding real value v of a parameter from its internal l bit representation by interpreting the l bits as a binary number i representing the ith gridpoint from the left endpoint (lower bound) of the parameter interval, and letting $v = lower\_bnd + i * resolution$.

To get a sense of the effect of an internal binary representation, consider the output produced on the 1-D landscape defined by $f(x) = x^2$ over the interval $[0.0, 5.0]$ with a resolution of 10^{-4}.

```
Simulation time limit (# births): 500
Random number seed (positive integer): 12345
Using a parabolic landscape defined on 1 parameter(s)
   with parameter initialization bounds of:
      1: 0.0  5.0
   and with hard parameter bounds of:
      1: 0.0  5.0
EA type: ga
Crossover: one_point
Using a genome with 16 binary genes.
Parent population size: 10; offspring population size: 10

Population data after 10 births (generation 1):
  Global fitness:  max =  21.02047, ave =   8.96513, min =   0.37711
  Local fitness:   max =  21.02047, ave =   8.96513, min =   0.37711
  Indiv  birthdate   fitness      gene values
    1        1        5.50103   0111100000010110
    2        2        4.25183   0110100110010011
    3        3        8.62828   1001011001100101
    4        4       14.35989   1100001000000101
    5        5        0.41238   0010000011100001
```

```
  6       6        12.75269   1011011011010111
  7       7        20.78745   1110100101110000
  8       8         0.37711   0001111101110001
  9       9        21.02047   1110101010111110
 10      10         1.56021   0011111111110100
```

In this case, we see that to achieve the desired range and resolution, 16-bit strings were required. An initial population of randomly generated bit strings was generated and fitness was calculated by interpreting each bit string as a real number in the interval $[0.0, 5.0]$. One-point crossover and bit-flip mutation are used at the string level to produce the next generation. Notice that small changes at the bit string level can result in rather large changes in the corresponding real number (e.g., flipping the leftmost bit). Continuing, we observe definite patterns emerging in the binary gene pool:

```
Population data after 80 births (generation 8):
  Global fitness:  max =  23.88882, ave =  16.86300, min =   0.03412
  Local fitness:   max =  22.52034, ave =  20.34158, min =  12.28837
  Indiv  birthdate   fitness       gene values
    1       71       21.45503   1110110100101000
    2       72       21.27589   1110110000101010
    3       73       12.28837   1011001101111011
    4       74       21.50737   1110110101110010
    5       75       22.38297   1111001000111011
    6       76       21.45503   1110110100101000
    7       77       22.52034   1111001011111001
    8       78       21.62713   1110111000011011
    9       79       21.34703   1110110010001111
   10       80       17.55663   1101011010001000


Population data after 240 births (generation 24):
  Global fitness:  max =  24.84080, ave =  17.78426, min =   0.03412
  Local fitness:   max =  24.73368, ave =  18.59314, min =  11.17597
  Indiv  birthdate   fitness       gene values
    1      231       23.16574   1111011001101110
    2      232       21.19713   1110101110111010
    3      233       11.17597   1010101100101010
    4      234       24.06290   1111101100101000
    5      235       21.72872   1110111010101010
    6      236       24.73368   1111111010100010
    7      237       12.31353   1011001110101010
    8      238       21.79706   1110111100001010
    9      239       11.70443   1010111100101010
   10      240       14.05220   1011111111101110
```

```
Population data after 470 births (generation 47):
Global fitness:   max =   24.94434, ave =   17.66376, min =    0.05648
Local fitness:    max =   24.65861, ave =   21.53086, min =   10.52465
Indiv   birthdate   fitness        gene values
  1       461       24.65861   1111111000111111
  2       462       20.20855   1110011000101010
  3       463       23.11069   1111011000100011
  4       464       10.52465   1010011000011010
  5       465       24.63286   1111111000011101
  6       466       23.13123   1111011000111111
  7       467       23.87465   1111101000101100
  8       468       23.12756   1111011000111010
  9       469       18.17187   1101101001000010
 10       470       23.86794   1111101000100011

Global best:   birthdate   fitness        gene values
                  346       24.944336   1111111110110111
```

For this particular 1-D landscape, the real numbers with high fitness are those at the right-most end of the interval $[0.0, 5.0]$. In binary form, these are real numbers whose binary string representations have lots of leading 1s, and the highest fitness is associated with the string of all 1s. Fairly early in the simulation we see 1s beginning to dominate the left-most gene positions, and we note that a near-optimal string is already encountered at time 346. Recall, however, that this GA is a generational model, so even the best individuals only live for one generation. After about 400 births this GA settles into a dynamic equilibrium in which the diversity provided by crossover and mutation is balanced by the selection pressure toward homogeneity.

An obvious question is whether there is any significant difference between using a binary or a real encoding. A detailed answer will have to be deferred to later chapters. However, it is easy to illustrate that there are significant differences. This can be seen in a number of ways. First, consider its effect on the average fitness of the population. Figure 3.9 compares the average fitness of a binary-coded GA (GA-B) with its real-coded equivalent(GA-R) on landscape L2. Notice how the larger steps that are possible in a binary GA provide some initial advantage, but then have a negative effect.

But, of course, average population fitness is only one aspect of evolutionary behavior. From a computation search perspective, best-so-far curves provide a better picture of search performance. Figure 3.10 illustrates this aspect for GA-B and GA-R on landscape L2. Notice how, in this case, we see just the opposite. In spite of lower average fitness, GA-B is able to find individuals with higher fitness faster than GA-R.

The interested reader can find many additional details about GAs in Goldberg (1989), Holland (1992), and Mitchell (1998).

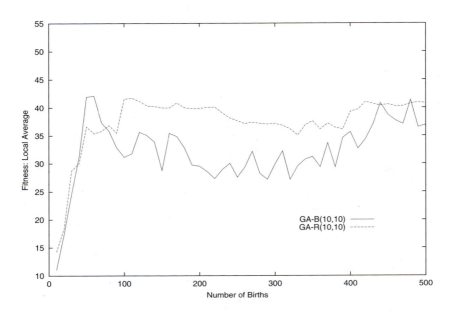

Figure 3.9: Average population fitness of real and binary coded GAs on landscape L2.

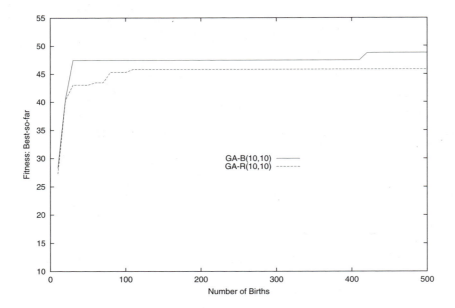

Figure 3.10: Best-so-far curves of real and binary coded GAs on landscape L2.

3.6 Summary

The canonical evolutionary algorithms EP, ES, and GA are important for several reasons. First, they have had a strong influence on the field of evolutionary computation as we see it today. A majority of the evolutionary computation applications that have been developed over the past 30 years have been strongly influenced by these canonical EAs. A second role that they play is to emphasize that there are a variety of ways in which interesting and useful evolutionary algorithms can be designed and used for problem solving. Finally, these canonical EAs serve as the basis for a more general framework that can help us build new and more effective evolutionary problem solvers. These ideas are explored more fully in the next several chapters.

Chapter 4

A Unified View of Simple EAs

From a biological point of view, the last three chapters have focused on fairly simple evolutionary systems: single species models with fixed population sizes, simplistic reproductive mechanisms, static fitness landscapes, etc. However, as we have seen, even these simple models can be instantiated in a variety of ways that can affect the observed behavior of a model in rather striking and sometimes unexpected ways.

From an evolutionary computation point of view, even these simple models exhibit surprising potential as adaptive search techniques. So, before moving on to more complex evolutionary models, the focus of this chapter will be on unifying the models we have discussed so far into a general framework that will serve as the basis for understanding the various ways evolutionary algorithms can be used as problem solvers. Then, in the later chapters we will use this framework as the starting point for exploring the properties of more complex evolutionary models.

4.1 A Common Framework

If we look back at the various evolutionary algorithms (EAs) discussed in the previous chapter, the following general pattern for modeling the evolutionary dynamics emerges. In each case:

- a population of constant size m is evolved over time,

- the current population is used as a source of parents to produce n offspring, and

- the expanded population is reduced from $m + n$ to m individuals.

In addition to choosing particular values for m and n, an EA must specify a method for selecting the parents to be used to produce offspring, and a method for selecting which individuals will survive into the next generation . As we have seen, these choices can and do vary quite widely and can significantly affect EA behavior. There is now a large body of experimental and theoretical work that makes it clear that there are no universally optimal methods. Rather, if we are to apply EAs successfully to difficult computational problems, we need to make intelligent and frequently problem-specific choices. Clearly, we have some historically important examples of useful choices made by the developers of the EP, ES, and GA paradigms. However, describing the population dynamics in this more general way also makes it clear that there are many other possible choices one could make. Is it possible to make informed decisions based on an understanding of the role the various choices play in the overall behavior of an EA? The answer is an unequivocal yes, and we will explore these roles in this chapter.

However, in addition to specifying the population dynamics, an EA must specify how individuals are represented internally, and how the reproductive process works (i.e., how an offspring's internal representation is derived from its parents). Again, we have seen a variety of historical choices and can imagine many additional possibilities. Are there design principles involved as well? Absolutely, as we will see.

These insights into the nature of EAs are the result of a large body of experimental and formal analysis that has accumulated over the last 30 years. In this chapter our goal is to gain an intuitive understanding of EA design issues that we can use in the next chapter when applying EAs to specific classes of problems. A more substantial and a more formal analysis of these issues will be provided in chapter 6.

4.2   Population Size

An important first step toward a deeper understanding of EAs is to focus on population-sizing issues. How big should the population be? How many offspring should be produced per generation al cycle? What role do these sizes play? Is the choice of values critical to problem solving performance? If so, how does one choose appropriate values?

4.2.1   Parent Population Size m

Intuitively, the parent population size m can be viewed as a measure of the degree of parallel search an EA supports, since the parent population is the basis for generating new search points. For simple landscapes, like the 1-D and 2-D parabolic landscapes we have seen so far, only small amounts of parallelism are required. However, for more complex, multi-peaked landscapes, populations of 100s or even 1000s of parents are frequently required.

A simple illustration of this can be obtained by making a small, but subtle change to L2, the 2-D parabolic landscape used in the previous chapters. Recall that this landscape involved individuals represented by a feature vector $< x1, x2 >$ in which each feature was a real number in the interval [-5.0,5.0] with a fitness function $f2(x1, x2) = x1^2 + x2^2$. If we break the symmetry of this landscape by changing the interval to $[-5.5, 4.5]$, we now have a landscape L2a with four peaks and a unique optimal fitness of approximately 60 at $< -5.5, -5.5 >$ as shown in figure 4.1.

With this simple change in the fitness landscape, it is now quite easy to observe the behavioral changes in simple EAs due to changes in the parent population size m. Consider, for example, $EV(m, 1)$ with an offspring population of size $n = 1$ and a Gaussian mutation operator $GM(1.0)$ with an average step size of 1.0. Figure 4.2 plots the best-so-far curves for $m = 10$, $m = 40$, and $m = 100$. However, there is an important difference in these graphs

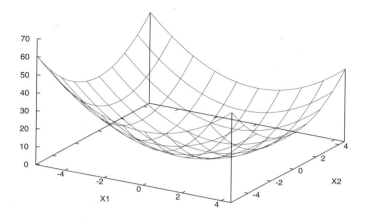

Figure 4.1: L2a, a 2-D parabolic objective fitness landscape with multiple peaks and a unique maximum of 60 at $[-5.5, -5.5]$.

from those presented in the earlier chapters. The illustrative examples so far have typically involved observing some aspect of an EA on a *single* run. While this is satisfactory for simple EA properties, it is important never to lose sight of the fact that EAs are *stochastic* algorithms. As such, observed EA behavior can vary considerably from one run to another in which the only change is the seed used to initialize the underlying pseudo-random number generator. Hence, to make more precise statements about the behavior of a particular EA we must observe it over multiple runs using different random number seeds and describe its behavior in terms of averages, variances, etc.

In this particular case, each best-so-far curve is the point-by-point average of five best-so-far curves obtained using a pre-chosen set of five different random number seeds. Using this approach we can see that the *average* behavior of $EV(10, 1)$ is quite good initially, but then fades, reflecting the fact that it frequently converges to a suboptimal peak. By contrast, $EV(40, 1)$ starts out more slowly but invariably converges to the global optimum (of 60). As $EV(100, 1)$ illustrates, increasing m further on this particular landscape provides no additional advantage and only serves to slow down convergence considerably.

As we will see in the next chapter, another important consideration when using EAs as problem solvers is the amount of variance possible from run to run. For example, if one uses an EA to evolve a solution to a complex VLSI layout problem, a natural question is whether a quite different solution would be obtained simply by running the EA again with different random number seeds. In this context, a reduction in variance from one run to the next is often desirable from a user's perspective, in the sense that a single broader global search is

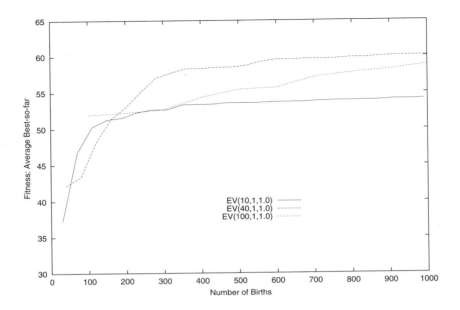

Figure 4.2: The effects of parent population size on average best-so-far curves for landscape L2a.

preferred over having to repeat a series of more localized searches. In this case m plays an important role in controlling the breadth of the search, particularly in the early stages of evolution. Increasing the initial breadth of the search increases the likelihood that regions containing global optima will be explored, and hence serves as a mechanism for reducing the variance due to convergence to local optima.

This aspect is illustrated quite clearly in figure 4.3. Here the point-by-point standard deviations of the best-so-far curves of figure 4.2 have been calculated and plotted as vertical "error bars". Notice the rather dramatic reduction in variance exhibited by $EV(m,1)$ on this particular landscape as we increase m from 10 to 40. As one might expect, significantly larger values of m are required to obtain similar reductions in variance on more complex, multi-peaked landscapes.

4.2.2 Offspring Population Size n

By contrast, the offspring population size n plays quite different roles in an EA. One important role relates the exploration/exploitation balance that is critical for good EA search behavior. The current parent population reflects where in the solution space an EA is focusing its search, based on the feedback from earlier generations. The number of offspring n generated is a measure of how long one is willing to continue to use the current parent population as the basis for generating new offspring *without* integrating the newly generated high-fitness offspring back into the parent population. From a control theory perspective,

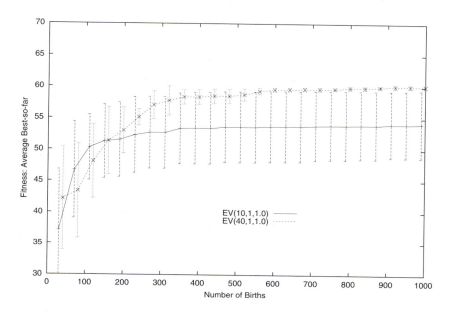

Figure 4.3: The effects of parent population size on best-so-far variance for landscape L2a.

n represents the delay in a feedback loop. From a financial point of view, n represents the time delay in compounding interest.

So, why not adopt a strategy of maximal exploitation of new information (i.e., $n = 1$)? If you had a choice, would you not choose a bank that offers daily compounding of interest over one that compounds interest monthly? To see why this is not necessarily the case for EAs, recall that the simple EAs we are currently studying all maintain a fixed parent population size. Hence, feedback in a simple EA necessarily involves replacing current individuals in the parent population with new individuals. As we saw in the earlier chapters, this can result in the premature removal of individuals before they have had a chance to produce any offspring at all. This, in turn, can result in a premature reduction in parent population diversity (parallelism), and an increase in the likelihood of converging to a sub-optimal solution.

This effect can be seen quite clearly if we keep the parent population size m constant and increase the offspring population size n. Figure 4.4 illustrates this for $EV(10, n)$ on the asymmetric 2-D landscape L2a. Notice how increasing n improves average performance in this case, but in a quite different way than increasing the parent population size. Here the effect is an increase in the initial convergence rate at the cost of relatively little further progress because of the loss of population diversity.

There are several other roles played by the offspring population size n in simple EAs, but they are best explained in the context of the next few sections.

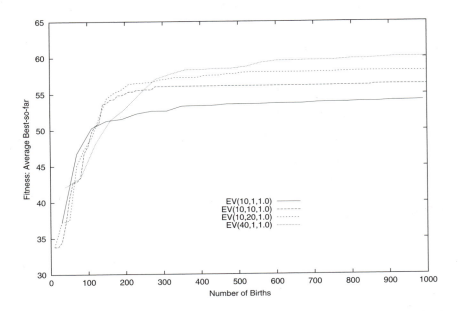

Figure 4.4: The effects of offspring population size on average best-so-far curves for landscape L2a.

4.3 Selection

As noted earlier, these simple EAs all maintain a population of size m by repeatedly:

- using the current population as a source of parents to produce n offspring, and

- reducing the expanded population from $m + n$ to m individuals.

Regardless of the particular values of m and n, both steps involve selecting a subset of individuals from a given set. In step one, the required number of parents are selected to produce n offspring. In step two, m individuals are selected to survive. So far, we have seen several examples of the two basic categories of selection mechanisms: *deterministic* and *stochastic* selection methods.

With *deterministic* methods, each individual in the selection pool is assigned a fixed number that corresponds to the number of times they will be selected. So, for example, parent selection in EP is uniform and deterministic. Since there are m parents and $n = m$ offspring to be generated, each individual in the current population is selected *exactly once* to produce an offspring. Similarly, survival in an ES is via "truncation selection" in which the selection pool is sorted by objective fitness, and the top m survive (i.e., are assigned a value of 1) and the remaining individuals die (are assigned a value of 0).

With *stochastic* selection mechanisms, individuals in the selection pool are assigned a fixed probability p_i of being chosen. So, for example, in a GA parents are selected stochastically using a fitness-proportional probability distribution. In EV, offspring survive only if

EA	m	n	parent_sel	survival_sel
EP	< 20	$n = m$	deterministic	deterministic
ES	< 10	$n >= m$	stochastic	deterministic
GA	> 20	$n = m$	stochastic	deterministic

Table 4.1: Traditional EA selection categories.

they have higher fitness than a randomly selected member of the current population. As a consequence, when k selections are made, each individual i will be selected *on average* $k * p_i$ times. However, since selection is achieved by randomly sampling the given probability distribution, the actual number of times an individual is selected can vary significantly from the expected value.

Does it make any difference whether selection is implemented as stochastic or deterministic? In general, yes, it does make a difference, for two quite different reasons. First, statistical sampling theory tells us that small samples drawn from a probability distribution can and frequently do differ considerably from the average properties of the distribution itself. What that means for EAs is that when small populations are involved (i.e., values of m and/or n of less than 20), the actual selected subsets can differ quite significantly from the expected ones. So, for example, if we use a uniform probability distribution to select m parents from a population of size m, the best individual in the population may never get chosen and the worst individual selected multiple times. On the other hand, using a deterministic algorithm forces each individual to be chosen exactly once.

Given all this, is there any reason to use stochastic selection? As we will see in the next chapter, the answer is yes. In some cases, stochastic selection can be used to add "noise" to EA-based problem solvers in a way that improves their "robustness" by decreasing the likelihood of converging to a sub-optimal solution. In fact, we have already seen indirect evidence of this in the choices made by the designers of the canonical EAs we surveyed in the previous chapter and summarized in table 4.1.

However, more important than whether selection is stochastic or deterministic is how a particular selection mechanism distributes selection pressure over the selection pool of candidate individuals. As we have already seen, the range of possibilities is quite wide, varying from rather elitist "truncation selection" strategies in which only the best individuals are chosen, to much more egalitarian "uniform selection" strategies in which anyone can be chosen. There are several useful ways of comparing and contrasting selection techniques. The simplest way is just to visualize how a particular technique distributes selection probability over the selection pool. Since most selection schemes are based on fitness, the differences are easiest to see if we imagine the selection pool to be sorted from left to right by decreasing fitness values. Figure 4.5 illustrates this for three of the selection mechanisms commonly used in simple EAs: truncation, linear ranking, and uniform.

Notice how truncation selection assigns all of the probability mass to just a few individuals (in this case, the top 20%), while linear ranking and uniform selection distribute the probabilities across the entire population. Since selection is used in EAs to narrow the focus

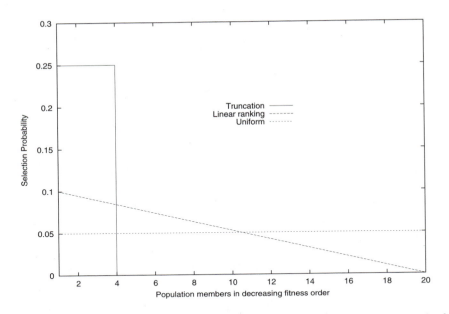

Figure 4.5: The distribution of selection probability mass over a selection pool of size 20, sorted by fitness.

of the search, shifting probability mass away from low fitness individuals and toward high fitness individuals increases the "exploitation" pressure. Using more traditional computer science terminology, this corresponds to increasing the "greediness" of EA-based search, which can be helpful on simpler fitness landscapes, but detrimental on more complex ones.

A more formal analysis of selection methods will be provided in chapter 6. However, it is easy to get a sense of their effects on behavior by simply running an EA with the reproductive variation operators disabled (i.e., no mutation or crossover). Under these conditions, after the initial randomly generated population, no novel individuals are ever created – only clones of existing parents are produced. If we then plot the average fitness of the parent population over time, we can see the compounding effects of repeated applications of a particular selection algorithm sel. Figures 4.6 and 4.7 illustrate this using $EV(10, 10, sel)$ with 10 parents producing 10 clone offspring, and all 20 individuals competing for survival using the survival selection mechanisms of truncation, linear ranking, and uniform selection.

Under truncation selection, the "takeover time" of the best individual in the initial population is extremely rapid, resulting in a homogeneous population after just a few generations. As we might have expected, switching to a less greedy linear ranking selection method slows down the rate of convergence, but the end result is the same: a homogeneous population after approximately 10 generations. And, under uniform selection, the only changes in average fitness are the minor variations due to sampling errors.

Perhaps the most surprising aspect of this example is that, as illustrated in figure 4.7, even under uniform (neutral) selection $EV(10, 10, sel)$ converges to a homogeneous popu-

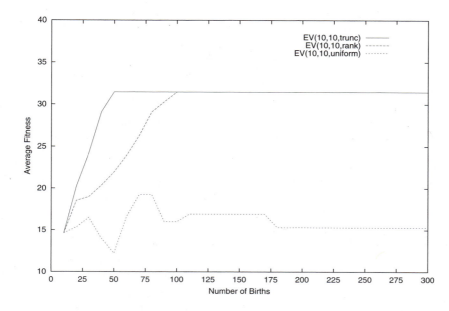

Figure 4.6: Average fitness of $EV(10, 10, sel)$ population under different selection pressures.

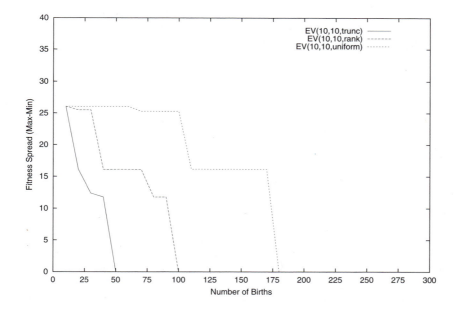

Figure 4.7: Fitness spread of $EV(10, 10, sel)$ population under different selection pressures.

lation in less than 20 generations. The reason is straightforward: with a finite population, *any* stochastic selection method is likely to result in a loss of diversity simply because of sampling error. This is a well-understood phenomenon in biology and results in populations exhibiting "genetic drift". In our example, having disabled reproductive variation, this effect is magnified and its compounding effects result in a loss of all but one genotype in less than 20 generations.

There are two other commonly used selection techniques, tournament selection and fitness-proportional selection, that can be characterized in a similar manner. Tournament selection involves randomly selecting k individuals using a uniform probability distribution, and then selecting the best (or worst) individual from the k competitors as the winner (or loser). If n individuals need to be selected, n such tournaments are performed (with replacement) on the selection pool. The effect is to implicitly impose a probability distribution on the selection pool without explicit calculation and assignment of probabilities. In the case of binary tournaments ($k = 2$), the implicit distribution can be shown to be equivalent (in expectation) to linear ranking, and produces curves identical to the linear ranking curve in figure 4.6. If we increase the tournament size to $k = 3$, the implicit probability distribution changes from linear ranking to quadratic ranking with more probability mass shifted toward the best. With each increase in the tournament size k, selection becomes more elitist.

More difficult to characterize is fitness-proportional selection, in which each individual in the selection pool is assigned the probability f_i/f_{sum}, where f_i is the fitness of individual i, and f_{sum} is the total fitness of all the individuals in the current selection pool. The result is a *dynamically changing* probability distribution that can be quite elitist in the early generations when there is a wide range of fitness values, and typically evolves to a nearly flat uniform distribution in the later stages, as the population becomes more homogeneous and the range of fitness values is quite narrow.

As we will see in chapter 6, it can be shown formally that the various selection schemes can be ranked according to selection pressure strength. Of the ones we have discussed so far, the ranking from weakest to strongest is:

- uniform

- fitness-proportional

- linear ranking and binary tournament

- nonlinear ranking and tournaments with $k > 2$

- truncation

4.3.1   Choosing Selection Mechanisms

How do we use this knowledge about selection mechanisms when designing an EA? There are two places in simple EAs where selection occurs: when choosing parents to produce offspring, and when choosing which individuals will survive. The cumulative effect is to control the focus of search in future generations. If the combined selection pressure is too strong, an EA is likely to converge too quickly to a suboptimal region of the space. As we saw in the previous section, even an EA with uniform parent selection and linear ranking

EA	m	n	parent_sel	survival_sel
EP	< 20	$n = m$	uniform	truncation
ES	< 10	$n >= m$	uniform	truncation
GA	> 20	$n = m$	fitness-prop	uniform

Table 4.2: Traditional EA population selection mechanisms

survival selection produces fairly strong selection pressure and rapid rates of convergence. The compounding effects of two non-uniform selection steps generally produces far too strong a selection pressure. As a consequence, one of the two selection mechanisms (i.e., either parent or survival selection) is generally chosen to be uniform (neutral) as illustrated in table 4.2. This observation is frequently used to simplify EA design, in that the overall selection pressure can be controlled by using a uniform selection method for one of the mechanisms (e.g., parent selection) and varying the choice of the non-uniform selection method for the other (e.g., survival).

4.3.2 Survival Selection: A Special Case

So far there has not been any discussion regarding exactly which individuals are competing for survival. The answer differs depending on whether a particular EA implements an *overlapping*- or *non-overlapping*-generation model. With non-overlapping models, the entire parent population dies off each generation and the offspring only compete with each other for survival. Historical examples of non-overlapping EAs include "generational GAs" and the "μ, λ" variation of ESs.

In non-overlapping models, if the offspring population size n is significantly larger than the parent population size m (e.g., traditional ESs), then competition for survival increases. Hence, we see another role that increasing offspring population size plays, namely, amplifying non-uniform survival selection pressure.

However, a much more significant effect on selection pressure occurs when using an EA with an overlapping-generation model such as a "steady-state GA", a "$\mu + \lambda$" ES, or any EP algorithm. In this case, parents and offspring compete with each other for survival. The combination of a larger selection pool $(m + n)$ and the fact that, as evolution proceeds, the m parents provide stronger and stronger competition, results in a significant increase in selection pressure over a non-overlapping version of the same EA.

These effects can be easily demonstrated using the same approach that was used for figure 4.6, namely, by plotting the average fitness of a population being evolved only by selection and cloning. For example, if we are using uniform parent selection and linear ranking survival selection, we can increase overall selection pressure just by switching from a non-overlapping model to an overlapping one. Figure 4.8 illustrates this using ES(10,20).

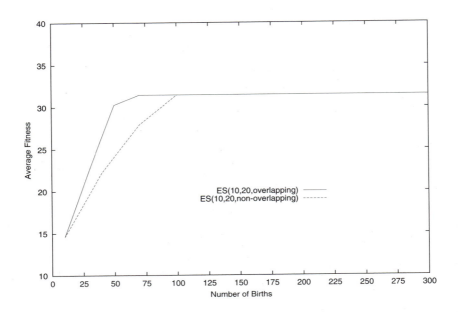

Figure 4.8: Average fitness of $ES(10, 20)$ population using non-overlapping and overlapping generations on landscape L2a.

4.3.3   Selection Summary

Having now surveyed a number of different selection mechanisms, it is tempting to ask what the "best" combination of selection mechanisms is to achieve optimal EA performance. Unfortunately, there are no simple answers, since selection is just one of a number of key EA components that interact in highly nonlinear ways. At the same time, there are some qualitative guidelines that can be used for effective EA design.

As we have noted before, a critical performance issue is achieving a balance between exploration and exploitation. For problems that exhibit highly multi-modal (rugged) fitness landscapes or landscapes that change over time, too much exploitation generally results in premature convergence to suboptimal peaks in the space. Conversely, performance on relatively smooth, time-invariant landscapes with a small number of peaks can be enhanced by increasing exploitation. Since most of the exploitation in a simple EA is due to the choice of selection mechanisms, an EA designer can adjust relatively easily the level of exploitation (greediness) by switching to alternative selection procedures and/or (non-)overlapping-generation models.

Alternatively, one can change the exploration/exploitation balance by adjusting the level of exploration. Since most of the exploration in a simple EA results from to the variation introduced by the reproductive operators, significant changes in performance can be obtained as well by switching to different reproductive operators.

It should come as no surprise then that EAs using strong selection pressure generally counterbalance that with more explorative reproductive operators, while EAs that use weaker forms of selection pressure invariably use much less explorative reproductive operators. Good examples of this contrast are ESs that typically use truncation selection and strong doses of mutation, and GAs that typically use fitness-proportional selection and 1- or 2-point crossover combined with weak doses of mutation. To understand this better we need to look at reproductive mechanisms in more detail.

4.4   Reproductive Mechanisms

We have already seen examples of the two basic classes of reproductive mechanisms: an asexual (single parent) mutation operator and a sexual (more than one parent) recombination operator. Although we have only seen examples so far of two-parent sexual reproduction, one can imagine (and in fact we will study in later chapters) cases in which more than two parents are used.

4.4.1   Mutation

The classic one-parent reproductive mechanism is mutation that operates by cloning a parent and then providing some variation by modifying one or more genes in the offspring's genome . The amount of variation is controlled by specifying how many genes are to be modified and the manner in which genes are to be modified. These two aspects interact in the following way. It is often the case that there is a natural distance metric associated with the values that a gene can take on, such as Euclidean distance for the real-valued parameter landscapes used in many of the examples in this book so far. Using this metric, one can then quantify the exploration level of mutation operators based on the number of genes modified and the amount of change they make to a gene's value.

The Gaussian mutation operator $GM(0, s)$ used in the earlier chapters is a good example of this. Recall that it was defined to stochastically modify *on average* 1 of the L genes in a genome , and each gene's value was changed *on average* by an amount s. Hence, the distance between parents and children is *on average s*. Increasing either the average number of genes modified or the step size s increases this distance (and the amount of variation). If we want to increase mutation variation, does it matter how we do it? In general, yes. Keeping the number of genes that are modified low (e.g., one gene) and increasing the step size s biases the exploration along the axes of the search space in a way quite similar to traditional "line search" algorithms. This bias is quite effective when the genes (parameters) are relatively independent with respect to their contributions toward fitness (i.e., low epistasis), but can cause difficulties when genes interact, since in such cases improvements in fitness require simultaneous mutations to multiple genes.

Up to this point, the simple parabolic landscapes we have been using have been sufficient to illustrate the points under discussion. However, they are examples of linearly separable functions on which "line search" algorithms work well. In order to illustrate the effects of epistasis we need to add to our collection of example landscapes some additional functions with nonlinear parameter interactions. A classic benchmark of this type from the function optimization literature is the deceptively simple two-dimensional Rosenbrock function

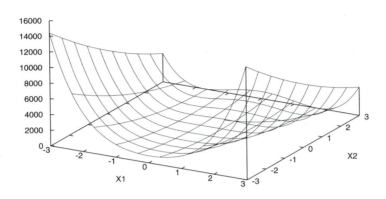

Figure 4.9: Rosenbrock 2D landscape.

$f(x_1, x_2) = 100 * (x_1{}^2 - x_2)^2 + (1 - x_1)^2$ (De Jong, 1975). Its global minimum can be seen by inspection of the closed form to be at $< 1.0, 1.0 >$, but lies along a deep parabolic valley as illustrated in figure 4.9.

Such a topology is very difficult for "line search" algorithms since they are constantly exploring directions unaligned with the path of descent to the global optimum. As a consequence, if we use our Gaussian mutation operator $G(0, s)$ that modifies on average $1/L$ genes, it struggles to make progress on such landscapes. By contrast, if we make a simple change to $G(0, s)$ so that it modifies *all* genes, we see a significant improvement in performance as illustrated in figure 4.10.

However, as L increases, modifying all genes is generally too disruptive. Rather, one would prefer to make simultaneous changes to those subsets of genes that interact epistatically. The difficulty, of course, is that we seldom know *a priori* which genes (if any) interact with each other. Since, as the length L of the genome increases, the number of possible subsets of K interacting genes grows combinatorially as $\begin{pmatrix} L \\ K \end{pmatrix}$, it is not feasible in practice to attempt to dynamically discover and exploit more than very low order interactions (e.g., pairwise covariance estimates used in some ESs).

Similar issues arise with binary representations. In this case, Hamming distance is the natural metric to measure how far children are from their parents. The standard "bit-flip" mutation operator changes the value of a gene (one bit) to its complement and so the mutation step size s is always equal to 1. Hence, for binary representations, the expected distance between a child and its parent is determined by a single parameter, namely how

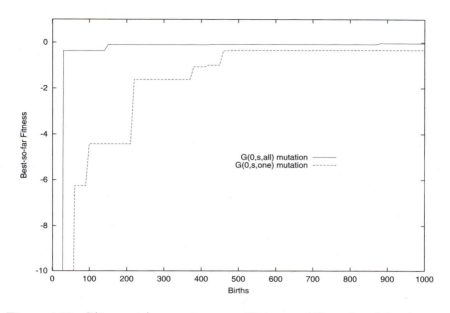

Figure 4.10: $G(0, s, rate)$ mutation on a 2D inverted Rosenbrock landscape.

many genes are modified. The bit-flip mutation operator that we have used so far in our examples has modified on average $1/L$ bits, which is the equivalent of line search in Hamming space.

Just as we saw for real-valued representations, increasing the mutation rate on binary representations will improve performance on landscapes with epistatic interactions. However, as we will see in more detail later in this chapter, there is an important difference. Binary representations require a mapping between genospace and phenospace. Whether or not small distances in genospace correspond to small changes in phenospace depends on the properties of the mapping. For many of the standard mappings (e.g., simple binary encodings), the average distance between parents and children in phenospace, produced by a $1/L$ bit-flip mutation operator, is quite large. As a consequence, historically, we see EAs that use a binary representation with bit-flip mutation running with much lower mutation rates (in terms of the number of genes modified) than ones using real-valued representations with Gaussian mutation.

4.4.2 Recombination

The classic two-parent reproductive mechanism is recombination in which subcomponents of the parents' genomes are cloned and reassembled to create an offspring genome . For simple fixed-length linear genome representations, the recombination operators have traditionally taken the form of "crossover" operators, in which the crossover points mark the linear subsegments on the parents' genomes to be copied and reassembled. So, for example, a 1-

point crossover operator would produce an offspring by randomly selecting a crossover point between genes i and $i + 1$, and then copying genes $1...i$ from parent 1 and genes $i + 1...L$ from parent 2:

```
Parent1:   A B C D E F
             |                 Child:    A B c d e f
Parent2:   a b c d e f
```

Similarly, a 2-point crossover operator randomly selects two crossover points and copies segments one and three from parent 1 and segment two from parent 2:

```
Parent1:   A B C D E F
             |     |           Child:    A B c d e F
Parent2:   a b c d e f
```

For these kinds of reproductive operators, the amount of variation introduced when producing children is dependent on two factors: how many crossover points there are and how similar the parents are to each other. The interesting implication of this is that, unlike mutation, the amount of variation introduced by crossover operating on fixed-length linear genomes diminishes over time as selection makes the population more homogeneous. (As we will see in chapter 7, this is not true when recombination is applied to variable-length genomes.)

This dependency on the contents of the population makes it much more difficult to estimate the level of crossover-induced variation. What can be calculated is the variation due to the number of crossover points. One traditional way of doing this is to calculate the "disruptiveness" of a crossover operator (Holland, 1975). This is done by calculating the probability that a child will inherit a set of K genes from one of its parents. Increasing the number of crossover points increases variation and simultaneously reduces the likelihood that a set of K genes will be passed on to a child. Even the 1- and 2-point crossover operators described above, which are the ones used in canonical GAs, can be shown to introduce adequate amounts of variation when the parent population is fairly heterogeneous.

One of the difficulties with these traditional crossover operators is that, by always choosing a fixed number of crossover points, they introduce a (generally undesirable) distance bias in that genes close together on a genome are more likely to be inherited as a group than if they are widely separated. A simple extreme case are the two genes on either end of a linear chromosome undergoing 1-point crossover. They have no chance of being inherited together, while any two adjacent genes are highly likely to be inherited. This distance bias can be reduced by increasing the number of crossover points, but at the cost of increasing disruptiveness.

A solution to this dilemma is to make the *number* of crossover points a stochastic variable as well. One method for achieving this is to imagine flipping a coin at each gene position. If it comes up heads, the child inherits that gene from parent 1; otherwise, the child inherits that gene from parent 2. Hence, a coin flip sequence of TTHHHH corresponds to a 1-point crossover, while a sequence of HHTTTH corresponds to a 2-point crossover operation:

```
Parent1:    A  B  C  D  E  F
                  |
            T  T  H  H  H  H       Child:    A  B  c  d  e  f
                  |
Parent2:    a  b  c  d  e  f



Parent1:    A  B  C  D  E  F
                  |     |
            H  H  T  T  T  H       Child:    A  B  c  d  e  F
                  |     |
Parent2:    a  b  c  d  e  f
```

Depending on the coin flip sequence, anywhere from zero to $L - 1$ crossover points can be generated. If the probability of heads is 0.5, then the average number of crossover points generated is $L/2$ and has been dubbed "uniform crossover" (Syswerda, 1989).

The key feature of uniform crossover is that it can be shown to have no distance bias. Hence, the location of a set of genes on a genome does not affect its heritability. However, uniform crossover can be shown to have a much higher level of disruption than 1- or 2-point crossover, and for many situations its level of disruption (variation) is too high. Fortunately, the level of disruption can be controlled *without* introducing a distance bias simply by varying from 0.0 (no disruption) to 0.5 (maximum disruption) the probability of a heads occurring. This unbiased crossover operator with tunable disruption has been dubbed "parameterized uniform crossover" (Spears and De Jong, 1991) and is widely used in practice.

This can be nicely illustrated on the Rosenbrock landscape using a standard GA with a binary representation and bit-flipping mutation. Figure 4.11 shows the effect that varying the crossover operation has on best-so-far performance. Notice how the lack of a distance bias improves things initially. However, in this case, a 0.5 uniform crossover operator introduces too much variation to continue to be effective. On this landscape, running parameterized uniform crossover at a rate of 0.2 reduced the variation to a more productive level. In general, a value of 0.2 is frequently seen in practice to be a good choice.

A frequent question that arises with all crossover operators is whether they should produce one or two children since, for a given set of crossover points, a second child can be easily produced by copying the odd numbered segments from parent 2 and the even numbered segments from parent 1. In general, one finds that producing both children results in a slight performance improvement over producing a single child. A more formal analysis of why this is true will be deferred to chapter 6. The informal explanation is as follows. Both the standard mutation and crossover operators are themselves stochastic in the sense that, given particular parents, the resulting children are only probabilistically determined. So,

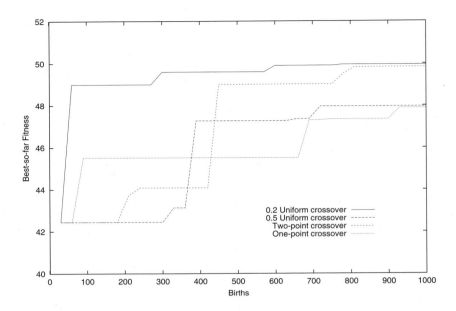

Figure 4.11: The effects of varying crossover on a 2D inverted Rosenbrock landscape.

the production of a single child consists of one sample from the underlying probability distribution, and is a rather limited assessment of a parent's ability to produce useful progeny. Increasing the "brood size" gives parents more opportunity to do so. This observation relates directly to our earlier discussion of the role of the child population size n. In addition to the other roles, increasing the child population size can smooth the effects of stochastic reproduction operators by allowing parents more opportunities to produce useful offspring.

4.4.3   Crossover or Mutation?

A question that arises repeatedly is whether crossover or mutation is the "better" way to produce useful offspring (Spears, 1992). This is a complex issue about which much has been written. The simplest answer is that neither of the reproductive strategies is universally better than the other one. Each embodies a quite different reproductive "heuristic" that complements the other one. A geometric interpretation of mutation and crossover can help clarify this idea. If we think of a parent as a point in an N-dimensional gene space, then the children produced by mutation can be visualized as forming a cloud around the parent that decreases in density with distance from the parent. By contrast, since crossover only swaps parental genes, the children it produces correspond to the vertices of the N-dimensional rectangle defined by the two parents. The overall effect is one of crossover exploring a discrete lattice of points defined by the gene values of the parents in the current population, but unable to introduce new gene values and change the underlying lattice itself. Mutation, on the other hand, continuously introduces new gene values, but because it is undirected, it is unable to take the larger directed steps that crossover can. The goal is to design a system in which mutation provides a continuous source of useful gene values while crossover explores the lattice they define.

At a higher level, the goal is to find an effective balance between further exploration of unexplored regions of the search space and exploitation of the regions already explored. As we noted in the previous section, selection is the primary source of exploitation in an EA and therefore the level of exploitation can be controlled directly by the choice of selection mechanisms. Similarly, reproductive variation is the primary source of exploration in an EA, and the level of exploration can be controlled directly by the choice of reproductive mechanisms.

What that means is that as EA designers we are now in a position to tune the overall system balance in an informed manner. Suppose, for example, we decide to replace the fitness-proportional selection mechanism in a canonical GA with rank-proportional selection. We know from the previous section that by doing so we have significantly increased selection pressure, which will in turn increase the rate at which the population is becoming more homogeneous. While this has no effect on the level of variation produced by mutation, the variation produced by crossover diminishes rapidly as the population homogeneity increases, resulting in a further shift toward exploitation. This may actually result in improved performance on simple landscapes, but is likely to result in convergence to a local peak on more complex, multi-peaked landscapes. But, as we saw above, we have tuning knobs available for both mutation and crossover that allow us to increase the variation they produce, to counterbalance the increased selection pressure, and increase the likelihood of convergence to a global peak.

4.4.4 Representation Issues

So far in the discussion of reproductive operators, representation issues have, for the most part, been ignored. The discussion was restricted to fixed-length linear representations because variable-length and nonlinear representations introduce considerably more complexity and will be treated separately in chapter 7. However, even in the fixed-length linear case, there are representation issues that need to be addressed, the most important of which is the choice between *genotypic* and *phenotypic* representations.

The classic example of a genotypic representation is the binary string representation used by canonical GAs. In this case the natural distance metric is Hamming distance, that is, the number of bit positions in which two individuals differ. Hence, the exploration level of a mutation operator that clones a parent and then randomly flips some bits to produce an offspring can be controlled directly by specifying the number of bits on average that are flipped. Similarly, the exploration level of a recombination operator can be controlled directly by specifying the number of subsegments (or equivalently in this case, the number of crossover points) to be used to produce an offspring. As discussed in the previous section, we can easily control the amount of genetic variation by tuning our reproductive operators.

However, there are cases where no amount of tuning appears to help. To see how this might happen, recall the way in which real-valued parameter spaces were mapped into binary strings in canonical GAs in section 5 of chapter 3). Each parameter interval (e.g., [-5.0,5.0]) was discretized into a uniform set of grid points, with each grid point assigned in left-to-right order the binary values of 00...000 to 11...111. In this case, although the most natural measure of variation at the genotype level is Hamming distance, the most natural measure of variation for real-valued parameter spaces is Euclidean distance.

It should be clear that small changes in Hamming distance can result in a wide range of change in Euclidean distance, depending on whether the low order or high order bits are being modified. Conversely, small changes in a parameter's value in Euclidean space can produce large changes in its bit string representation in Hamming space. The classic example of this is that of two adjacent real numbers in the center of a parameter interval, the first of which is represented internally by 0111...11 and the second by 1000...00, which are maximally distant in Hamming space.

It is this lack of correlation between variation at the genotype level and variation at the phenotype level that can cause problems. A well designed EA must maintain useful variation at both levels, and the particular choice made for mapping between the phenospace and the genospace can seriously affect the ability to do so. For example, a frequent alternative to the simple binary encoding of real-valued parameters is to use a Gray code that significantly increases the variation correlation (De Jong, 1975).

An alternative approach is to ignore the geno/phenospace distinction altogether and use an internal phenotypic representation. The advantage, of course, is that one can focus on achieving useful variation at just this one level. Good examples of this are the real-valued parameter problems we have been using as examples so far. The natural phenotypic representation is to represent each parameter internally as a real number and a set of parameters as a vector of real numbers. In this case, Gaussian mutation operators and/or crossover operators that swap one or more genes are natural reproductive operators that produce useful variation and the level of variation easily controlled as discussed above.

The disadvantage to phenotypic encodings is that our reproductive operators can now become problem-specific. Suppose, for example, we want to use an ES to solve traveling salesperson problems. The standard phenotypic representation involving vectors of real numbers and Gaussian mutation are useless for this problem class. Rather, a new representation and reproductive operators must be designed and, to achieve the same degree of design control as before, we must be able to analyze and tune the variation produced by the new operators.

4.4.5   Choosing Effective Reproductive Mechanisms

So far, in the discussion of reproductive operators, we have used the term "useful variation" in a fairly loose and intuitive sense. It can be made more precise by considering the fitness correlation between parents and offspring. Intuitively, one can not expect a reproductive operator to produce, on average, highly fit offspring from low-fitness parents. Conversely, we expect the offspring from highly fit parents to have, on average, high fitness as well. Of course a cloning operator produces a perfect (positive) fitness correlation, so correlation alone is not the goal. Hence, operators that produce useful variation are those that promote genotype/phenotype diversity while maintaining a high level of fitness correlation. Unfortunately, the ability of an operator to do so is a function of the particular fitness landscape being explored (Jones, 1995) and can even vary during the course of evolution.

The message for EA designers is clear. There is no *a priori* best representation and/or

EA	m	n	parent_sel	survival_sel	mutate	crossover	repres
EP	< 20	$n = m$	uniform	truncation	yes	no	pheno
ES	< 10	$n >= m$	uniform	truncation	yes	no	pheno
GA	> 20	$n = m$	fitness-prop	uniform	yes	yes	geno

Table 4.3: Characterization of traditional EAs.

reproductive operators. Rather, there are EA design goals that must be met: namely, achieving an appropriate exploration/exploitation balance and doing so using reproductive operators that exhibit good fitness correlation. This can be seen clearly by looking at the canonical EAs as illustrated in table 4.3. Each represents a well-tuned EA but is based on quite different sets of design choices.

4.5 Summary

So, now we have it: a unified view of simple EAs. A simple EA consists of the following basic elements:

- a parent population of size m,

- an offspring population of size n,

- a parent selection method,

- a survival selection method,

- a set of reproductive operators, and

- an internal method for representing individuals.

As we have seen in this chapter, there are many different ways these basic elements can be instantiated. By understanding the role each element plays in the overall behavior and performance of an EA, it is possible to make informed choices about how the elements should be instantiated for a particular application.

At the same time, it is clear that these components interact with each other so as to affect the behavior of simple EAs in complex, nonlinear ways. This means that no one particular choice for a basic element is likely to be universally optimal. Rather, an effective EA is one with a co-adapted set of components. The canonical EAs studied in chapter 3 are historically important examples of well-balanced EAs and are frequently used "as is" for various EA applications. However, as we will see in the next chapter, the wide range of potential EA applications pushes canonical EAs beyond their limits. We will see that adopting this unified view helps considerably in understanding such limitations and encourages the design of new and more effective EAs.

Chapter 5

Evolutionary Algorithms as Problem Solvers

In the previous chapters the focus has been on the properties of biologically motivated evolutionary algorithms (EAs) as dynamical systems, primarily concerned with how their trajectories over time and their convergence properties are affected by choices of population size, selection pressure, and so on. In this chapter the focus shifts to computer science and engineering issues relating to how EAs can be used to solve difficult computational problems. That does not mean that the biological and dynamical systems perspectives will be abandoned. Rather, as we will see, these perspectives will serve as a source of ideas for ways to build effective evolutionary computation systems.

5.1 Simple EAs as Parallel Adaptive Search

The EAs discussed so far are best described as simulation models of simple evolutionary systems. They were not specifically designed with any computer science or engineering applications in mind, or even with any notion of what it means to produce an answer. On the other hand, it does not take much imagination to interpret a simple EA as a parallel adaptive search procedure not unlike a swarm of ants exploring a landscape in search of food. Initial random individual movement gives way to more focused exploration, not as the result of some pre-planned group search procedure, but rather through dynamic reorganization as clues regarding food locations are encountered. Mathematically, one can view individuals in the population as representing sample points in a search space that provide clues about the location of regions of high fitness. The simulated evolutionary dynamics produce an adaptive, fitness-biased exploration of the search space. When the evolutionary process is terminated, the results of that search process (e.g., the best point found) can be viewed as the "answer" to be returned by an EA.

Viewing simple EAs as parallel adaptive search procedures immediately opens up a wide range of potential application areas in science and engineering. In order to obtain solutions to problems involving complex nonlinear component interactions, one is frequently faced with two choices: either to make simplifying linearity assumptions that permit analytical solutions, or to develop effective computational search procedures for finding solutions to the nonlinear systems.

In this context, simple EAs can be viewed as a problem-independent paradigm for designing effective search procedures. As such, in order to be applied to a particular problem, this abstract notion of an EA-based parallel adaptive search procedure must be instantiated by a series of key design decisions involving:

- deciding what an individual in the population represents,

- providing a means for computing the fitness of an individual,

- deciding how children (new search points) are generated from parents (current search points),

- specifying population sizes and dynamics,

- defining a termination criterion for stopping the evolutionary process, and

- returning an answer.

Appropriate choices for each of these design decisions is a function of both general, domain-independent issues and the specific properties of a particular application area. In this section the focus will be on the more general, domain-independent aspects of these design decisions. These issues will be revisited later in the chapter in the context of specific problem domains.

5.1.1 Representation

The first question I ask myself when considering using an EA to solve a problem is: what space do I want the EA to search? The simplest answer, of course, is to have the EA search *solution spaces*, i.e., to have individuals in the population represent potential solutions to the problem at hand, and to have the fitness of an individual defined in terms of the quality of the solution it represents or in terms of its proximity to a solution. So, for example, if we want to maximize the throughput of a manufacturing process, individuals in the population might represent the many alternative ways the manufacturing process could be configured, and the fitness of a particular configuration could be determined by estimating its throughput via a simulation of the manufacturing process.

There are, of course, other possible scenarios. The population as a whole could represent a solution. For example, each individual could represent a decision rule, and the population could represent the current set of rules being evaluated collectively for its decision-making effectiveness, as is the case with Holland's classifier systems (Holland, 1986). Alternatively, we might develop a hybrid system in which individuals in the population represent the initial conditions for a problem-specific local search procedure, such as the initial weights used by an artificial neural network backpropagation procedure.

For simplicity, the initial focus of this chapter will be on on EAs that search *solution spaces*, deferring until the later sections discussions about alternative scenarios. However, having committed to searching solution spaces still leaves open the question of how to represent that space internally in an EA. In most cases, problems can be represented in more than one way, some of which may be more amenable to evolutionary techniques than others.

As we saw in the previous chapter, there are two primary approaches one might take in choosing a representation: a phenotypic approach in which individuals represent solutions internally exactly as they are represented externally, and a genotypic approach in which individuals internally represent solutions encoded in a universal representation language. Both approaches have their advantages and disadvantages. A phenotypic approach generally allows for more exploitation of problem-specific properties, but at the expense of more EA software development time. A genotypic approach encourages rapid prototyping of new applications, but makes it more difficult to take advantage of domain knowledge. The choice of which approach to take depends strongly on the particular properties of the solution space to be searched.

5.1.1.1 Fixed-Length Linear Objects

The simplest and most natural internal representation for an EA involves individuals that consist of fixed-length vectors of genes. Hence, solution spaces that are defined as N-dimensional parameter spaces are the simplest and easiest to represent internally in an EA since solutions are described by fixed-length vectors of parameters, and simple internal representations are obtained by considering each parameter a "gene". In this case the only decision involves whether individual parameters are internally represented phenotypically (i.e., as is) or encoded genotypically (e.g., as binary strings). The advantages and disadvantages of both approaches are explored in more detail in the section on parameter optimization later in this chapter.

However, there are many problems whose solutions are not naturally expressed as linear, fixed-length parameter vectors. For example, one might want to solve job shop scheduling problems whose solutions can vary considerably in length, or one might want to evolve both the size and shape of an artificial neural network. How should one represent such objects internally in an EA?

5.1.1.2 Nonlinear Objects

Just as with linear objects, in considering how best to represent nonlinear objects, one can think in terms of either a phenotypic or genotypic representation.

A genotypic approach looks for ways to "linearize" nonlinear objects so that a standard internal representation can be used. So, for example, if the objects to be evolved are $M \times N$ matrices, they are easily linearized by just lining up the rows (or columns) end-to-end, resulting in an internal vector representation of length $M * N$. To complete the task, one must have effective reproductive operators as well. In this particular case, standard mutation operators can be used without modification. However, recombination operators like 1- and 2-point crossover generally yield disappointing results. To see why, recall that, intuitively, one wants recombination to exchange semantically meaningful subassemblies. In a connection matrix, a row represents all the connection weights leading out from a particular node, and a column represents all the connection weights leading into a particular node. Both are semantically important subunits, but linearizing fragments either one or the other. This can be alleviated to some extent by using parameterized uniform crossover which, as we saw in the previous chapter, does not have the representation bias that standard n-point crossover operators have.

Alternatively, one can adopt a phenotypic approach in which individuals in the population *are* $M \times N$ matrices, and concentrate on devising reproductive operators that modify matrices in interesting and useful ways. So, for example, mutation and crossover operators that manipulate entire rows or columns are natural candidates for matrix representations.

A similar but more complicated situation arises if solutions are naturally represented as graph structures, as is the case if we want to evolve trees, neural network structures, finite-state machines, molecular structures, and so on. In such cases the focus is on arriving at a solution of the appropriate size and shape. Genotypic approaches are possible here as well, in that there are standard techniques for linearizing graph structures. Having done so, however, the EA designer is confronted with a much more challenging task in constructing effective reproductive operators. Cutting, splicing and mutating linearized representations of graph structures with standard crossover and mutation operators is likely to result in inviable offspring, since most linearization processes discard significant amounts of syntactic and semantic information.

By contrast, a phenotypic approach would adopt a more natural internal representation such as a connection matrix or an adjacency list. Here again, the primary issue is designing reproduction operators that manipulate such representations effectively. For most graph structure representations, a mutation operator that adds and deletes links between nodes is fairly straightforward. However, the design of effective crossover operators requires more thought, since the most natural subassemblies to be swapped are subgraphs. So, for example, a crossover operator that swaps rows and/or columns of connection matrices is easy to implement, but corresponds to swapping all the links going into (or out of) a node, an operation that is in most cases semantically less useful than swapping subgraphs.

5.1.1.3   Variable-Length Objects

Solutions (objects) that can vary in length also require careful thought as to how best to represent them internally. Generally, objects that are viewed naturally as variable-length lists of items, such as sets of rules or action sequences, are the easiest to deal with. In this case the items in a list can be thought of as "genes" and fairly natural extensions of the standard crossover and mutation operators can be developed. In the case of mutation, in addition to modifying the value of genes, inserting new genes and/or deleting existing genes is often quite useful. Standard crossover operators can generally be used "as is" with the minor modification that the subsequences being exchanged can reside in different locations on the genome and may possibly be of different lengths.

One complication that will be discussed in more detail later in this chapter involves the "execution semantics" of these list structures, that is, how they are interpreted as a solution. If these list structures are "read" sequentially from, say, left to right, then the position and order of "genes" is semantically important. This means that even relatively small changes to the genome can result in arbitrarily large changes in an object's behavior and fitness. As a consequence, care must be taken to assure that reproductive operators have reasonable levels of "fitness correlation". By contrast, if the variable-length lists being evolved are interpreted as unordered sets of items, they are semantically much less "brittle" and it is easier to devise effective reproductive operators for them.

5.1.1.4 Nonlinear, Variable-Length Objects

Generally, the most difficult representation issues involve objects that are both nonlinear and of variable length. Suppose, for example, we want to evolve graph structures of varying sizes and shapes. As we saw earlier, adding and removing links between existing nodes is fairly straightforward for most graph representations. Now suppose we need to add and delete nodes as well. For connection matrix representations, deleting state i is achieved by removing the ith row and ith column, and relabeling and removing links as appropriate so as to obtain a consistent $n - 1$-dimensional connection matrix. Similarly, adding a state consists of appending a new row and column with some nonzero elements.

While this does not seem inordinately complex on the surface, the key difficulty is designing reproductive operators with good fitness correlation. As the complexity of the objects to be evolved increases, it becomes increasingly difficult to design reproductive operators that produce offspring that are valid structures, much less structures with high fitness.

One approach is not to worry about creating invalid structures and just allow competition to weed them out. This strategy works fine for structures that need to satisfy a relatively small number of constraints, but can be a serious problem for more tightly constrained structures, since almost all offspring are invalid and little progress, if any, is made toward finding more fit structures.

An alternative approach explored in chapter 7 introduces a process of morphogenesis. Taking its inspiration from nature, this approach focuses on genotypic representations that represent the *plans* for building complex phenotypic structures through a process of morphogenesis. The rationale here is that it is easier to represent and manipulate the plan for a complex object than the object itself. So, for example, the size and shape of an offspring is determined indirectly by inheriting the genes that are responsible for controlling their development during the growth process. Readers familiar with Dawkins' work will recognize that this is how his "biomorphs" were evolved (Dawkins, 1986).

5.1.2 Reproductive Operators

It was noted repeatedly in the previous section that closely tied to EA design decisions about representation are the choices made for reproductive operators. If our EA is searching solution spaces, we need reproductive operators that use the current population to generate interesting new solution candidates. With simple EAs we have two basic strategies for doing so: perturb an existing solution (mutation) and/or hybridize existing solutions (recombination). As we saw in the last chapter, there is no *a priori* reason to choose one or the other. In fact, these two reproductive strategies are quite complementary in nature, and an EA that uses both is generally more robust than an EA using either one alone.

However, the specific form that these reproductive operators take depends heavily on the choice made for representation. If, for example, we choose to evolve molecular structures using an internal graph structure representation, then we need to carefully consider how to perturb and recombine graph structures in useful and interesting ways. On the other hand, if we choose to map molecular structures into a universal string representation, then we need to think carefully about how to encode molecular structures in a way that our universal mutation and crossover operators produce interesting molecular variations. As we will see later in this chapter, both approaches have been used to build effective EA-based problem solvers.

At this level of abstraction, advice about choosing reproductive operators is a bit like the proverbial advice for making money in the stock market: buy low and sell high! The difficulty is always in figuring out how to apply this advice to specific situations. Fortunately, in the case of reproductive operators, EA theory provides some additional high-level guidance to help the practitioner. First, EA theory tells us that a smoothly running EA engine has reproductive operators that exhibit high fitness correlation between parents and offspring. That is, reproductive operators are not expected to work magic with low fitness parents, nor are they expected to produce (on average) poor quality offspring from high fitness parents. While fitness correlation does not give specific advice on how to construct a particular reproductive operator, it can be used to compare the effectiveness of candidate operators (see, for example, Manderick et al. (1991)).

Operators that achieve good fitness correlation are those that effectively manipulate semantically meaningful building blocks. This is why the choices of representation and operators are so closely coupled. If I want to evolve matrices effectively with an EA, I need to think about how to perturb them (mutate the building blocks) and how to swap subunits (recombine building blocks) in meaningful ways. Since matrices can represent many different kinds of problem solutions (weights of artificial neural networks, assignments for transportation problems, magic squares, etc.), the choice of representation and reproductive operators can potentially be different in each case.

Finally, in order for mutation and recombination operators to manipulate building blocks effectively, the building blocks must not in general be highly epistatic; that is, they must not interact too strongly with each other with respect to their effects on the viability of an individual and its fitness. So, for example, if improvements in fitness are obtained only by manipulating a set of five building blocks simultaneously, then reproductive operators that, with high probability, manipulate only a subset of these building blocks are not likely to be effective (i.e., exhibit good fitness correlation).

5.1.3   Objective Fitness Evaluation

Another advantage of having individuals in the population represent entire problem solutions is that it frequently simplifies the design of the objective fitness evaluation process. In many problem domains, there are fairly natural measures of solution quality that are easy to encode in a fitness function. So, for example, for shortest-path problems like traveling salesman problems, path length is a simple and natural measure of fitness. However, natural measures of fitness can also be bad choices for EA fitness functions. When trying to solve constraint satisfaction problems such as Boolean satisfiability problems, the natural measure is 1 (True) if all conditions are satisfied, and 0 (False) otherwise. If we adopt this as our fitness measure, we are asking our EA to solve a "needle in a haystack" problem in the sense that, while the search process is in progress, the current population of candidate solutions all have a fitness of zero, and thus provide no useful selection differential for biasing the search in promising directions. So, while having natural objective fitness measures is a desirable goal, the more important feature is that fitness must provide constructive feedback.

A related issue that comes up frequently is how best to handle situations in which the objective fitness can only be estimated and not calculated precisely. For example, the objective fitness evaluation process of checker-playing strategies may involve playing a certain number of games against a set of opponents. In general, playing more games will improve the estimate of the fitness of a particular strategy but can increase significantly the cost of evaluating the fitness of a single individual. Alternatively, one might reduce the number of games played per fitness evaluation in order to explore more of the strategy space for the same overall cost. How best to make this tradeoff is an open question in general. In practice we find that EA search is relatively insensitive to imprecise (noisy) objective fitness functions, allowing us to spend less time obtaining precise fitness measures and more time exploring the solution space.

Finally, note that these simple EAs assume that the fitness of a particular individual can be calculated independent of the other members of the current population. There are interesting alternative EAs for which this is not the case, which are described in more detail in chapter 7. For now, however, by choosing to search solution spaces, we simplify the objective fitness evaluation process in that many problem domains have a context-independent notion of the quality of a solution.

5.1.4 Population Sizes and Dynamics

As we saw in the last chapter, the size of the parent population sets an upper limit on the degree of parallelism of the evolutionary search process, in the sense that each parent represents an independent agent exploring a particular area of the solution space. Alternatively, one can conceptualize the population as a set of samples from which one can draw statistical inferences about the solution space. In either case, when attacking a particular problem with a simple EA, how does one choose a population of the appropriate size?

In general, the answer is problem-dependent. If the fitness landscape is a simple, convex surface, even parent populations of size 1 may suffice, such as the well-studied $(1 + 1)$-ES (Schwefel, 1995). However, as the surfaces become more complex with multiple peaks, discontinuities, etc., more parallelism is required, and, as we will see later in the chapter, population sizes can be as high as several thousand for very difficult problems. In practice, EA search is not highly sensitive to moderate changes in parent population size, so many EA-based systems default to a value in the 25–75 range.

Recall also from the last chapter that the size of the offspring population reflects the delay in the exploration feedback loop. After new points in the search space are generated and evaluated, a reallocation of resources occurs in the form of competition for survival. If the offspring population size is too large, resources will be wasted by continuing to produce offspring from soon-to-be-deleted low fitness parents. If the offspring population is too small, there is insufficient opportunity for high fitness parents to reproduce. How to set this balance to be most effective is in general an open question. In practice, EAs with small parent population sizes tend to have higher offspring:parent ratios and EAs with larger parent population sizes generally have lower offspring:parent ratios. So, for example, a typical ES might be $ES(10, 70)$, a 7:1 ratio, while a typical GA might be $GA(50, 50)$, a 1:1 ratio. Fortunately, EA-based search is not highly sensitive to the particular values chosen and is frequently performed with default values.

For many problem domains the cpu time required to solve a problem is dominated by the cost of evaluating the fitness of an individual. If computing the fitness of points in solution spaces is an independent process, then there is an obvious opportunity for using parallel computing hardware to speed up the overall search process via parallel fitness evaluation. In such cases population sizes are often adjusted to take advantage of particular hardware configurations.

Finally, as we saw in the last chapter, the selection mechanisms used in an EA determine the "greediness" of the search process: the willingness to focus on short term gains at the risk of incurring long term losses. Strong selection pressure results in rapid, but possibly premature, convergence. Weakening the selection pressure slows down the search process, not unlike the annealing schedule in simulated annealing, but increases the likelihood of finding global solutions. Finding the appropriate rate of convergence is problem-dependent and requires some experimentation in practice. If running an EA several times on the same problem produces substantially different answers each time, the selection pressure is too strong (premature convergence) and needs to be weakened. An EA with very slowly rising best-so-far curves suggests the selection pressure is too weak.

5.1.5   Convergence and Stopping Criteria

The terms convergence and stopping criteria have been used fairly loosely up to this point. In order to implement an effective problem-solving EA we need to be more precise. As we have seen in the preceding chapters, there are a number of EA properties that one can potentially use as indicators of convergence and stopping criteria. Ideally, of course, we want an EA to stop when it "finds the answer". For some classes of search problems (e.g., constraint satisfaction problems) it is easy to detect that an answer has been found. But for most problems (e.g., global optimization) there is no way of knowing for sure. Rather, the search process is terminated on the basis of other criteria (e.g., convergence of the algorithm) and the best solution encountered during the search process is returned as "the answer".

The most obvious way to detect convergence in an EA is recognizing when an EA has reached a fixed point in the sense that no further changes in the population will occur. The difficulty with this is that only the simplest EAs converge to a static fixed point in finite time. Almost every EA of sufficient complexity to be of use as a problem solver converges in the limit as the number of generations approaches infinity to a probability distribution over population states. To the observer, this appears as a sort of "punctuated equilibrium" in which, as evolution proceeds, an EA will appear to have converged and then exhibit a sudden improvement in fitness. So, in practice, we need to be able to detect when an EA has converged in the sense that a "law of diminishing returns" has set in.

As we saw earlier, from a dynamical systems point of view homogeneous populations are basins of attraction from which it is difficult for EAs to escape. Hence, one useful measure of convergence is the degree of homogeneity of the population. This provides direct evidence of how focused the EA search is at any particular time, and allows one to monitor over time an initially broad and diverse population that, under selection pressure, becomes increasingly more narrow and focused. By choosing an appropriate measure of population homogeneity (e.g., spatial dispersion, entropy, etc.) one typically observes a fairly rapid decrease in homogeneity and then a settling into a steady state as the slope of the homogeneity measure approaches zero.

A simpler, but often just as effective measure is to monitor the best-so-far objective fitness during an EA run. Best-so-far curves are typically the mirror image of homogeneity curves in that best-so-far curves rise rapidly and then flatten out. A "diminishing returns" signal can be triggered if little or no improvement in global objective fitness is observed for g generations (typically, 10–20).

Both of these measures (population homogeneity and global objective fitness improvements) are fairly robust, problem-independent measures of convergence. However, for problem domains that are computationally intensive (e.g., every fitness evaluation involves running a war game simulation), it may be the case that one cannot afford to wait until convergence is signaled. Instead, one is given a fixed computational budget (e.g., a maximum of 10,000 simulations) and runs an EA until convergence or until the computational budget is exceeded.

A natural and important question that one asks of any computational procedure is: what guarantee does one have regarding the properties of the solutions found? For example, if we design an EA-based global optimization procedure, will it find a global optimum? Will it find all of them? If there exists at least one feasible solution for a constraint-satisfaction problem, will an EA-based procedure find it? Will it find all feasible solutions?

Such questions can not be answered at this level of generality. They depend on the problem domain, on how solutions are represented and manipulated inside an EA, and on the termination criteria. What can be said is that most of the difficult computational search problems are known to be NP-hard, i.e., the only algorithms that can make strong global guarantees about solution properties require unacceptably high (non-polynomial) amounts of computational time. For such problems the focus is on heuristic procedures: ones that provide satisfactory answers in an acceptable amount of computer time.

5.1.6 Returning an Answer

A final benefit of having a simple EA search solution spaces is that the process of returning an answer is fairly straightforward: whenever the stopping criterion is met, the individual with the best objective fitness encountered during the evolutionary run is returned. Of course, there is nothing to prohibit one from returning the K most fit solutions encountered if that is perceived as desirable.

This raises the issue of how an EA "remembers" the most fit K individuals encountered during an entire evolutionary run. One solution is to use an EA with an elitist policy that guarantees that the best K individuals will never be deleted from the population. An example of this type of EA is the $(\mu + \lambda)$-ES discussed in chapter 3, in which parents and children compete with each other for survival and only the top μ survive into the next generation. In this case, when the termination criterion is met, the answer is simply read from the contents of the current population.

At the other end of the spectrum are "generational" EAs in which parents only survive for one generation. For such EAs the best solutions encountered over an entire run may not be members of the population at the time the stopping criterion is met, and so an additional "memo pad" is required to record the list of the top K solutions encountered.

Does it matter which of these two approaches one uses? In general, the answer is yes. The more elitist an EA is, the faster it converges, but at the increased risk of not finding the best solution. In computer science terms, increasing the degree of elitism increases the "greediness" of the algorithm. If we reduce the degree of elitism, we slow down the rate of convergence and increase the probability of finding the best solution. The difficulty, of course, is that if we slow down convergence too much, the answer returned when the stopping criterion is met may be worse than those obtained with more elitist EAs. As noted earlier, appropriate rates of convergence are quite problem-specific and often are determined experimentally.

5.1.7   Summary

In this section I have argued that a solid conceptual starting point for EA-based problem solving is to conceive of a simple EA as a heuristic search procedure that uses objective fitness feedback to explore complex solution spaces effectively. As we have seen, in order to instantiate this notion for a particular class of problems, a number of design decisions needs to be made, and the implications of these design decisions on the behavior of EA-based search procedures are quite well understood conceptually. However, in order for these procedures to be effective, these design decisions must also reflect the properties of the particular class of problems to which they are being applied. Historically, this has not been difficult to achieve and, as a result, an EA-based approach has been surprisingly effective in a wide range of problem areas. Some of the more common applications are described in the following sections.

5.2   EA-based Optimization

The application area that has unquestionably received the most attention is the area of optimization, and for good reasons. There is an incredible variety of optimization problems, both discrete and continuous, for which no analytic methods exist to solve them. Rather, considerable effort has been invested in computational procedures for producing (approximate) solutions. Furthermore, as we saw in the earlier chapters, EAs convey a strong sense of objective fitness optimization in that the fitness-biased selection procedures of EAs result in population sequences of increasing fitness and decreasing diversity. Hence, if the individuals in the population represent potential solutions to an optimization problem, and their fitness is directly related to the given optimality criterion, then we observe an EA-generated population sequence that leads to increasingly better solution candidates and terminates with a (possibly optimal) solution.

5.2.1   OPT-EAs

If we take our favorite EA and apply it as is to an optimization problem, generally the result is an optimization procedure that is passable, but nothing to get excited about. This situation can usually be improved by making a few simple changes to EAs in order to make them more robust and more effective as optimizers. To emphasize this I will refer to these modified EAs as OPT-EAs.

The simplest change is due to the fact that EAs maximize fitness while optimization problems can be expressed as either a minimization or a maximization problem. One approach for handling this is to require the user to state an optimization problem as a maximization problem. However, it is quite simple and more convenient for the user if this is handled internally. So, for maximization problems, one typically defines the internal OPT-EA fitness of individual x as $fitness(x) = optimality(x)$, and for minimization problems $fitness(x) = -optimality(x)$.

5.2.1.1 Fitness Scaling

This distinction between the internal OPT-EA fitness and the external optimality criterion is important for several reasons. First, it creates an abstract interface that allows a single OPT-EA procedure to be applied to a wide variety of optimization problems. At the same time, it provides an opportunity to manipulate internal fitness values in order to improve OPT-EA effectiveness. There are two particular cases that come up frequently enough to warrant further discussion.

The first case involves OPT-EAs that use fitness proportional selection procedures. Recall that fitness proportional selection procedures dynamically assign a selection probability at time t to each individual x in the current population via:

$$select\_prob(x, t) = fitness(x, t)/population\_fitness(t)$$

where $population\_fitness(t)$ is simply the sum of the fitnesses of all the individuals in the current population. Note that there is an unstated assumption that fitness values are non-negative since, of course, probabilities must lie in the range $[0, 1]$. Since most optimization problems make no such assumption, a standard method for handling this is to simply add a constant k to the internal fitness, which is sufficient to keep everything non-negative:

$$fitness(x, t) = optimality(x) + k$$

Since in general an appropriate value for k is not known *a priori*, a simple solution is to assign k the minimum optimality value in the current population. Hence,

$$fitness(x, t) = optimality(x) + pop\_min(t)$$

A potentially negative side effect of this approach is that, particularly for smaller population sizes, the internal fitness of the same individual can vary considerably from one generation to the next. A standard approach in this case is to "smooth" the process of assigning values to k by using the minimum value observed over the past g generations or possibly over all preceding generations.

A second case in which internal fitness values are frequently modified are situations in which one might want to change EA selection pressure without changing selection algorithms. For example, when using fitness-proportional selection, squaring the internal fitness will magnify fitness differentials and may improve the rate of convergence to a solution, but may also increase the likelihood of convergence to a suboptimal solution. Alternatively, as the population becomes more homogeneous, one might choose to re-scale the fitness values in the current population, in order to maintain sufficient selective differential between the best and the worst individuals in the population and sustain reasonable convergence rates (see, for example, Goldberg (1989)).

5.2.1.2 Convergence and Elitism

So far I have been talking about an OPT-EA converging to an answer without being very precise about what I mean by that. How does an OPT-EA know that it has found the answer to an optimization problem and can terminate? Unfortunately, unless an OPT-EA (or any other optimization procedure for that matter) has specific *a priori* information about an optimization problem, there is no way to know when a global optimum is found.

The alternative is to have one or more (generally user-specified) stopping criteria. As noted earlier in this chapter, the most natural stopping criteria involve monitoring the dynamics of the OPT-EA process and inferring that the law of diminishing returns has set in. A standard criterion of this type is to keep track of the best solution found so far. If that solution remains unchanged for g generations (typically, 10–20), then terminate and return the best solution found. For real-valued optimization problems, a slightly more robust criterion that is used frequently is to terminate if the best solution has changed less than ϵ in g generations.

As noted earlier, the homogeneity of the population is also a useful and general purpose indicator of convergence. From an optimization point of view, this means that an OPT-EA is tightly clustered around an optimum (either local or global) and if allowed to run longer, is not likely to discover another optimum somewhere else in the space.

It is also simple and straightforward to impose an *a priori* fixed stopping criterion such as setting a limit on the number of simulated generations. In general, however, it is difficult to choose appropriate limits unless one needs to set an upper bound on the running time of an OPT-EA for other reasons.

In any case, when a stopping criterion is met, the result returned is typically the best solution found during the entire run. As noted earlier in this chapter, an interesting and important question is: where does an OPT-EA accumulate this result during a run? A fairly standard approach is to adopt some sort of "elitist" policy that guarantees that the best individuals are never deleted from the population. Hence, the best individuals in the final population are also the best of the entire run.

Pure elitist OPT-EAs that delete only the worst individuals in the population have the pleasing property of fitness monotonicity (population fitness never decreases) and this in turn simplifies considerably the formal proofs of convergence and rates of convergence that are traditional in the optimization literature. However, from an algorithmic point of view, elitism is very closely related to the notion of hill climbing, which has both good and bad features. The primary advantage is rapid convergence to the top of the hill being climbed. The main disadvantage is a decrease in the probability that the global optimum will be found.

An alternate approach is to save the best solution observed so far in a location outside the population, thus removing the necessity for some form of an elitist policy. An OPT-EA of this sort has a quite different, non-monotonic behavior, namely one of exploring various peaks but allowing fitness to decrease temporarily in order to move on to other potentially more interesting peaks. As we have seen in the previous chapter, this is easily achieved by making survival selection probabilistic rather than deterministic. It can also be achieved in a more dramatic fashion by using non-overlapping-generation models, such as the canonical GA or the (μ, λ)-ES, in which individuals only live for one generation.

Non-elitist OPT-EAs are more likely to find the global optimum when there are multiple local optima, but at the price of slower rates of convergence. They are also much more difficult to analyze formally (see, for example, Schwefel (1995)).

5.2.1.3   Summary

In this section the focus has been on general ways in which EA search procedures can be specialized to serve as EA optimization procedures. To be effective, however, an OPT-EA must also take into account specific properties of the optimization problems to which they are being applied. The following sections focus on how that can be done for some of the more common classes of optimization.

5.2.2   Parameter Optimization

One of the most frequently encountered types of optimization problem is that of parameter optimization: finding one or more combinations of parameter values that optimize a given performance measure. Optimization problems of this type are generally formalized as a function optimization problem, i.e., given a function f of n arguments, $x_1...x_n$, find the values for $x_1...x_n$ that maximize (or minimize) f. Of course, if the function is available in closed form and is not too complex, the optimal values for $x_1...x_n$ can often be determined analytically. More often than not, this is not the case, and computational procedures are developed to find the desired optimal parameter settings.

Of all the various classes of optimization problems, parameter optimization is the easiest to attack using an EA-based approach. The reason for this should be obvious. Linear vectors of n parameter values map directly onto our intuitive notions of genes and chromosomes, and permit a very simple mapping between points in an n-dimensional vector space and individuals in the population. This gives us maximum leverage in terms of successfully using ideas from evolutionary systems to build a problem solver. As a consequence, this is one of the most pervasive and successful EA application areas (see, for example, Schwefel (1995)).

Exactly how one designs an EA-based parameter optimization technique depends on the particular type of parameter optimization problem being addressed. One important property is whether the parameter values are constrained in any way. If there are no constraints or if the only constraints are those specifying upper and/or lower bounds on the values of the parameters, then simple mappings between genes and parameters apply, and reproductive operators like mutation can be applied to genes independently of each other. Problems with more complex constraints require more complex EA techniques. For simplicity, we will assume the problems to be unconstrained or lightly constrained, and will address the more complex case later in this chapter.

What remains, then, is to consider how points in n-space are represented in an EA and which kinds of reproductive operators can be used to produce interesting new points in n-space. Recall that there are two basic approaches one might take: a phenotypic approach and a genotypic approach. We explore both approaches in some detail.

5.2.2.1   Phenotypic Representations and Operators

With a phenotypic approach, individuals in the population correspond directly to points in the solution space, which means that individuals are parameter vectors and the individual parameters themselves are the genes, the basic inheritable units. In this case, our standard notions of mutation and recombination are easily translated into mutation operators that perturb the values of inherited parameter values, and recombination operators that select the parameter values to be inherited from multiple parents.

For example, many function optimization problems are stated as real-valued parameter optimization problems. As we have seen in the previous chapters, stochastic mutation operators like the Gaussian mutation operator $G(0, s)$ are generally quite effective, in the sense that they capture an intuitive bias toward making small perturbations in parameter values. In addition, if necessary, the magnitude s of the perturbation is easily adapted to the varying scales and ranges of the values of individual parameters.

The simplest and most generic recombination operator for parameter vectors is the parameterized uniform crossover operator described in the previous chapter. In this case decisions about from which parent a child will inherit a parameter is made by flipping a coin, the bias of which is controlled by a parameter p that varies from 0.0 (all heads) to 0.5 (even chance for heads or tails).

5.2.2.2   Genotypic Representations and Operators

A genotypic approach involves encoding parameter vectors using some type of a universal code. For computer objects, a natural code to use is a binary code consisting of strings of 0s and 1s. In this case, if a parameter can take on V distinct values, then a string of $log_2(V)$ bits are sufficient to encode it. In order to encode real numbers, they must be discretized, and so one must additionally specify the degree of precision required (e.g., 10^{-6}). Having converted each of the individual parameters into a fixed-length binary encoding, the entire parameter vector can be represented by concatenating the individual parameter codes into one long string.

Having done that, the natural interpretation of a gene is a single bit (or, more generally, a single character) in the string encoding. As a consequence, mutation simplifies considerably to flipping bits (or, more generally, modifying coding characters). Parameterized uniform crossover can be implemented exactly as before but is now operating at a finer level of granularity.

The effect of choosing a (binary) genotypic representation is that the trajectory a population follows through parameter space is quite different from the trajectories produced using a phenotypic representation, and that can affect the solutions found. It is quite simple to see why this is the case. Consider first the effects of a single mutation. With a phenotypic representation, this results in a perturbation of a single parameter value which with high probability is a small perturbation. With a genotypic representation, this involves flipping one of the bits of an encoded parameter value. If a simple binary encoding is used, flipping a bit can produce either a small or a large perturbation depending on whether low-order or high-order bits are flipped.

Similarly, crossover at the binary gene level can result in the creation of new parameter values by combining some of the bits from one parent with bits from the other. At the phenotypic level this is not possible. Crossover selects among parameter values but does not create new ones.

5.2.2.3 Choosing Representations and Operators

Neither the phenotypic nor the genotypic approach can be declared to be better than the other with respect to representing parameter optimization problems. Each approach has its own strengths and weaknesses. Often the decision hinges on the specific properties of the parameter optimization problem to be solved. We explore this in more detail in the following sections.

5.2.2.4 Real-Valued Parameter Optimization

The most prevalent type of parameter optimization problem is that in which all the parameters are real-valued, as are the values returned by the fitness evaluation process. This type of problem is, of course, exactly what has been used as examples in the first four chapters of this book.

As has been noted on several earlier occasions, choosing a phenotypic representation allows one to exploit domain knowledge more readily. For real-valued function optimization problems, there are a variety of properties that are potentially exploitable. As we have seen in the preceding chapters, the Gaussian mutation operator $G(0, s)$ exploits the notion of continuity: small changes in parameter values producing small changes in fitness. Maintaining different step sizes s for different parameters allows one to deal with significant differences in parameter scales. *A priori* and/or dynamically acquired knowledge about parameter interactions can be used to target particular genes for coupled mutations. In addition to the standard notions of crossover, when dealing with real-valued genes, it is also possible to consider a blending version of recombination in which children inherit a linear combination of their parents' genes, rather than choosing among them (Schwefel, 1995).

In a similar manner, choosing a genotypic representation for real-valued parameter optimization problems also allows for exploitation of domain knowledge. A standard approach in this case is to use the binary string encoding technique described earlier, in which the values of each parameter are discretized and represented as fixed-length binary strings. In order to perform discretization, additional information concerning upper and lower bounds and resolution must be provided for each parameter. This constitutes a rather significant *a priori* bias in that the search space is now bounded and contains only a finite number of points.

One concern with a standard binary encoding of real-valued parameters is that it is not distance-preserving, i.e., small changes in a binary string (Hamming distance) can result in small or large changes in the real number it represents (Euclidean distance), and vice versa. This makes it difficult to design a mutation operator that simultaneously makes small changes in binary strings and in the real numbers they represent. As a consequence,

Gray code binary representations are often preferred because they have the property that adjacent discretized real numbers have binary representations that differ in only a single bit (Whitley, 2000).

Once the individual parameters have been discretized, the individual bit strings are generally concatenated together into a single seamless bit string to which the reproductive operators are applied. This makes it difficult to incorporate more traditional parameter-oriented heuristics into the reproductive operators, but at the same time provides an opportunity for interesting alternatives, such as making multiple mutations to a single parameter (e.g., flipping the second and the ninth bit), or using a crossover operator that creates new parameter values not by averaging the parental values, but by recombining the parental bit strings representing a parameter.

OPT-EAs that incorporate such features, whether they be of a phenotypic or genotypic nature, introduce a bias in the way in which the adaptive search takes place. This means that such EAs exhibit improved performance on problems that match their built-in biases, but at the expense of poorer performance on problems that do not match well. The key for the EA practitioner is to understand the implications of such biases and to design EA-based optimizers accordingly.

To get a better sense of how this all plays out in practice, we will look at several illustrative examples. Suppose we are confronted with a black box parameter optimization problem, i.e., a problem consisting of n real-valued inputs and one real-valued output and no additional information about this function, including any knowledge about continuity, the existence of derivatives, and so on. This is a classic situation in which an EA-based search procedure is a likely candidate for finding the optimum by adaptively searching the parameter space.

As a first example, suppose our black box optimization problem is a five-parameter problem BBF1. We might begin by trying a canonical ES procedure, say $ES(5, 25, 0.1)$, that uses a phenotypic representation, a Gaussian mutation operator, without crossover, and with a parent population of size 5 and an offspring population of size 25 (i.e., a 5:1 ratio). Recall that a canonical ES uses truncation selection, a very strong elitist policy, to reduce intermediate populations of $5 + 25$ back to 5 parents. Since we have so little information to go on, we arbitrarily set the stopping criteria to 5000 samples, and we specify the initial randomly generated parents to be in the 5-D cube bounded by $[-10.0, 10.0]$.

If we run this OPT-EA several times using different random number seeds on BBF1, we obtain best-so-far plots of the sort illustrated in figure 5.1.

We can immediately observe that our $OPT - ES(5, 25)$ is converging very consistently to a value of 50.0 after sampling about 1500 points in parameter space. Additional sampling after that produces nothing better. The only change from one run to the next is due to the variance in the randomly generated initial populations. If we also look at the answers produced, i.e., the best parameter values found during each run, we observe:

Run	Optimum	Parameter values				
1	50.000000	-0.00001	0.00042	-0.00058	-0.00000	0.00048
2	50.000000	-0.00012	0.00078	-0.00034	-0.00092	-0.00052
3	50.000000	0.00103	-0.00039	-0.00070	-0.00020	-0.00020
4	50.000000	0.00002	0.00016	-0.00024	0.00096	0.00050
5	49.999996	-0.00031	0.00144	0.00100	-0.00053	-0.00031

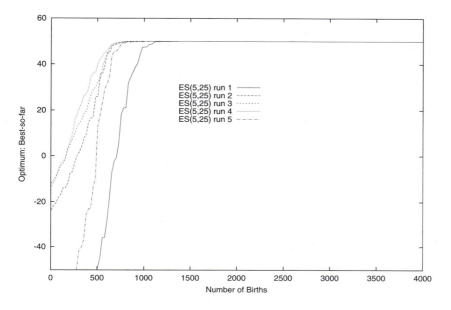

Figure 5.1: Individual runs of $OPT - ES(5, 25)$ on BBF1.

To see if the bounds for generating the initial set of randomly generated parents are biasing the results, we can try additional runs with different initial bounds. So, for example, on BBF1 if we set the bounds to $[1.0, 20.0]$, we obtain results such as

$$50.000000 \qquad -0.00045 \quad 0.00028 \ -0.00008 \quad 0.00022 \ -0.00069$$

which are quite similar to the earlier ones obtained.

Of course, this could be a local optimum since we have still biased the initial samples to be near the origin. So we might try a broader search by increasing the initial bounds to $[-100.0, 100.0]$ and increasing the parallelism by switching to a $(15 + 15)$-ES. Figure 5.2 plots the results of doing so.

In this particular case we observe nothing new. The only effect of increasing the initial bounds and the parallelism is the slowing down the rate of convergence. As a consequence it seems quite likely that BBF1 has an optimum centered at the origin surrounded by a large basin of attraction.

Suppose, by contrast, we decide to attack BBF1 using a genotypic approach. In this case, we need to provide additional information regarding how to discretize the space to be searched. So, for example, we might search the 5D cube bounded by $[-10.0, 10.0]$, discretized to a resolution of 10^{-5}. If we use a canonical binary string GA with a population size of 15, 2-point crossover, and bit-flip mutation, we observe the results presented in figure 5.3.

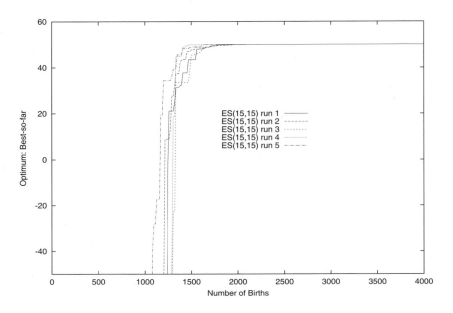

Figure 5.2: Individual runs of $OPT - ES(15, 15)$ on BBF1.

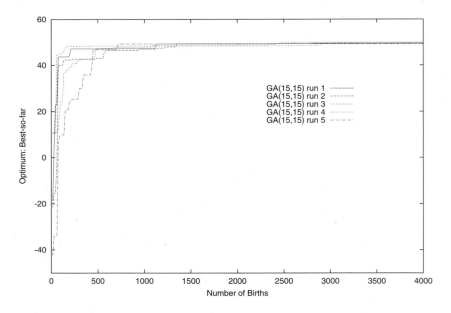

Figure 5.3: Individual runs of $OPT - GA(15, 15)$ on BBF1.

Notice how in this case the ability of the binary string crossover and mutation operators to produce larger exploratory jumps than the Gaussian mutation operator $G(0, 0.1)$, used with the phenotypic representation, resulted in faster initial convergence. On the other hand, the weaker fitness-proportional selection pressure of a canonical GA using non-overlapping generations slows down the rate of final convergence in comparison to the truncation selection used in a canonical ES. However, in general, the end results are the same. If we look at the answers returned, we see:

```
Run   Optimum     Parameter values
 1    49.439293   011111111111111101 100000110110010010 011110101000001011
                  100001100101101010 100000110010001111
 2    49.266201   011101111011011111 100000100010101011 011111110010111010
                  100000000000011100 100001101100110101
 3    49.474438   100000101100110110 100000100011110010 100001111001100011
                  011111000010111101 011111110000001000
 4    49.873871   011111110101000000 100000000001000000 100000000000001000
                  011110111001111111 011111101111101100
 5    49.200005   100001000110100100 100001100010111101 100001111001010101
                  011111111010110101 011111000000011110
```

To make sense of this, note that discretizing the interval $[-10.0, 10.0]$ with a resolution of 10^{-5} requires 18 bits, and that there are a total of 5 such strings, one for each parameter. Since the interval is symmetric about the origin and since a simple binary encoding is being used, as we approach the origin from the left (negative numbers), the encoded bit strings are of the form 01111..., and as we approach the origin from the right (positive numbers) the encoded bits strings have the form 10000.... As a result we see a large amount of genotypic diversity in the answers produced, but if we interpret them phenotypically, we see results similar to those produced when using a phenotypic representation:

```
Run   Optimum     Parameter values
 1    49.439293   -0.0002288   0.2650451  -0.4288482   0.4963684   0.2452850
 2    49.266201   -0.6470489   0.1692962  -0.0639343   0.0021362   0.5313873
 3    49.474438    0.2189636   0.1747131   0.5934906  -0.2980804  -0.0775146
 4    49.873871   -0.0537109   0.0048828   0.0006103  -0.3418731  -0.0796508
 5    49.200005    0.3445434   0.4831695   0.5924225  -0.0252532  -0.3102111
```

However, if we now change the parameter bounds to $[1.0, 20.0]$ as we did before, we get quite different results:

```
                  (genotype)
43.866692   000000110000011111 000000001000100011 000000010100011000
            000000010011010010 000000010001010101
```

```
                  (phenotype)
43.866692   1.2249031   1.0396461   1.0945129   1.0894394   1.0803795
```

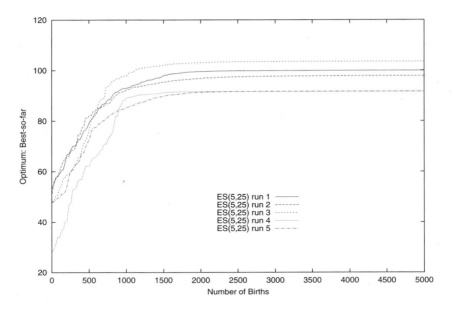

Figure 5.4: Individual runs of $ES(5,25)$ on BBF2.

This is, of course, due to the fact that, for the simple, fixed-length genotypic encoding technique being used, these bounds represent global constraints on the search, not just constraints on the initially generated individuals. Depending on the context, this can be viewed as good news or bad news. The advantage of the phenotypic approach is that an OPT-EA can often overcome poorly chosen user-specified initial bounds on the parameters. The advantage to the genotypic approach is that naturally occurring parameter bounds are automatically incorporated into an OPT-EA without the need for additional code to check for constraint violations.

To illustrate these and other issues further, consider another situation in which we are confronted with a similar 5-parameter black box optimization problem, BBF2. But in this case, the problem domain itself restricts the parameter settings to $[-4.0, 5.0]$. If we adopt a phenotypic approach, we now have to decide how to detect and handle the situation in which mutation produces a parameter setting outside of these bounds. One approach is to modify mutation to produce only legal values. An alternate approach is to assign very low fitness to such individuals. How best to deal with this is a complex question that is addressed in more detail in the section on constrained optimization. For now we adopt the simplest approach, namely, any attempt by mutation to produce values that violate the constraints is treated as a failed mutation attempt and the gene value remains unchanged.

Having incorporated this notion of "hard" boundaries into our OPT-ES and applying our $OPT - ES(5,25)$ as before with initial bounds of $[-4.0, 5.0]$, we observe the results presented in figure 5.4.

Notice how the individual runs of $OPT - ES(5,25)$ on BBF2 exhibit considerably more

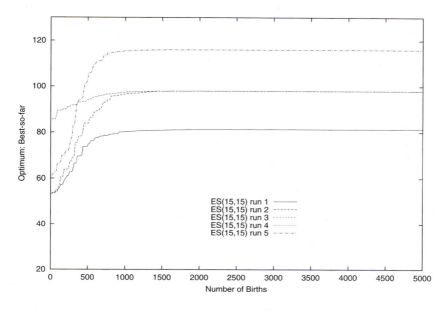

Figure 5.5: Individual runs of $ES(15, 15)$ on BBF2.

variance than on BBF1. This is an indication of a more complex function with multiple optima. This becomes immediately clear if we look at the answers produced by the individual runs:

Run	Optimum	Parameter values				
1	99.909042	5.00000	4.23191	-4.00000	-4.00000	5.00000
2	97.835976	-0.53776	4.74837	4.99999	5.00000	4.99999
3	103.496666	-4.00000	5.00000	5.00000	5.00000	-3.53506
4	91.677269	-4.00000	5.00000	5.00000	5.00000	-0.82296
5	91.721130	3.11787	-4.00000	-4.00000	5.00000	5.00000

Changing bounds does not make much sense since they are a fixed part of the problem definition, and running the OPT-EA for a longer time period seems fruitless since each individual run appears to converge in less than 2000 evaluations. What does make sense in this case is an increase in the amount of parallelism. So, for example, switching to $OPT - ES(15, 15)$ results in the discovery of a new peak

Optimum	Parameter values				
116.000000	5.00000	5.00000	5.00000	5.00000	-4.00000

as illustrated in figure 5.5.

At the same time, we continue to observe considerable variance from run to run even with $OPT - ES(15, 15)$. This suggests that the selection pressure is too strong for this

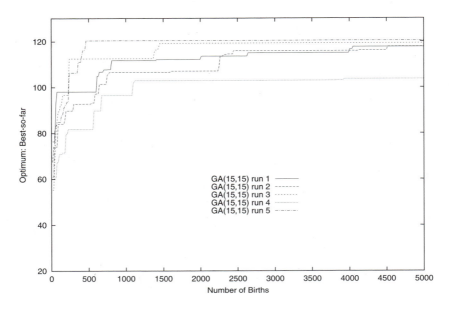

Figure 5.6: Individual runs of $GA(15, 15)$ on BBF2.

multi-peaked function, resulting in convergence to different local optima on each run. Suppose, instead, we had adopted a genotypic approach as we did on BBF1 by using an $OPT - GA(15, 15)$ with much weaker selection pressure. In this case, the bounds of $[-4.0, 5.0]$ are automatically incorporated into the binary string representation, so no additional constraint checking is required. Using the same discretization factor as before, we run $OPT - GA(15, 15)$ on BBF2 multiple times and obtain the results illustrated in figure 5.6.

As we saw before, the weaker selection pressure of a canonical GA slows down the rate of convergence. On BBF2 this is an advantage in that it reduces the likelihood of converging to a local optimum. This improvement is also reflected in the answers returned:

```
Run    Optimum      Parameter values
  1    117.644371   4.933189   4.885811   4.949737   4.921036   4.551964
  2    117.720505   4.649811   4.980430   4.73777    4.995193   4.88842
  3    119.249512   4.970337   4.953994   4.765716   4.862465   4.862877
  4    103.575897  -3.991142   4.892746   4.897964  -3.846809   4.991966
  5    120.415413   4.907509   4.982902   4.973701   4.674598   4.991279
```

including a new optimum found near $< 5.0, 5.0, 5.0, 5.0, 5.0 >$.

Of course, there are many other things one could try. The canonical ES and GA algorithms used in these examples were chosen to illustrate the effects that different design choices can have on the performance of OPT-EAs. The benefit of a unified view is that it provides an informed framework for designing OPT-EAs to match the characteristics of a particular application better. Rather than choosing among a small set of historically developed EAs, the OPT-EA designer thinks in terms of a parameterized family of algorithms that can be effectively tuned by making adjustments to parameters such as:

- parent population size

- offspring population size

- parent selection pressure

- survival selection pressure

- representation

- reproductive operators

For example, one can generally obtain improvements in an OPT-ES on problems like BBF2 by switching to non-overlapping generations and/or adopting a weaker form of survival selection such as linear ranking. Similarly, one can frequently obtain OPT-GA improvements by introducing some degree of generational overlap and/or a stronger form of parental selection pressure such as linear ranking.

Having a tunable optimization procedure can also be viewed as a disadvantage in that considerable time might have to be spent finding the right parameter settings for our OPT-EA, a parameter optimization problem in its own right! Fortunately, the situation is not as bad as it sounds. Most OPT-EAs have a fairly large "sweet spot" for their parameter settings, in the sense that robust and effective performance is obtained with "in the ballpark" parameter settings, and come with appropriately chosen defaults. In addition, as we will see in chapter 7, progress continues to be made on developing EAs that are capable of self-adapting their parameters.

5.2.2.5   Integer-Valued Parameter Optimization

Less frequently encountered, but equally difficult, are parameter optimization problems in which the parameters are integer-valued. One strategy for solving such problems that immediately comes to mind is to consider them as a special case of real-valued problems. This can be done in several ways, the simplest of which is to embed the discrete integer solution space in a real-valued solution space and treat it as a real-valued parameter optimization problem. In order for this to work, the function to be optimized must be extendable, in some reasonably natural way, to the larger real-valued solution space. Having done so, the optima found using a real-valued optimization technique are likely to be associated with non-integral parameter values. Hence, an additional procedure is required to find the nearest integer-valued solutions.

Such strategies are often possible if the function is available in closed form, but do not make much sense when the function is defined implicitly (e.g., via a simulation) and only integer arguments make sense (e.g., the number of crew members assigned to a plane). In such cases one needs an effective way to search integer-valued solution spaces directly. Adapting techniques that were designed to search real-valued spaces is often difficult since they frequently take advantage of notions of continuity and derivative information. By contrast, it is not difficult to adapt a real-valued OPT-EA to handle integer-valued problems.

In the case of phenotypic representations, the most obvious change required is replacing the mutation operator $G(0, s)$ with one that perturbs parameters in integer step sizes. A simple and effective approach is simply to discretize $G(0, s)$ by rounding up to the nearest integer value. Alternatively, one can choose familiar discrete distributions (e.g., multinomial) that have similar properties of favoring small perturbations. Discrete recombination operators are indifferent to the data type of the parameters and thus require no modification. Discretized versions of blending crossover operators that average parental parameter values can also be used but are generally less effective in this form.

In the case of genotypic representations, no significant changes are required to handle integer-valued parameters. Recall that real-valued parameters needed to be discretized in order to produce a binary string representation. For integer-valued problems, this step is not necessary, since the parameter values are already discrete. Everything else is identical to the real-valued case.

As an illustration of all this, consider how we might use an OPT-EA to solve N-MATCH problems, which are often used in the literature as simple examples of discrete optimization problems. N-MATCH problems are a family of functions having N discrete-valued arguments. For integer-valued versions of N-MATCH, the arguments typically take on a range of integer values, such as from 0 to K. The objective fitness function is defined by picking a target point in the space, such as the point $< 4, 4, ..., 4 >$, and the function value of every point in the space is defined in terms of how closely it matches the (unknown) target point. For integer-valued N-MATCH problems, a natural measure of closeness of match is simply Euclidean distance.

It is quite straightforward to solve such problems with an OPT-EA in a variety of ways. One possibility is to use a phenotypic encoding, in which each gene is an integer, together with a simple delta or Gaussian mutation operator that adds/subtracts integer values and respects the $[0, K]$ parameter bounds. Alternatively, one might choose a standard binary genotypic encoding with a bit-flip mutation operator. In either case the standard crossover operators can be used without modification. For simplicity we express the problem as a maximization problem, i.e.,

$$fitness(x) = -Euclidean\_distance(x, target)$$

so that points away from the target have negative fitness and a perfect match has a fitness of 0.0. Figure 5.7 illustrates the results of several simulation runs on a 10-parameter N-MATCH problem with parameter bounds of $[0, 31]$ and an (unknown) target of $< 4, 4, ..., 4 >$.

In this particular case, the simulation runs used a generational GA with a population size of 50 and parameterized uniform crossover operating at a 0.2 rate. The only difference in the runs was the choice of representation and the mutation operator. On these particular runs, the integer representation produced better results initially, but stagnated toward the end, while the binary representation resulted in slower but steady progress to the target value.

In general, just as in the real-valued parameter optimization case discussed earlier, the choice of a particular EA representation (whether phenotypic or genotypic) and reproductive

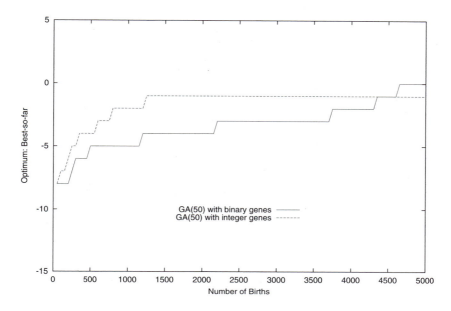

Figure 5.7: Individual runs of $GA(50)$ on N-MATCH(10,0,31) using binary and integer encodings.

operators introduces a bias into the search procedure that may match up well with some integer-valued parameter optimization problems and not with others. As we will see in the next chapter, EA theory provides us with some guidance and intuition about matching EAs and problems. However, the current state of the theory is weak in terms of making strong predictions relating search biases and problem characteristics. As a consequence, in practice, good matches are obtained by "getting in the ballpark" via theory and then fine tuning an OPT-EA experimentally.

Many integer-valued parameter optimization problems involve more complex constraints than just the bounds on parameter values. In general, choices for a particular parameter value can restrict the choices for other parameter values in complex, nonlinear ways. A discussion on how to handle such constraints is provided in the section on constrained optimization later in this chapter.

5.2.2.6 Symbolic Parameter Optimization

Both the real-valued and integer-valued parameter optimization problems have the property that the values that parameters can take on have a natural linear ordering, so it makes sense to talk about increasing or decreasing the value of a parameter. However, there are many situations in which the parameter values have no natural order, such as a Boolean-valued parameter (true or false) or choices of automobile color (red, white, etc.). Clearly, one can adopt a strategy of mapping unordered parameter value sets onto a set of integers and

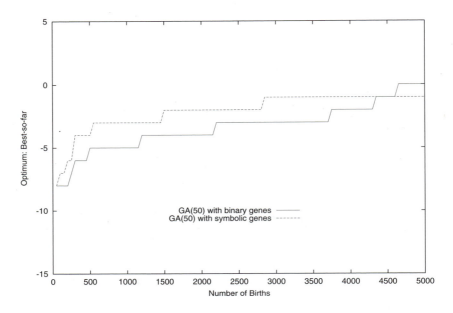

Figure 5.8: Individual runs of $GA(50)$ on N-MATCH(10,0,31) using binary and symbolic encodings.

treating it as if it were an integer-valued parameter optimization problem. The effectiveness of this approach, however, can vary significantly from problem to problem.

The alternative is to represent and manipulate unordered parameter values directly. In the case of OPT-EAs this is a simple and straightforward process. If we are using a phenotypic representation, the Gaussian and delta mutation operators need to be replaced by a mutation operator that selects a new parameter value randomly using a uniform probability distribution defined over the set of legal parameter values. All other aspects of the OPT-EA are unaffected.

In the case of a genotypic representation, nothing needs to be changed. The parameter values are already discrete and can be mapped directly into internal coded strings. Figure 5.8 illustrates this on the same 10-parameter N-MATCH problem as before, except that the closeness of points to the target is calculated simply as the number of mismatched symbols, since Euclidean distance measure can no longer be used.

Not surprisingly the results look quite similar to the integer parameter example shown in figure 5.7. This is a clear illustration of the robustness of an OPT-EA approach. With relatively few changes, an OPT-EA designed for solving integer optimization problems can be adapted to one capable of solving symbolic optimization problems. We will see more examples of this important property in the remainder of this chapter.

5.2.2.7   Non-homogeneous Parameter Optimization

Perhaps one of the biggest OPT-EA parameter optimization payoff areas is the situation frequently encountered in practice, in which the parameters of an optimization problem have non-homogeneous data types. For example, suppose I am interested in tuning the parameters of a complex engineering design or a military wargame simulation. In such cases it is most likely that the parameters will be a mixture of real numbers (e.g., beam thickness), integers (e.g., number of floors), and nominal parameters (e.g., facade type). Generally, mathematical optimization techniques require one to "embed" such problems into a real-valued space by converting everything to real numbers, which can lead to messy issues relating to continuity and derivative calculations involving the pseudo-real-valued parameters.

By contrast, it is relatively easy to modify an OPT-EA to handle non-homogeneous parameters. In the case of genotypic representations, nothing new is required except an indication of the data type of each parameter, since the mapping between internal (binary) strings and external parameter values is now dependent on the data type of each parameter. Once converted, all of the standard reproduction operators can be used.

If the internal representation is phenotypic, the standard crossover operations can still be used as is. However, mutation must now be generalized to handle different parameter data types. But, as we have seen in the previous sections, there are simple mutation operators for each of the three data types. So, for non-homogeneous problems, the parameter data type determines which mutation operator to use.

5.2.3   Constrained Optimization

So far, there has been a tacit assumption that, while solving a parameter optimization problem, the values of individual parameters can be changed independently of one another. In practice, however, there are frequently complex, nonlinear interdependencies between parameters that constrain the search space and must be dealt with in one form or another by any parameter optimizer, EA-based or otherwise.

One standard approach to handling constraints is to embed the constrained space in an unconstrained space and augment the objective function with a "penalty function" for points outside the constrained space. As a simple example, suppose that the solution space to be searched is a two-dimensional unit circle centered at the origin. This means that in order to stay within the boundary of the unit circle, both parameters must simultaneously satisfy $x_1{}^2 + x_2{}^2 <= 1$ and hence cannot be changed independently of each other. However, if we embed the unit circle in the unit square and extend the objective function to the boundaries of the rectangle via a penalty function, we can now use our favorite unconstrained parameter optimization technique.

The effectiveness of this approach depends a great deal on the form of the penalty function used and the ratio of the size of the constrained space to that of the unconstrained space. For example, a simply implemented penalty function assigns the worst objective function value possible (e.g., negative infinity) to all points outside the constrained space. If we do that for the two dimensional circle/square problem, things work reasonably well. However, as we increase the dimensionality of the problem, the ratio of the volume of the hyper-sphere to that of the corresponding hyper-cube approaches zero. Hence, a randomly generated initial population is unlikely to contain any points in the constrained space and the flat penalty function provides no information about where the constrained subspace is located.

One obvious alternative is to replace a flat penalty function with one that provides directional information. So, for example, we might define a penalty function whose penalty gets worse the farther a point is from a constraint boundary, thus providing a "gradient" for a search procedure to follow. This approach can be quite effective for problems in which the constraints are not too complex. However, as the complexity of the constraints increases, so does the difficulty of constructing a penalty function with the desired properties.

With OPT-EAs, a frequently used alternative is to modify the reproductive operators to "respect" the constraints. Operators like mutation and crossover are defined so that infeasible points are never generated so that only the constrained space is searched. This works quite well when the constrained space is convex and connected. However, for non-convex and/or disconnected spaces it is often more effective to allow infeasible points to be generated so as to be able to take advantage of "shortcuts" through infeasible regions to higher fitness feasible regions.

An elegant, but often difficult to achieve, approach is to construct a one-to-one transformation of the constrained space onto an unconstrained one. For the unit circle problem introduced earlier, the alert reader will, of course, have noted that one can easily convert this particular constrained optimization problem into an unconstrained one simply by switching to polar coordinates. For more complex constraints, finding such a transformation is a much more difficult task.

Since there is a large and readily available body of literature on the various ways EAs can be adapted to solve constrained parameter optimization problems (see, for example, Michalewicz and Schoenauer (1996)), we will not restate the many detailed results here. Rather, we end this section with an example from the field of discrete (combinatorial) optimization that involves searching permutation spaces, and use it to reemphasize the basic strategies for solving constrained optimization problems with EAs.

The classic example of this type of problem is the Traveling Salesperson Problem (TSP), in which N cities are to be visited exactly once, but the order in which they are to be visited is discretional. The goal is to identify a particular order that minimizes the total cost of the tour.

It is fairly easy to conceive of this as a constrained N-dimensional symbolic parameter optimization problem in which parameter 1 corresponds to the first city visited, parameter 2 the second city, and so on, with the constraint that once a city has been assigned to a parameter it cannot be used again. So, for example, allowable tours for a 7-city problem can be represented as:

```
Tour 1:    A B C D E F G
Tour 2:    B A C D E F G
Tour 3:    E F G A B C D
```

The cost of a tour is calculated using an (N+1) by (N+1) cost matrix c specifying the cost of traveling from city i to city j, including the home city of the salesperson. So, for example, the cost of Tour 1 above is given by $c(home, A)+c(A, B)+c(B, C)+...+c(F, G)+c(G, home)$.

One can easily map permutation spaces into an unconstrained parameter space by embedding them in the space of all combinations of N cities with the aid of a penalty function for tours that visit a city more than once and exclude others. So, for example, strings like AACDEFF and BBBBBBB are legal combinations of city names, but are not legal tours. The difficulty with this approach is that, as the number of cities N increases, the ratio of legal tours to illegal ones rapidly approaches zero and search efficiency drops off accordingly.

A plausible alternative is to modify the reproductive operators so that only legal tours are created. For TSP problems, this is a bit of a challenge. A useful way to proceed is to think of mutation as a perturbation operator and recombination as a mechanism for swapping subassemblies. From this perspective the simplest perturbation is to swap the order of two adjacent cities. More aggressive mutations might involve inverting the order of longer segments such as:

```
Parent:  A B C D E F G     ==>   Child:  A B E D C F G
           |_____|                          |_____|
```

or swapping the positions of non-adjacent cities.

For recombination, the obvious subassembly to be exchanged is a subtour, i.e., a subset of adjacent cities:

```
Parent 1:  A B C D E F G        Child 1:  A B E D C F G
             |_____|                         |_____|
                             ==>
Parent 2:  E D C A B F G        Child 2:  C D E A B F G
             |_____|                         |_____|
```

With reproductive operators like this we now produce legal offspring. What remains is to verify that these operators provide useful variations, i.e., that the offspring inherit useful subassemblies from their parents. Formal methods for assessing this will be presented in the next chapter. For now, an intuitive notion is that good reproductive operators induce a correlation in fitness between parents and offspring. For these particular operators, the correlation is not ideal and has lead to considerable exploration of other operators and representations (see, for example, Whitley (1989b) or Manderick et al. (1991)).

It turns out that there are also one-to-one mappings between permutation spaces and binary string spaces (De Jong, 1985). This means that a genotypic approach to solving TSP problems is also possible, and has the distinct advantage that no new operators need to be invented. Unfortunately, the known mappings are not distance preserving, so that small changes in string space can result in large changes in permutation space and vice versa. As a consequence, genotypic representations based on this mapping have only met with moderate success.

5.2.4   Data Structure Optimization

So far in this chapter we have been focusing on the "easy" case, in which optimization problems are naturally represented as fixed-length parameter optimization problems which, as we have seen, can be mapped quite naturally onto one of the standard EAs. However, there are many important optimization problems in which solutions are most naturally represented as matrices, trees, sets, etc.. In some cases there is a fairly natural way to "linearize" a given class of data structures, e.g., linearizing matrices by row or by column. In such cases the parameter optimization EAs discussed earlier in this chapter can be applied directly, but with caution, since linearization procedures in general result in the loss of higher-dimensional spatial relationships represented in the original structures. For example, linearizing the weight matrix of an artificial neural network by rows preserves horizontal node proximity information at the expense of vertical proximity, while linearizing by columns has the reverse effect. Whether this is important or not for EA-based optimization depends directly on whether the standard reproductive operators like crossover and mutation can be effective (i.e., good fitness correlation) in the absence of this higher-level information.

The alternative is to adopt a more phenotypic representation in which the members of the population are simply the data structures themselves (e.g., matrices). However, this can require significant additional effort in developing new and effective reproductive operators for these nonlinear structures, and are in general quite problem specific.

As as example, consider the general problem of representing graph structures and evolving them over time. The simplest problems of this type involve a fixed number of nodes N, and the goal is to find a set of connections (arcs) that optimize a (typically unknown) objective function. A simple and straightforward approach is to search the space of all possible $N \times N$ connection matrices C in which $C(i, j)$ is a 1 if there is a connection from city i to city j, and a 0 if not.

The next step is to decide how to represent C internally in our EA and which reproductive operators should be used to create new and interesting offspring Cs from existing parent Cs. The first thought that immediately comes to mind is to linearize Cs (either by row or by column) into a bit string of length N^2, and then use a standard GA involving standard crossover and mutation operators. The issue at hand, of course, is whether this is a good idea and, if so, is there any difference between linearizing by row vs. by column?

Figure 5.9 gives an illustration of how this plays out in practice by comparing the performance of two nearly identical GAs on a "black box" graph structure problem. graph structures The only difference is that GA-row linearizes C by rows and GA-col linearizes C by column. Notice the negative effect that column linearization has on performance. This is due to the fact that the graph structure problem was deliberately designed to have an (unknown) row bias in which the optimal C is given by:

$$111111\ldots$$
$$000000\ldots$$
$$111111\ldots$$
$$000000\ldots$$
$$\ldots\ldots$$

So, by choosing a row linearization we (unknowingly) improve the effectiveness of the stan-

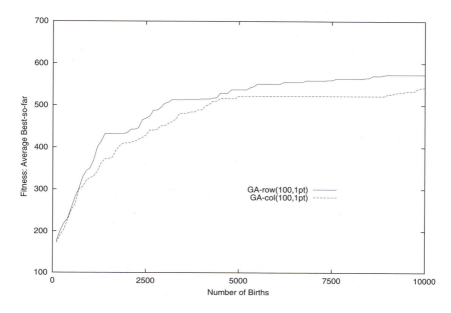

Figure 5.9: Average performance of GA-row and GA-col on a black box graph structure problem using 1-point crossover.

dard 1-point crossover operator, while choosing a column linearization has the opposite effect.

In cases such as this, where *a priori* information about such biases is not available, one can often reduce the effects of potential bias mismatches by using parameterized uniform crossover (Spears and De Jong, 1991) rather than the more traditional 1-point or 2-point operators. Figure 5.10 illustrates this by rerunning GA-row and GA-col on the same graph problem using parameterized uniform crossover (0.2). Notice how the observed performance is mostly independent of the choice of row/column representation and, in this particular case, the use of parameterized uniform crossover also resulted in better overall performance than was observed with 1-point crossover.

Clearly, any algorithm should perform better if it is able to take advantage of additional problem-specific knowledge. For the graph problem at hand, *a priori* knowledge about the row bias would allow us not only to pick GA-row, but also modify the crossover operator to encourage row swapping. Of course, it is quite possible for problems to have multiple biases (e.g., both rows and columns). In such cases it is usually impossible to find a linearization that is simultaneously matched to each bias. Rather, an EA is more likely to be effective by adopting a phenotypic representation (e.g., matrices) and specialized operators designed to exploit the known biases (e.g., swap rows, swap columns, etc.).

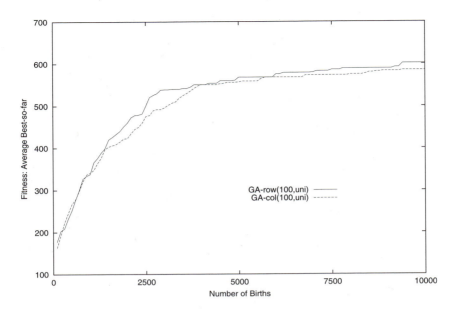

Figure 5.10: Average performance of GA-row and GA-col on a black box graph structure problem using parameterized uniform crossover.

5.2.4.1   Variable-Length Data Structures

Additional thought is required to decide how best to apply EA-based techniques to problems in which solutions are naturally represented as variable-length data structures. Classic examples are job shop scheduling problems, path planning, and set covering problems. The key, of course, is to focus on the design of effective reproductive operators. In particular, standard reproductive operators are length-preserving, resulting in no additional length variability beyond that found in the initial population. Typical extensions involve insert/delete operators, and crossover operators that swap variable-length segments. The form such operators take tends to be quite problem specific (see, for example, Reeves and Yamada (1998) or Bierwirth and Mattfeld (1998)).

As an example, consider the graph structure problem discussed in the previous section. For many such problems, the optimal connection matrix C is quite sparse. In such cases, switching to an adjacency list representation results in a much more compact but variable-length representation. The positive effect of this change is an EA representation that better reflects the problem bias. The difficulty is that it is hard to linearize adjacency list representations in such a way that the more traditional reproductive operators are effective. Rather, a phenotypic representation is more likely to be effective in conjunction with specialized reproductive operators that insert/delete items from adjacency lists, swap entire adjacency lists, etc.

5.2.5 Multi-objective Optimization

So far in this chapter, the focus has been on optimizing a single objective function. However, most real-world engineering problems involve attempting to simultaneously optimize multiple objectives (such as good gas mileage and acceleration capabilities). A standard technique for handling such problems is to convert them to a single objective problem: optimize $F(x) = w_1 F_1(x) + w_2 F_2(x) + \ldots + w_n F_n(x)$.

This, of course, requires that someone choose the weights to properly reflect the relative importance of the individual objective functions. The clear advantage to doing this is that the standard EA-based optimization techniques discussed earlier in this chapter can be applied directly.

The more challenging case is when such weights are difficult or impossible to obtain. In such cases, rather than "guesstimate" the unknown weights, a preferred approach is to provide the engineerer with a set of "tradeoff" solutions, from which particular solutions can be selected based on other external factors. Problems of this sort have been studied extensively under the label "Pareto Optimality", in which the tradeoff solutions of interest are the "non-dominated" solutions, i.e., solutions for which any attempt to improve their optimality with respect to one or more objectives results in a decrease in optimality with respect to one or more other objectives.

For simple sets of objectives, this set of non-dominated solutions is a surface, the details of which can be derived analytically. In general, however, such problems are analytically intractable, and require computational techniques to solve them. If EA-based techniques are to be used, then there are two related issues to be addressed: 1) how does an EA find a single non-dominated solution, and 2) how does an EA find a useful set of non-dominated solutions?

The EC community has been quite active in attempting to answer these questions, resulting in a large number of publications in this area (see, for example, Fonseca and Fleming (1995), Deb (1999), or Zitzler et al. (2000)). The interested reader is encouraged to explore this extensive literature in more detail. For our purposes, I will summarize a few of the main techniques.

Since individuals in the population are now associated with vectors of objective values produced by the set of objective functions, the first thing that needs to be addressed in designing a "Pareto EA" is an appropriate definition of fitness. Since the goal is to find non-dominated solutions, an intuitively appealing approach is to define the fitness of individuals in terms of the number of individuals they dominate. However, since this cannot in general be determined analytically, such assessments must be based on observations made during the evolutionary process. One of the earliest approaches developed was to estimate dominance-based fitness using the current contents of the population (Goldberg, 1989) by ranking individuals based on how many population members they dominate. This is quite similar to the competitive fitness techniques used to co-evolve entities (e.g., game playing programs) for which there is no readily available explicit measure of fitness. The problem is that such relativistic measures of fitness can result in highly varying estimates of the same individual's fitness from one generation to the next, and lead to oscillatory dynamics, stagnation, etc.

A common next step is to introduce into a Pareto EA some sort of "hall of fame" mechanism to keep track of good individuals from previous generations (see, for example, Zitzler and Thiele (1998)). Fitness is then a function of the ability to dominate the individuals in the current population *and* the ability to dominate current members of the hall of fame. This has the effect of reducing oscillation and stagnation by providing a dynamically increasing standard by which fitness is assessed, and can be quite effective in locating non-dominated solutions that, with high probability, are members of the Pareto-optimal set.

Still to be addressed is how multiple elements of the Pareto-optimal set are found. A quick-and-dirty approach is just to run your favorite algorithm (EA or otherwise) multiple times and collect in a single set the results from each run. Here, it would seem, there is a potential advantage to EA-based approaches in that multiple (possibly all) solutions can be found in a single EA run. Unfortunately, our standard optimization-oriented EAs are designed to converge to a single peak in the landscape, and are thus likely to produce only one or a few closely related members of the Pareto-optimal set. However, there are standard EA modifications such as fitness sharing (Goldberg, 1989) that are designed to promote and maintain diversity in the population. Adding this to a Pareto EA significantly improves its ability to evolve multiple and diverse members of the Pareto-optimal set during a single run (see, for example, Horn et al. (1994)).

Unless there is a strong elitist policy for survival from one generation to the next, many EAs have the property that good (possibly optimal) individuals can exist for a while and then disappear. For Pareto EAs that base their answer on the contents of the final population, this means that it is quite possible that the final answers produced may be missing Pareto-optimal individuals produced in earlier generations. Switching to an elitist policy solves this problem but results in significant loss of diversity. Fortunately, this is easily addressed by mechanisms like the hall-of-fame discussed earlier by providing a repository for the accumulating set of candidate Pareto-optimal solutions external to the current population.

A final thing we might demand of a Pareto EA is that it finds a set of solutions that represent a reasonably uniform coverage of the entire Pareto-optimal surface. This is the most difficult thing to achieve, since Pareto-optimal surfaces can range from simple concave surfaces to complex, multi-modal and even discontinuous surfaces. In fact, it is even difficult to construct a measure of uniform coverage without requiring additional problem-specific information (see, for example, Deb (1999)).

There are, of course, many other things that could or have been done to improve the performance of Pareto EAs. The interested reader can find these ideas developed in much more depth in the open literature, including two excellent books on the subject by Deb (2001) and Coello et al. (2002).

5.2.6   Summary

Given the many optimization methods already in existence, one can legitimately ask what additional benefits are provided by EA-based approaches. The ones most frequently cited are:

- The ability to apply EAs to a wide range of discrete and continuous optimization problems, and even to problems involving a mixture of both discrete and continuous components.

- In the case of continuous optimization problems, EAs do not require any constraints on derivatives (such as bounds). In fact there are no requirements that derivatives of any order even exist.

- EAs make no *a priori* assumptions about the shape of the surface (e.g., convexity).

- EAs are relatively insensitive to noisy optimization problems where the optimality values can only be estimated to a less than precise level (e.g., the optimality of a particular chess strategy).

- EAs have an inherent notion of parallelism that make them easy to parallelize.

That does not mean that EA approaches are uniformly better than traditional optimization techniques. Any algorithm that is designed to exploit specific properties of a particular subclass of problems (e.g., derivatives exist and are bounded) should on that subclass outperform other algorithms that do not make such assumptions. However, it is generally the case that such algorithms also tend to exhibit "brittleness", in the sense that their performance degrades rapidly on problems that do not satisfy their built-in assumptions.

It is also the case that many traditional methods were designed to be run on serial machines and require considerable recoding to take advantage of parallel architectures, while population-based EAs can be parallelized quite simply and naturally. The overall effect is that EAs and more traditional mathematical optimization techniques complement each other quite nicely, and collectively they allow one to solve a wider range of parameter optimization problems.

5.3 EA-Based Search

Closely related to optimization are problems that require procedures capable of efficiently searching solution spaces looking for solutions that satisfy a set of specified criteria. The EA-based optimization procedures discussed in the previous section can be viewed as a special case of this, searching a space for solutions that satisfy optimality criteria. However, there are many problems for which the notion of optimality may not make sense. Constraint satisfaction problems are good examples of problems for which the goal is to find *any* solution that satisfies a set of constraints (e.g., classroom scheduling problems). If there is more than one solution, no particular solution is generally viewed as preferable over another, and of course it is possible that, for a particular set of constraints, there are no solutions at all.

We could attack such problems with a SEARCH-EA, in which the objective function is simply a membership function that takes on only two values: 0 (not a solution) and 1 (a solution). The problem with this approach is that the most interesting and difficult constraint satisfaction problems are those in which there are a relatively few number of solutions. For such cases we have presented our SEARCH-EA with a needle-in-a-haystack problem for which, in general, there is no more effective search procedure than systematic enumeration of the entire search space. This may be acceptable for small search spaces, but it rapidly becomes computationally infeasible as the search space increases in size.

If we expect a SEARCH-EA to do better than this, the objective fitness function must provide more selective differential among potential solutions. Ideally, one would prefer a landscape similar in shape to one that is formed by draping a bed sheet over the spikey needle-in-a-haystack landscape. In other words, from an EA point of view, the best strategy is to turn these more general search problems into optimization problems and use an OPT-EA to find the required solutions.

At first glance, this does not seem particularly difficult, since at least intuitively this draped bedsheet surface could be achieved by a fitness function based on the number (or percentage) of constraints satisfied. However, since constraints can be redundant and can have different priorities associated with them, it is difficult to see how one can develop such fitness functions in a problem-independent way.

Boolean satisfiability (SAT) problems are good examples of these issues. In this case, the task is: given a Boolean function of N variables with no restrictions on the number or the size of the clauses that make up the function, find true/false assignments for the N variables that make the value of the entire function true. In this case a particular vector of true/false assignments is either a solution or not. If there is more than one solution, no one solution is viewed as preferable over another, and of course it is possible that for a particular Boolean function there are no solutions at all.

SAT problems are a member of a well-studied class of problems in computer science called NP-complete problems. These problems share the common property that as one increases the size of the problem (in this case, the number of Boolean variables N), the upper bound on the amount of cpu time required to find a solution for all known algorithms is exponential in the size of the problem. In practical terms that means, for example, that even SAT problems involving 20 variables can potentially require weeks of cpu time. As a consequence, there is a lot of interest in developing heuristic procedures for NP-complete problems that can, with high probability, find solutions in bounded time.

From an EA point of view, the choice of internal representation and reproductive operators for SAT problems could hardly be simpler. An individual (a candidate solution) is simply a fixed-length string of 0s and 1s representing the true/false assignments to each of the N variables, and the standard binary string mutation and crossover operators seem quite plausible. However, if an EA is to serve as an effective SAT heuristic, it must have a useful objective fitness function as well. Simply returning the value of the function 0 or 1 is clearly not sufficient since it produces a needle-in-the-haystack fitness landscape. Fitness functions based on the number of clauses satisfied provides some improvement, but generally not enough to produce an EA-based heuristic that is competitive with other approaches.

An example of a more complex but more effective objective fitness function is the work by Spears (1990). In his case, all fitness values were real numbers in the range $[0.0, 1.0]$ obtained by propagating the truth values 0 (false) and 1 (true) from the leaf nodes of the parse tree of the Boolean function using the rules:

```
fitness( (AND exp1 exp2 ... expn)) = AVE( fitness(exp1), ...),
fitness( (OR  exp1 exp2 ... expn)) = MIN( fitness(exp1), ...), and
fitness( (NOT exp) = 1.0 - fitness(exp).
```

As a result, a fitness of 0.0 represented the case in which no clauses were satisfied and 1.0 represented a solution to a given SAT problem. Intermediate values represented an estimate of how much of the parse tree was satisfied. The result was a rather effective heuristic for solving SAT problems.

Using EAs as search procedures for this large class of search problems has the additional benefit of making direct contact with a large and well-established body of computer science literature on search algorithms, and allows one to compare and contrast EA approaches with other, more traditional approaches. As is the case with optimization algorithms, there is no single search procedure that is uniformly best. Rather, each has its own strengths and weaknesses. The features that make EA-based search attractive include:

- SEARCH-EAs are relatively easy to parallelize.

- SEARCH-EAs have a convenient built-in resource management facility in the sense that the internal fitness-biased competition for parenthood and for survival naturally distributes cpu cycles and focus of attention to the more promising parts of a search space.

- SEARCH-EAs are relatively easy to port from one application to another without having to start from scratch.

5.4 EA-Based Machine Learning

Machine learning (ML) is another closely related class of problems for which there has been considerable interest in EA-based approaches. Although there are many forms of learning, for our purposes the focus in this section will be on the ability of a system to improve future task-specific performance as a result of related present and past activities. So, for example, we spend time on the driving range hoping to improve our golf handicap, and we read and experiment on paper with a new options-trading scheme before we risk real money. In machine learning, this typically takes the form of being given a set of training examples to "practice" on until sufficiently high performance levels are obtained, and then, with learning turned off, performance is measured on a set of previously unseen examples.

At this level of abstraction, the learning process can be viewed as one of inductive generalization in which the features relevant to good performance are identified and integrated into a model general enough to produce acceptable performance on both training and testing examples. Rote memorization, while easy to implement, is seldom sufficient because of the dynamic complexity and continual novelty of most task domains. Rather, a more general model is required, and in machine learning these models often take the form of a decision tree, a set of decision rules, an artificial neural network, etc.

A fairly standard machine-learning approach is to adopt a "bottom up" strategy and try to construct an appropriate model directly from the training examples. One's ability to do so effectively depends heavily on the kinds of tasks involved and the types of models to be constructed. For example, learning classification tasks, such as recognizing and categorizing objects described by feature vectors, appears to be quite amenable to "bottom-up" approaches, while learning sequential decision tasks, such as robot navigation, does not.

Alternatively, one can view the machine learning process as more of a "top-down" process in which one searches a model space for models that work well on the training examples and are of sufficient generality to have a high probability of success on not yet encountered examples. The concern with this approach is most often one of efficiency, since spaces of models of sufficient descriptive power are generally so large as to prohibit any form of systematic search. However, as we discussed in the previous section, EAs can often be used to search large complex spaces effectively, including the model spaces of interest here.

Consequently, ML-EAs tend to adopt a more top-down approach of searching a model space by means of a population of models that compete with each other, not unlike scientific theories in the natural sciences. In order for this to be effective, a notion of model "fitness" must be provided in order to bias the search process in a useful way. The first thought one might have is to define the fitness of a model in terms of its observed performance on the provided training examples. However, just as we see in other approaches, ML-EAs with no other feedback or bias will tend to overfit the training data at the expense of generality. So, for example, if an ML-EA is attempting to learn a set of classification rules using only training set performance as the measure of fitness, it is not at all unusual to see near-perfect rule sets emerge that consist of approximately one rule per training example!

Stated another way, for a given set of training examples, there are a large number of theories (models) that have identical performance on the training data, but can have quite different predictive power. Since, by definition, we cannot learn from unseen examples, this generality must be achieved by other means. A standard technique for doing so is to adopt some sort of "Occam's razor" approach: all other things being equal, select a simpler model over a more complex one.

For ML-EAs this typically is achieved by augmenting the fitness function to include both performance of the training data and the parsimony of the model. Precise measurements of parsimony can be quite difficult to define in general. However, rough estimates based on the size of a model measured in terms of its basic building blocks have been shown to be surprisingly effective. For example, using the number of rules in a rule set or the number of hidden nodes in an artificial neural network as an estimate of parsimony works quite well.

Somewhat more difficult from an ML-EA designer's point of view is finding an appropriate balance between parsimony and performance. If one puts too much weight on generality, performance will suffer and vice versa. As we will see in a later section in this chapter, how best to apply EAs to problems involving multiple conflicting objectives is a challenging problem in general. To keep things simple, most ML-EAs adopt a fairly direct approach such as:

$$fitness(model) = performance(model) - w * parsimony(model)$$

where the weight w is empirically chosen to discourage overfitting, and parsimony is a simple linear or quadratic function of model size (Smith, 1983; Bassett and De Jong, 2000).

Just as was the case in the previous sections, applying EAs to machine-learning problems is not some sort of magic wand that renders existing ML techniques obsolete. Rather, ML-EAs complement existing approaches in a number of useful ways:

- Many of the existing ML techniques are designed to learn "one-shot" classification tasks, in which problems are presented as precomputed feature vectors to be classified as belonging to a fixed set of categories. When ML-EAs are applied to such problems, they tend to converge more slowly than traditional ML techniques but often to more parsimonious models (De Jong, 1988).

- ML-EAs can be used effectively for other kinds of ML problems, particularly "sequential decision problems" like navigation and game playing that involve a coordinated series of decisions extending over time (Smith, 1983; Grefenstette et al., 1990).

- Most ML problems of interest involve significant amounts of computation time. Hence, ML approaches that lend themselves to parallel implementations are desirable.

5.5 EA-Based Automated Programming

The dream of automating the frequently tedious job of computer programming has been with us since the early days of computer science and artificial intelligence. It should come as no surprise that this was also on the minds of the early pioneers of evolutionary computation. As noted in chapter 2, in the early 1960s Fogel and his colleagues were motivated by the goal of producing intelligent artificial agents, not by hand-crafting them, but by evolving them. As a starting point they chose to use finite-state machines (FSMs) as their programming language and called their techniques for evolving FSMs "Evolutionary Programming" (Fogel et al., 1966).

Similarly, we find in Holland's early writing a description of his "broadcast language", a parallel programming language designed to facilitate manipulation by GAs and modeled loosely on gene-level mechanisms of protein production (Holland, 1975).

Since then there has been considerable interest in evolving programs expressed in a wide variety of languages, including rule-based systems (Smith, 1983; De Jong, 1987), artificial neural networks (Harp et al., 1989; de Garis, 1990), Lisp code (Fujiki and Dickinson, 1987; Koza, 1992), and even assembly language (Cramer, 1985; Ray, 1994). In each case the ability to do so effectively depends critically on two important issues: 1) how a PROG-EA represents and manipulates programs, and 2) how to assess the fitness of a candidate program. These issues are explored in more detail in the following sections.

5.5.1 Representing Programs

The simplest and most straightforward approach to representing programs is in terms of a fixed set of parameters. That is, we have a particular class of programs in mind that vary only with respect to their parameter settings, and we want to find the particular program instance whose execution behavior is optimal with respect to some objective criteria (such as execution speed, correctness of the output, etc.). The advantage to such an approach is that it immediately places us on the familiar terrain of parameter optimization, and we can use a variety of the techniques discussed earlier in this chapter to evolve programs.

It is tempting at first glance to dismiss this approach as trivial and not at all representative of what is usually meant by automatic programming. But it is important to note that, although the kinds of structural changes that can be made is quite limited, even modest changes in parameters can result in significant behavioral changes during program execution. Samuel's checker-playing program (Samuel, 1959) is a striking example of this. And, one can view the unified EA model developed in the previous chapter as a parameterized description of a class of algorithms that exhibit a wide range of behaviors.

However, there are many situations in which more significant structural changes must be made to programs in order to achieve the desired performance. The next step up the complexity ladder is the set of programs whose behavior is controlled by a data structure such as a tree or a graph. Hence, automatic programming in this case consists of evolving data structures that result in optimal program performance. For example, in addition to tuning the weights of an artificial neural network, one may also need to change the physical structure on the network (e.g., the number of nodes, the number of layers, etc.).

As with the case of parameter tuning, achieving automatic programming by evolving data structures puts us again in familiar EA territory. As discussed in an earlier section of this chapter, there is a significant amount of existing knowledge and experience regarding data structure optimization. However, as we have seen, evolving data structures is generally a more difficult and less well understood process than parameter optimization.

The final, and most difficult, situation is when automatic programming involves making structural changes at the most fundamental level: the executable code itself. If we expect to be successful at evolving programs at this level, we must consider whether some programming languages are more suitable than others for use with EAs. In particular, we must be able to define reproductive operators (like crossover and mutation) that have high fitness correlation to insure that the offspring of useful programs are also useful. However, for many programming languages this can be difficult to achieve because of their many syntactic and semantic constraints. For example, a simple mutation operator that changes a semicolon to a left parenthesis can turn a highly fit Java program into one that does not even compile correctly.

As we saw in the earlier section in this chapter on constrained optimization, one way of dealing with this is to devise new (language-specific) reproductive operators that preserve the syntactic integrity of the programs being manipulated, and hopefully some semantic integrity as well. Unfortunately, the complexity of the syntax and semantics of many traditional programming languages makes this a difficult and challenging task.

The good news is that there are a few programming languages that seem reasonably well-suited for EA-based techniques: low level machine languages (Cramer, 1985; Ray, 1994), Lisp (Fujiki and Dickinson, 1987; Koza, 1992), and rule-based languages (Holland, 1975; Smith, 1983; Grefenstette, 1989). In each case the syntactic and semantic constraints are sufficiently simple to permit the design of effective reproductive operators. However, as one might expect, the form that the reproductive operators take is quite language specific. It is beyond the scope of this book to explore these various approaches in more detail. The interested reader is encouraged to explore the extensive literature that is readily available, particularly the genetic programming (GP) literature that has historically focused on Lisp, and the rule-based approaches (classifier systems, Pitt approach, etc.)

5.5.2 Evaluating Programs

Regardless of how a PROG-EA represents the programs being evolved, it must assign differential fitness to programs in order to bias the evolutionary process in the direction of useful programs. A few minutes of thought should make it clear how difficult this can be in general. A static analysis of a program, as illustrated by most of today's compilers, can detect most syntactic and some semantic deficiencies. Biologically, we can think of this as a form of infant mortality, in the sense that programs that are not able to be successfully compiled never get a chance to be executed.

However, for those programs that are compilable, their fitness should reflect how accurately they perform the desired task (e.g., sorting, classification, navigation, etc.). This means executing a program one or more times in order to estimate its fitness, and raises several interesting questions. First, it is well known in computer science that if a programming language is of sufficient descriptive power, namely equivalent to a Turing machine, we are immediately confronted with the halting problem: our inability to always know for sure if the execution of a program will terminate in finite time. In practice this is generally handled by setting upper bounds on the expected amount of computation time required to solve a problem. Programs that exceed this time limit are simply terminated and assigned low fitness value.

For those programs that terminate normally within the specified time constraints, we still have the problem of how to assign fitness. For simple tasks, it may be possible to test a program exhaustively on all possible inputs, and have fitness be a function of output accuracy (and perhaps speed). However, for most programming tasks, the input space is far too large to be searched exhaustively, and so validation must be based on the performance of a "test set" which, ideally, will reflect how well a program will do on untested inputs.

If this sounds a lot like our earlier discussion on machine learning, it should! The task here is to evolve programs that perform well on both seen and unseen inputs, and the same issues arise regarding the generality of the programs being evolved. Without any form of parsimony pressure, the length of evolving programs increases indefinitely over time for two reasons: the tendency of evolving programs to overfit (memorize) the test data, and the tendency of evolving programs to collect harmless junk code that has no effect on test set performance. This phenomenon has been dubbed "bloat" in the evolutionary computation community and appears to have rather similar features to biological systems, in the sense that, as we decode more and more of naturally occurring genomes, we are continually surprised at how much of a genome consists of "non-coding" regions.

Is bloat a negative feature from a computational point of view? There is increasing evidence that, while unrestricted bloat significantly slows down and negatively affects the evolutionary search process, a little bloat is often a good thing. There are several hypotheses as to why this is the case. One hypothesis comes out of the related field of complex adaptive systems (of which EAs are an instance). A frequently observed phenomenon in complex adaptive systems is a phase transition – a relatively rapid shift of a system from one state to another. An avalanche on a mountainside is a classic example of a naturally occurring phase transition. In the case of programs (or other complex objects), the concern is one of ease of evolvability. As we increase parsimony pressure to remove bloat, we often observe a phase transition in which the ability to evolve the desired program drops off dramatically.

Biologically, these hypotheses take the form of workspace arguments: evolution needs some scratch areas in the genome to try out new things without negatively affecting fitness. A nice example of this is described in Ramsey et al. (1998) in which it was shown that, for a constant level of parsimony pressure, the average length of evolved programs changed in direct proportion to changes in mutation rates.

5.5.3 Summary

It should be clear by now that evolving programs is one of the most difficult and challenging areas of EC, since it invariably involves variable-length structures, syntactic and semantic constraints, multiple objectives, and complex, time-consuming fitness evaluation techniques. While we have made significant progress in the last twenty years, there is much more to be done.

5.6 EA-Based Adaptation

A final paradigm to be discussed in this chapter is that of using evolutionary algorithms to design systems capable of adapting to a changing environment. Problems of this type are quite different from the ones we have been discussing in that there has been an implicit assumption that the fitness function (landscape) is static and the job of an EA is to explore that landscape and find areas of high fitness. Adaptive systems, however, make just the opposite assumption: the fitness landscape is subject to constant change and areas of high fitness today may be areas of low fitness tomorrow. For example, consider the task of writing an effective stock market trading program. A good fixed strategy today may turn into a poor one as market conditions change. An effective adaptive strategy is one that maintains performance over time by self-tuning.

In order to consider an EA-based solution, several issues need to be addressed. The first issue is that of relative time scales: how fast the environment is changing relative to the evolutionary system's clock. Clearly, if the environment is changing so rapidly that it is impossible to evaluate in a consistent manner the fitness of even a single generation of individuals, an EA-based approach is not likely to be effective. At the other end of the spectrum are systems that are static for long periods of time with occasional abrupt transitions to a new relatively static phase. Such situations can be usefully viewed as a series of static optimization problems, in which a standard EA optimizer is invoked when a phase transition is detected in order to retune the system.

The interesting problems in adaptation are those that fall in between these two extremes, where for example the landscape may change slowly but continuously over time. In these cases a key issue is the ability of an EA to maintain sufficient diversity in the population so as to be able to track a dynamically changing landscape (De Jong, 1999). For example, selection methods such as truncation or ranking selection that are frequently used in OPT-EAs often exert too much selection pressure for an ADAPT-EA.

The second issue to be addressed in designing an ADAPT-EA is the distinction between "online" and "offline" fitness evaluation. The overall measure of effectiveness of an adaptive system is its performance over time as the environment changes. A key element of an EA is the notion of improving fitness in the long run by creating children that are variations of their parents and discarding (probabilistically) the ones with low fitness. If the only way to assess the fitness of a child is to try it out in the "real" system, then the observed behavior of the system will be quite erratic as individuals of varying quality are evaluated, and the overall time-average of system performance will drop.

This issue can be dealt with in several ways. The first is to tone down the reproductive operators so that the differences between parents and offspring are less dramatic. This has the effect of improving online performance initially but, if taken too far, it can slow down evolutionary convergence and also decrease online performance. A preferred, but not always available, alternative is to perform fitness evaluation in an offline manner while running the online system with the best settings available at the time. One way of accomplishing this is to evaluate fitness using a simulation model. So, for example, we might choose to evaluate new stock market trading strategies by testing them out on recent market data. If we find a strategy that outperforms the one currently in use, the new one is uploaded to the online system. This approach, using offline evolution to accomplish online adaptation, has been used quite successfully in a number of areas including evolutionary robotics (Grefenstette, 1996).

5.7 Summary

As we have seen in this chapter, viewing EAs as parallel adaptive search procedures immediately opens up a wide range of potential application areas, including optimization, machine learning, and automated programming. In each case a good deal of effort has been put into developing and refining an appropriate set of EAs. This in turn has served as a catalyst for the further development of EA theory to help understand existing systems and to guide the design of future systems. In the next chapter we provide a unified view of current EA theory.

Chapter 6

Evolutionary Computation Theory

6.1 Introduction

As we have seen in the preceding chapters, when developing a new application an EC practitioner is confronted with a variety of design decisions such as:

- choosing a particular EA paradigm that is well-suited for the application,

- choosing an appropriate internal representation,

- choosing an appropriate set of reproductive operators,

- choosing an appropriate population size,

- choosing appropriate selection mechanisms, and

- choosing an appropriate measure of fitness.

For many application areas, there is a wealth of "common wisdom" to guide the practitioner in making these sorts of choices. In addition, as we have seen, most EAs are relatively insensitive to exact parameter settings (such as population size). Consequently, "in the ballpark" is sufficient for many applications. At the same time, we continue to make significant progress in EC theory, providing a solid foundation for the field and accumulating an increasing amount of theory-based guidance for the practitioner. In this chapter the unified framework introduced in the preceding chapters is used to organize and survey the important theoretical developments in the EC field.

In every field there is a tension (and a corresponding gap) between theory and practice. This tension/gap first appears during the process of constructing an abstract model of the object of study. This process involves ignoring some lower-level details while retaining those aspects believed to be important to the goals of the analysis. The gap frequently widens when the initial model proves too difficult to analyze. In this case additional abstractions and assumptions are often made that are motivated by the goal of improving analytical tractability rather than by properties of the underlying object of study. Classic examples of this are assumptions of linearity or independence of variables. Obviously, the wider the gap, the more concern there is as to whether the analytical results obtained from such models carry over to the "real" thing.

These issues confront us immediately in our attempt to develop useful abstract models of evolutionary computation methods. In order to be useful, these models must be capable of capturing the important algorithmic details of particular EAs. However, the inclusion of such details often leads to analytic intractability, since the important EA components interact with each other in complex, nonlinear ways.

Yet, if theory is to have any impact on practice, these gaps must be addressed. This can be done in a number of ways. First, we can require a particular theory to make predictions about the behavior of "real" EAs, and evaluate a theory's usefulness in terms of the accuracy of its predictions. However, for some theories, the gap is so wide that making practical predictions is not even reasonable or possible. These gaps can often be narrowed by *incrementally* removing some of the simplifying assumptions, and studying the effects they have on the earlier analyses. Another gap reduction technique is to perform experimental studies on the models that are mathematically intractable, not unlike the computational techniques used to "solve" nonlinear systems of equations. And, finally, one can perform experimental analyses of the EAs themselves in ways that can be generalized to other situations.

Consequently, as we survey the important theoretical results, we will perform some "gap analysis" as well. In the process we will obtain a better understanding of the current gaps that exist between EC theory and practice, and how they are being addressed.

There are a wide range of analytical tools one might use to develop a theoretical framework for EC. The ones that have proved most useful historically are:

- dynamical systems tools for characterizing EA population dynamics,

- Markov process tools for analyzing the stochastic properties of EAs,

- statistical mechanics tools for studying aggregate EA properties,

- analysis of algorithm tools for assessing the computational complexity of EAs, and

- mathematical tools for characterizing the optimization properties of EAs.

The fact that there is more than one set of tools and techniques for EC analysis is a reflection of the fact that most theories are designed to capture specific properties and answer specific questions. For systems of any complexity it is seldom the case that there is a single "unified" theory capable of addressing all interesting issues at all levels of abstraction. Rather, our overall understanding of complex systems emerges from a collection of theoretical models that complement one another.

In the case of EC theory, this collection of models falls into two broad categories: 1) application-independent theories that focus on understanding EA dynamics, and 2) application-dependent theories that focus on understanding EA problem-solving properties. The remainder of this chapter explores each of these categories in more detail.

6.2 Analyzing EA Dynamics

At the core of any EA is a population of individuals evolving over time. If we are able to capture this dynamic process in a mathematically tractable form, we will have made significant progress in obtaining a deeper understanding of how EAs work and in our ability to make behavioral predictions. In order to do so, we need to select an appropriate mathematical representation of an EA population evolving over time.

The usual place to start is with the internal representation that an EA uses to specify the individuals in a population, or more precisely, the underlying geno/phenospace of which every individual in the population must be a member. EAs that use genotypic representations are quite naturally modeled in terms of fixed-length individuals consisting of L genes, with each gene taking on only a discrete set of values. EAs that use phenotypic representations can sometimes be characterized this way as well, but more often than not phenotypes are of variable length and/or have infinite variety. What that suggests is that mathematical models of finite-genotype EAs may be simpler and more tractable than phenotypic EAs. So, that is the best place to begin.

Notationally, we let X represent the entire finite set of distinct genotypes with x representing a particular genotype. To simplify the mathematical notation, we assume that members of X can be uniquely identified by an integer index i that ranges from $1...r$, the cardinality of X. We let $P(t)$ represent the set of individuals in an EA population at time t. Since it is always possible for a population to have zero or more instances of a particular genotype, we let $c_i(t)$ express the frequency of genotype x_i. This allows us to describe the makeup of an EA population at time t as a vector over the genotype space:

$$P(t) \;=\; <c_1(t), c_2(t), ..., c_r(t)>$$

What is still needed is a characterization of how these population vectors change over time, expressed as a dynamical system of the form:

$$P(t+1) = evolve(P(t))$$

Since the $P(t)$ in these models are just the genotype vectors described above, it is sufficient to develop a set of r equations of the form:

$$c_i(t+1) = evolve_i(P(t)), \; i = 1 \, ... \, r$$

that characterize how the frequency of each genotype in the population changes from one generation to the next. In order to do that we must now focus on the details of the evolutionary process itself, namely, that each generation consists of three phases:

$$evolve(P(t)) \;=\; survival\_selection(reproduction(parent\_selection(P(t))))$$

Developing a model of this complexity can be both daunting and difficult, so one often adopts some simplifying assumptions. For example, if we assume a non-overlapping-generation model (i.e., one in which at each generation all the parents die and all the offspring survive), there is no notion of fitness-based survival_selection, resulting in a simpler model:

$$evolve(P(t)) \;=\; reproduction(parent\_selection(P(t)))$$

If we are willing to assume that there is no reproductive variation (i.e., only cloning), the model can be further simplified to:

$$evolve(P(t)) \; = \; parent\_selection(P(t))$$

These simple selection-only models are often referred to in the literature as describing the *replicator dynamics* of a system, and they are the basis of many evolutionary game theory models (see, for example, Maynard-Smith (1982) or Hofbauer and Sigmund (1998)).

Each of these simplifications improves the analytical tractability of the model, while simultaneously widening the gap between the model and "real" EAs. A useful way of understanding the implications of all this is to study the models in the opposite order presented here, namely, by starting with the simplest models, analyzing them, and then increasing their complexity.

However, before we do that, we need to understand the implications of an issue that will confront us at each step: whether to adopt a finite or infinite population model. This sounds rather strange at first since all implementable EAs involve finite populations. So introducing the notion of an infinite population would seem to be an unnecessary complication. However, infinite population models are often more mathematically tractable than finite population models.

With infinite population models, each $c_i(t)$ represents the fraction of the population consisting of genotype x_i. For example, the vector $< 1/r, ..., 1/r >$ represents an infinite population in which every genotype is present in equal proportions. In general, all $c_i(t)$ must satisfy $0 \le c_i(t) \le 1$, and the $c_i(t)$ of any particular infinite population vector must sum to 1.0, i.e.,

$$\sum_{i=1}^{r} c_i(t) \; = \; 1$$

This means that, for infinite population models, population vectors are just points in an $(r - 1)$-dimensional simplex, the vertices of which represent homogeneous populations consisting of a single genotype, and an evolving population can be viewed as a trajectory through that simplex.

For example, all infinite populations constructed from a simple genospace consisting of just two genotypes can be described by the single real-valued number c_1 (or equivalently c_2) in the interval $0 \le c_1 \le 1$. The two end points (vertices) represent the two possible homogeneous populations consisting entirely of genotype x_1 or x_2. A randomly generated initial population will determine the value of $c_1(0)$. The evolutionary dynamics control subsequent values of $c_1(t)$ which, if plotted in temporal sequence, produces a trajectory in this one-dimensional simplex. Similarly, all infinite populations constructed from a genospace with three genomes are described by a two-dimensional triangular simplex, and so on.

Thus, by adopting an infinite population model, we have an elegant mathematical model of population dynamics that allows us to leverage off a large body of existing mathematics to answer questions about whether such EA populations converge to a fixed point and, if so, what a fixed-point population looks like. However, infinite population models clearly present a gap between theory and practice. Hence, it is important to have a clear understanding of the extent to which results obtained from infinite population models carry over to "real" EAs.

The alternative is to construct finite-population models that are closer to "real" EAs, but may be less mathematically tractable. Notationally, the finite-population models are nearly identical to their infinite-population counterparts, namely:

$$P(t) \ = \ < c_1(t), c_2(t), ..., c_r(t) >$$

However, $c_i(t)$ now represents the number of copies of genotype x_i in a population of size m at time t. Hence, all $c_i(t)$ must satisfy $0 \leq c_i(t) \leq m$, and the elements of any particular population vector must sum to m. For example, the vector $< 50, 50, 0, ..., 0 >$ describes a population of size 100 that consists of exactly two genotypes, x_1 and x_2, in equal proportions.

Of course, we can always normalize such vectors by dividing each element by m so that finite-population vectors represent points in the same $(r - 1)$-dimensional simplex as the infinite population case. Note, however, that these normalized finite-population vectors can represent only a discrete subset of points in the simplex, and hence finite-population trajectories are restricted to visiting only this subset of points.

This normalization provides us with a useful mathematical view of the effect of increasing the population size m, namely, increasing in a uniform way the number of points a finite-population EA can visit in the $(r - 1)$-dimensional simplex. In particular, it puts us in the position of being able to characterize the extent to which the trajectories of finite-population EAs match up with the trajectories of infinite-population models as a function of m. A useful exercise for the reader at this point is to calculate how many unique populations of size m can be constructed from r genotypes.

Just as we did in the infinite-population case, since $P(t) =< c_1(t), ..., c_r(t) >$, we seek to develop a set of r dynamical equations of the form:

$$c_i(t + 1) = evolve_i(P(t)), \ i = 1 ... r$$

However, for finite population models, the c_i can only take on a discrete set of values of the form k/m where m is the population size and k is an integer in the range $0...m$. This creates difficulties mathematically since the most natural way to write down equations for $evolve_i$ involves the probabilities associated with the stochastic elements of an EA. Since these probabilities can take on arbitrary real values between 0.0 and 1.0, there is no easy way to guarantee c_i values of the form k/m. The simplest approach to dealing with this issue is to shift to "expected value" models in which the population update rules are of the form:

$$E[c_i(t + 1)] = evolve_i(P(t)), \ i = 1 ... r$$

and make predictions about the makeup of future finite populations "on average". In the simplex, trajectories of these models start at one of the finite-population points, but then are free to visit any point in the simplex.

The concern, of course, is the extent to which the trajectories of "real" EAs resemble these "average" trajectories. As we will see, they can and do vary quite dramatically from their expected trajectories. This does not mean that expected value models provide little in the way of additional insights into the behavior of actual EAs. Historically they have proved to be quite helpful.

The alternative to adopting an expected value model is to appeal to a more powerful (and more complex) stochastic analysis framework. The one most frequently used is a Markov chain analysis that allows one to characterize how entire probability distributions evolve over time rather than just the means of the distributions.

This is as much as can be said at this level of generality about modeling EA population dynamics. To go further, we must model specific aspects of EA components, namely how selection and reproduction are implemented. Since these EA components interact in complex, nonlinear ways, our strategy here will be to understand first the effects of selection and reproduction in isolation, and then analyze their interactions.

6.3   Selection-Only Models

If we remove reproductive variation from our models, then we are left with models of the form:

$$P(t+1) = evolve(P(t)) = survival\_selection(parent\_selection(P(t)))$$

There are two major categories to be considered: 1) non-overlapping-generation models in which all of the parents die and only the offspring compete for survival, and 2) overlapping-generation models in which both parents and offspring compete for survival. We explore both of these in the following sections.

6.3.1   Non-overlapping-Generation Models

In the case of non-overlapping-generation models, we can initially simplify things further by assuming that *all* of the offspring survive, i.e.,

$$P(t+1) = evolve(P(t)) = parent\_selection(P(t))$$

This is the standard interpretation of infinite-population models and is also true for non-overlapping finite-population models in which the sizes of parent and offspring populations are identical. As noted earlier, since $P(t) = < c_1(t), ..., c_r(t) >$, we seek to develop a set of r dynamical equations of the form:

$$c_i(t+1) = evolve_i(P(t)), \ i = 1 \ ... \ r$$

For parent-selection-only EAs this is quite straightforward:

$$c_i(t+1) = prob\_select_i(t), \ i = 1 \ ... \ r$$

since the number of x_i genotypes in the next generation is completely determined by the number of times x_i is chosen to be a parent.

The actual probabilities will be a function of two things: the frequency of the different genotypes in the current population, and the degree to which selection is biased by genotype fitness. The following subsections summarize these issues for the various forms of selection typically used in practice.

6.3.1.1   Uniform (Neutral) Selection

Consider the situation in which all genotypes have the same fitness. In this case, their probability of selection depends only on their frequency in the current population. For the infinite population models, this determines a set of r equations of the form:

$$c_i(t+1) \;=\; prob\_select_i(t) \;=\; c_i(t), \; i = 1 \ldots r$$

the dynamics of which are rather uninteresting in that every possible population is a fixed point. Hence, the population trajectories never move from their initial positions specified by $P(0)$.

   This is also true for finite-population models in which uniform parent selection is deterministic, i.e., each member of $P(t)$ produces exactly one offspring. However, if uniform selection is *stochastic*, the actual number of offspring produced by each parent can vary considerably for the same reason that twenty flips of a (fair) coin are unlikely to result in exactly ten heads and ten tails.

   If we assume our initial (finite) parent population consists of m distinct genotypes, then it is quite easy to see the implication of this over multiple generations. In the absence of reproductive variation, stochastic-uniform sampling can at best maintain this diversity, but frequently reduces it. In population genetics, this corresponds to the phenomenon of *genetic drift*. If we allow evolution to run indefinitely, this loss of genetic diversity continues to accumulate to the point where the population converges to a homogeneous fixed point.

   It is clear from the discussion above that infinite population models (and expected value models) cannot be used to model this phenomenon of genetic drift. On the other hand, genetic drift is quite naturally captured with a Markov model in which the states s_i of the systems are simply the number of unique genotypes in the population (see, for example, De Jong (1975) or Goldberg and Segrest (1987)). Hence we have m states and an $m \times m$ state transition matrix Q. Since the number of genotypes can never increase, $q_{ij} = 0$ for all $j > i$. For $i \geq j$, we have $\binom{i}{j}$ different ways to chose which set of j genotypes survive. For each such set, the probability of choosing exactly one copy of each genotype is:

$$j! \; \prod_{k=1}^{j} c_{j_k}$$

where c_{j_k} is the probability of selecting the kth genotype of the j survivors. These j survivors can be assigned to the offspring population in $\binom{m}{j}$ different ways. The probability of filling the remaining $m-j$ population slots with additional copies of the surviving genotypes is:

$$\left(\frac{\sum_{k=1}^{j} c_{j_k}}{m} \right)^{(m-j)}.$$

Putting this all together we have:

$$q_{ij} \;=\; \binom{i}{j} \binom{m}{j} \left(j! \prod_{k=1}^{j} \frac{(c_{j_k})}{m} \right) \left(\frac{\sum_{k=1}^{j} c_{j_k}}{m} \right)^{(m-j)}$$

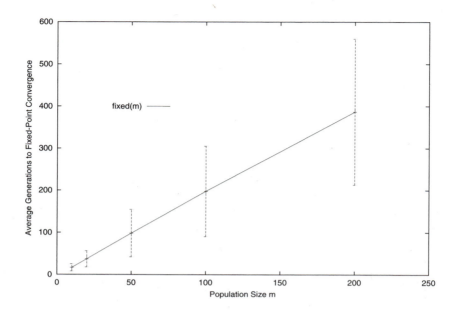

Figure 6.1: Average fixed-point convergence times due to drift in a non-overlapping-generation EA with parent population size $m =$ offspring population size n.

With the Markov model in place, we can now (in principle) calculate the expected length of time (number of generations) it will take to reach s_1 (a fixed point) starting from our initial state s_m:

$$fixed(m) \; = \; \sum_{j=0}^{\infty} j * prob_{m1}(j)$$

where $prob_{m1}(j)$ is the probability of first entry from s_m to s_1 in exactly j steps. This can be calculated from Q^t as follows:

$$prob_{m1}(j) \; = \; \sum_{k=1}^{j} q_{m1}(k) * q_{11}(m-k)$$

where $q_{ij}(t)$ is the ijth entry of Q^t.

Unfortunately, solving equations such as these in closed form is an extremely challenging task. Even solving them numerically requires considerable computational effort since, although suppressed in the equations above, the c_{j_k} are time dependent. For our purposes it will be sufficient to estimate $fixed(m)$ empirically by running a non-overlapping-generation EA with $m = n$, stochastic-uniform parent selection and no reproductive variation, and an initial population of m unique genotypes. Figure 6.1 shows the results. Each point on the curve represents the time to population fixed-point convergence averaged over 400 independent runs. The error bars represent one standard deviation.

It should not come as too much of a surprise to see that $fixed(m)$ is a linear function of m, since $m - 1$ genotypes must be lost to reach a fixed point. In this particular case $fixed(m) = 2m$ is a very close fit to the experimental data, meaning that on average one genotype is lost every two generations. What is more surprising is the size of the variance. A standard deviation of order m suggests that, even in this simplified context, expected value models tell us very little about individual evolutionary runs.

This linear relationship between loss of diversity and population size allows us to reduce the effects of drift by simply increasing m. However, as every EA practitioner is acutely aware, as the population size increases, so does the amount of computational time required to process each generation (on a serial machine). For most applications the processing time of an EA generation can be reasonably assumed to be a linear function of n, the number of new births in a generation. Using this approximation, the time to convergence (measured in births) when $m = n$ is simply $birth(m) = m * fixed(m) \simeq 2m^2$. So, linear improvements in drift effects are obtained at the price of quadratic increases in running time.

If we focus now on the trajectories of uniform-selection-only EAs in the simplex, the picture is quite clear. Unlike the infinite-population models whose initial population *is* the fixed point, finite-population EAs with stochastic-uniform selection produce trajectories that terminate (converge) at one of the vertices of the simplex (i.e., a population consisting of a single genotype). Since the drift effects are linear and uniform over all genotypes, the probability of converging to a particular vertex is proportional to its frequency in the initial population. If the initial genotype proportions are all equal (e.g., $1/m$), then convergence to every vertex is equally likely.

Since every genotype has a fitness associated with it, it is also instructive to analyze the average fitness of the fixed points. For stochastic-uniform selection, this is simply the average fitness of the members of the initial population. It is easy to illustrate this by reusing the data from figure 6.1 and plotting the average fixed-point fitness for the situation in which each genotype is assigned a unique fitness value uniformly from the interval $[0, 100]$, as indicated in figure 6.2.

Although conceptually simple, studying the special case of neutral selection allows us to better understand "genetic drift": the underlying pressure to reduce population diversity that is present in every EA that uses some form of stochastic selection. Its presence will be observed repeatedly in the remainder of this chapter. Drift effects can often be reduced by variance-reduction sampling techniques or avoided altogether by using deterministic selection methods. Opportunities for doing so will be discussed in the following sections.

6.3.1.2 Fitness-Biased Selection

Things get somewhat more interesting if we assume that in the initial population there is a genotype, say x_*, whose fitness is unique and maximal. In this case one can show that, if selection favors higher fitness, then an infinite-population parent-selection-only EA will converge to a population consisting of the single genotype x_*. Stated another way, starting from any initial population $P(0)$, the population trajectory $P(t)$ converges to the simplex vertex $< 0, 0, ..., 1, 0, 0, ..., 0 >$ that corresponds to x_*. The only difference that a particular selection algorithm makes is in the speed of convergence.

Under the same conditions, finite-population models also converge to a homogeneous fixed point. However, that fixed point is often not the same as the corresponding infinite-population model since it is possible for x_* to disappear from the population due to the drift effects analyzed in the previous section.

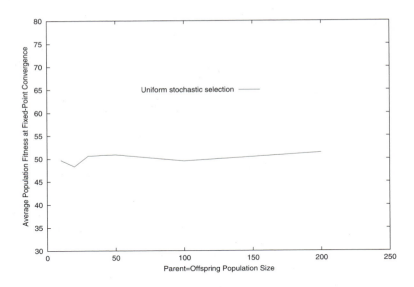

Figure 6.2: Average fixed-point fitness for stochastic-uniform parent selection in a non-overlapping-generation EA with $m = n$ and no reproductive variation.

This suggests a natural way to compare and contrast different selection algorithms: by studying which homogeneous populations they cause an EA to converge to, and by characterizing the time required to converge to a homogeneous population (see, for example, Goldberg and Deb (1990) and Bäck (1996)). For simplicity, these analyses assume an initial population containing m distinct genotypes in equal $1/m$ proportions and, in addition, that one of the genotypes has a unique, maximal fitness. The results are summarized in the following sections.

Truncation Selection

Truncation selection is intuitively one of the strongest (most elitist) forms of selection in that only the k most fit individuals are selected from a pool of individuals of size $r > k$, the most extreme case being when $k = 1$. Within the selected set of k individuals, there is no further selection differential. All are equally likely to be used. When truncation selection is used for parent selection, then $k < m$ individuals are selected for breeding purposes. Within the selected set of k individuals, there is no further selection differential. All individuals are equally likely to be used.

With an infinite-population model, the top k/m proportion of the population P(t) is selected and replicated m/k times to create population P(t+1). If we then focus on the proportion of the population taken up by the best genotype, it starts in generation 0 at $1/m$, and then increases each generation by a factor of m/k. So, at generation i, its proportion is $\frac{1}{m}\left(\frac{m}{k}\right)^i$. The expected takeover time is then given by the smallest value of i for which $\frac{1}{m}\left(\frac{m}{k}\right)^i \geq m$. Solving this for i yields $i \simeq ceiling(((log\ m)\ /\ (log(m/k)))$.

So, truncation selection leads to extremely rapid convergence. When $k = 1$, it takes only one generation and when $k = 2$, it takes only two generations.

For finite-population models, the top k individuals can be used to produce offspring either deterministically or stochastically. If breeding occurs deterministically, then offspring are produced in multiples of k. For non-overlapping-generation models with $m = n$, this restricts the choice of k to $k = m/b$ where b is the "brood size". Since only the offspring survive, everything is deterministic, resulting in convergence to the same fixed points and the same takeover times as the corresponding infinite population model in which the top k/m fraction are selected.

However, if the offspring population is created from the k parents using *stochastic-uniform selection*, then we have the additional effects of drift to account for. Although difficult to analyze mathematically, we can experimentally study this effect using the same experimental setup that we used to study drift by initializing the population with m unique genotypes and estimate the time, $fixed(m)$, it takes for a population of size m to converge to a fixed point. In addition, in keeping with the model assumptions, each genotype is assigned a unique fitness (arbitrarily chosen from the interval [0,100]).

Figure 6.3 presents these results for the case of $m = 50$ and contrasts them with the predicted values of the infinite population model. Notice how the effects of drift, namely faster convergence times, increase with k, which makes sense since increasing k in the absence of drift increases the number of generations before convergence and, as we saw in the earlier section, drift effects increase linearly with the number of generations.

Perhaps more important to note is that, in addition to faster convergence times, the finite population models are also converging to different (non-optimal) homogeneous fixed points than their infinite population counterparts. Figure 6.4 illustrates this for $m = 50$.

Rank-Proportional Selection

Another frequently used selection scheme that is based on sorting the members of a selection pool by fitness is one in which the probability of selecting a genotype is based linearly on its rank in the fitness-sorted selection pool. So, rather than have all of the probability mass assigned to the top k individuals, each genotype is assigned a selection probability, ranging from $(2/m) - \epsilon$ for the best fit genotype, to a probability of ϵ for the worst fit. By doing so, the total probability mass sums to 1.0 and ϵ controls the slope of the linear probability distribution by ranging from 0.0 to $1/m$. To be more precise, the probability of selecting a genotype of rank i is given by:

$$prob(i) = \left(\tfrac{2}{m} - \epsilon\right) - \left(\tfrac{2}{m} - 2\epsilon\right) * \tfrac{i-1}{m-1}$$

when the best genotype is assigned a rank of 1 and the worst a rank of m.

Clearly, when $\epsilon = 1/m$, the slope is zero and the distribution is uniform over the entire selection pool. The more interesting case is when ϵ approaches zero producing a maximal slope, in the sense that each genotype has a nonzero probability of being selected, but with maximum selection differential based on rank. To understand the selection pressure induced in this case, we again focus on p_t, the proportion of the population occupied by the best genotype at generation t. This corresponds to the set of genotypes with rank $i \leq p_t * m$, and so we have:

$$p_{t+1} = \sum_{i=1}^{p_t * m} prob(i)$$

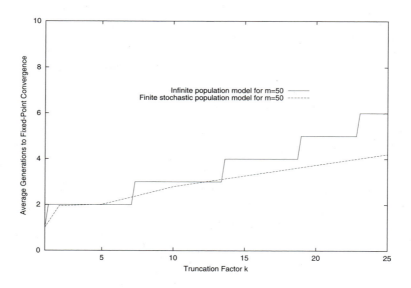

Figure 6.3: Average fixed-point convergence times for truncation selection with $m = 50$ in contrast to the infinite population model.

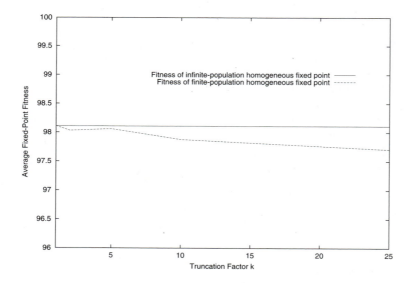

Figure 6.4: Average fixed-point fitness for truncation selection with $m = 50$.

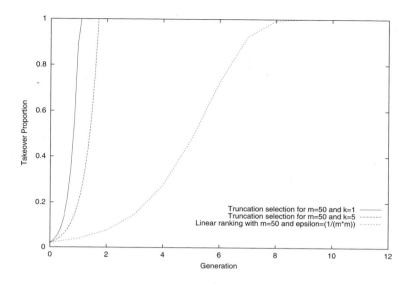

Figure 6.5: Takeover curves for truncation selection and linear ranking with $m = 50$.

which expands into:

$$p_{t+1} = \sum_{i=1}^{p_t * m} \left(\left(\frac{2}{m} - \epsilon \right) - \left(\frac{2}{m} - 2\epsilon \right) * \frac{i-1}{m-1} \right)$$

Solving this recurrence relation in general is difficult. However, the case in which $\epsilon = 1/m^2$ turns out to be mathematically more tractable and important for another reason, as we will soon see. In this case the recurrence relation can be simplified using straightforward (but tedious) algebraic manipulation to:

$$p_{t+1} = 2 * p_t - p_t^2$$

If we again assume $p_0 = 1/m$, then the takeover time is the first generation t for which $p_t \geq m$ can be shown to be of order $ceiling(log(m) + log(log(m)))$ (Goldberg and Deb, 1990). So, compared to truncation selection, linear ranking induces much weaker selection pressure.

One can see more clearly how linear ranking compares to truncation selection by plotting their respective "takeover curves", in which the proportion of the population taken over by the best genotype is plotted as a function of time (in generations) by using the recurrence relations directly without approximation. Figure 6.5 illustrates these takeover curves for both truncation selection and linear ranking when $m = 50$. One can clearly see both the qualitative and the quantitative differences between the two families of selection algorithms: truncation selection induces unrestricted exponential growth of the best genotype, while linear ranking induces a much softer, "logistics-like" growth.

Since linear rank selection necessarily involves stochastic sampling when used with finite population models, there are additional effects due to drift. This is easily seen by comparing the convergence times predicted by the infinite-population model and the observed

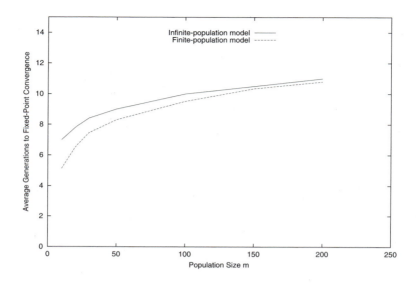

Figure 6.6: Predicted and observed takeover times for linear rank selection.

convergence times for the corresponding finite-population model. Figure 6.6 illustrates these effects for linear rank selection with $\epsilon = 1/m^2$. In particular, one can see how the effects of drift diminish as the population size increases.

Tournament Selection

A potential computational disadvantage to truncation and linear ranking selection methods is that they require the selection pool to be sorted by fitness. For large populations this computational overhead can be of concern to the EA practitioner. An interesting alternative is to leave the selection pool unsorted and use tournament selection, in which the individuals selected are those that "win" a tournament of size q. A tournament consists of picking q individuals from the selection pool using a uniform probability distribution with replacement and designating the winner of that tournament as the one with the best fitness (with ties broken randomly).

The standard infinite population model of tournament selection is based on a non-overlapping-generation model involving m unique genotypes with no reproductive variation. If we let p_t represent the proportion of the population taken up by the best genotype at generation t , then we have:

$$p_{t+1} = 1 - (1 - p_t)^q$$

since the only way the best genotype will not win a tournament of size q is if it is not picked to participate, and the probability of that happening is $(1 - p_t)^q$. If we further assume that $p_0 = 1/m$, then the expected takeover time is given by the smallest t, such that $p_t \geq 1.0$. This recurrence relation is quite difficult to solve in closed form but can be shown to be

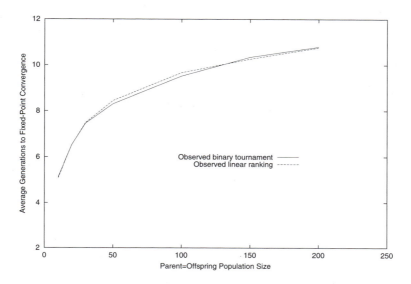

Figure 6.7: Observed takeover times for linear ranking and binary-tournament selection.

asymptotically approximated by $(log\ m + log(log\ m))\ /\ (log\ q)$ for sufficiently large m (Goldberg and Deb, 1990).

A special case of interest is binary-tournament selection ($q = 2$). In this case the general recurrence relation above simplifies to:

$$p_{t+1} = 1 - (1 - p_t)^2$$

which can be rewritten as:

$$p_{t+1} = 2 * p_t - p_t^2$$

Referring back to the previous section on linear ranking, we see that this is identical to the case where $\epsilon = 1/(m^2)$.

This rather surprising result immediately raises the question of whether this observation is also true for finite-population models. To show that this is true mathematically is difficult and beyond the scope of this book. However, this can be easily tested with our experimental analysis methodology. Figure 6.7 plots the fixed-point convergence times for each using a non-overlapping-generation EA with $m = n$, averaged over 400 independent trials. Figure 6.8 plots the average fitness of the fixed points of this same data set. In both cases we see that on average the two selection techniques produce the same results with the same degree of variance.

This is an important insight for the practitioner. It means that the two selection methods can be used interchangeably without any significant change in EA dynamics. So, for example, in moving from a centralized, single-machine EA architecture to a decentralized, multiple-machine EA architecture, one might prefer binary-tournament selection over linear ranking because it does not require any global actions (such as sorting).

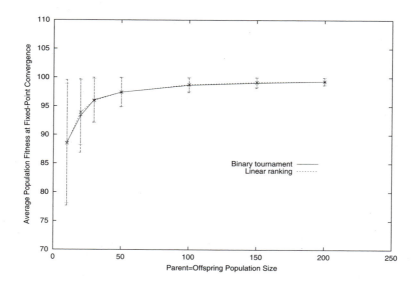

Figure 6.8: Average fixed point fitness for linear ranking and tournament selection.

Understanding this relationship also allows the EA designer to fill in the rather large gap we saw in figure 6.5 between the selection pressures induced by truncation and linear ranking. This is easily accomplished by increasing q as illustrated in figure 6.9.

The combination of these two features, the implementation simplicity and the ability to control selection pressure easily, has made tournament selection the preferred choice of many EA practitioners.

Fitness-Proportional Selection

The three selection methods that we have studied so far can be summarized as providing a wide range of selection pressures, from very strong (truncation) to moderate (tournament) to weak (linear ranking). Each method has a parameter that allows an EA designer to fine tune the selection pressure within these general categories. However, having chosen a particular selection method, the induced selection pressure is then constant for the entire evolutionary run. A natural question to ask is whether it is possible and useful to adapt the selection pressure during an evolutionary run. It is clearly possible and in fact rather easy to do so with the three selection methods we have studied so far by designing a procedure for dynamically modifying the method's tuning parameter. Whether this will be useful will depend on both the application domain and the particular update procedure chosen.

However, there is another selection method, fitness-proportional selection, that self-adapts the selection pressure without requiring the designer to write additional code. This is accomplished by defining the probability of selecting individual i at generation t to be $fitness(i)/total\_fitness(t)$. If we sample this distribution m times, the expected number of times individual i is chosen is simply $fitness(i)/ave\_fitness(t)$. In particular, if we focus

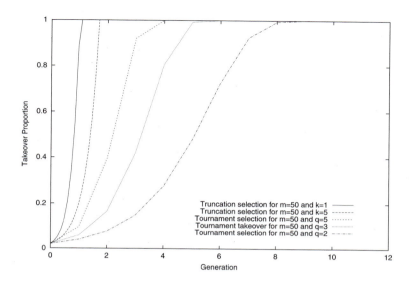

Figure 6.9: Growth curves for truncation and tournament selection method using a non-overlapping-generation EA with $m = 50$.

on the best individual, then it grows at a rate given by:

$$p_{t+1} = \frac{fitness(best)}{ave\_fitness(t)} * p_t$$

So, in the early generations with significant fitness diversity, the growth rate of the best individual is quite high. However, as the best individual takes over more of the population, the average fitness of the population increases and thus reduces the growth rate of the best individual. As the population approaches homogeneity, the selection pressure flattens out to become nearly uniform. The implication of all this is that the expected takeover time is a function of the properties of the fitness landscape, and in general is much longer than the fixed-pressure methods. For example, on polynomial and exponential landscapes the expected takeover time can be shown to be of order $m * log\ m$ (Goldberg and Deb, 1990).

As before, the finite-population case is much more difficult to analyze mathematically. We can, however, use our empirical methodology to provide comparative illustrations. Figure 6.10 illustrates the dramatic difference in convergence rates between fitness-proportional and binary-tournament selection, and also shows that, after an initial burst of high selection pressure, the long-term selection pressure of fitness-proportional selection is only slightly stronger than that of uniform selection.

One should be careful, however, not to place too much emphasis on average fixed-point convergence times alone. One obtains a quite different picture if one looks at the average fitness associated with the fixed point itself. Figure 6.11 illustrates this by plotting (from the same data set used for figure 6.10) the average fitness of the population fixed points as a function of both selection method and population size. The case of stochastic-uniform

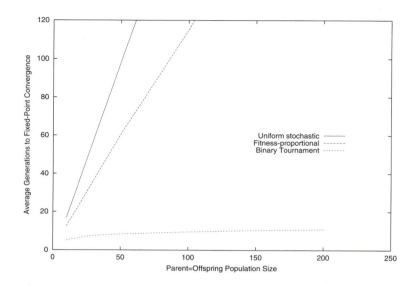

Figure 6.10: Average fixed-point convergence times for various parent selection methods in a non-overlapping-generation EA with $m = n$ and no reproductive variation.

selection (pure drift) is a bit surprising at first, but easy to understand. With neutral selection, all of the initial genotypes are equally likely to be lost, so the average fixed-point fitness is the same as the average fitness of the initial population (approximately 50.0).

As one would expect, when we switch to fitness-biased selection methods, we dramatically increase the likelihood of converging to high-fitness fixed points. The stronger the fitness bias, the higher the resulting fixed-point fitness. At the same time, both binary tournament and fitness-proportional selection are themselves stochastic sampling techniques and are subject to sampling errors as well (i.e., drift). The effects of this drift can be seen quite clearly in figure 6.11, in that lower convergence fitness is obtained as the population size m decreases.

So, is this self-adaptive selection pressure of fitness-proportional selection good or bad? The answer, of course, depends on a number of things, including the application domain. As we will see in chapter 7, softer and adaptive forms of selection are helpful when the fitness landscape is itself changing during an EA run. On the other hand, if one is given a fixed computational budget to find a reasonable solution to an optimization problem, stronger and more aggressive forms of selection are necessary.

6.3.1.3 Non-overlapping-Generation Models with $n \neq m$

Of course, many EAs are run with a parent population size of m and a different offspring population size n, so it is important to understand how this affects EA dynamics. For non-overlapping-generation EAs, the only interesting case is $n > m$. In this case one needs to specify both a parent selection method and a survival selection method to select the m

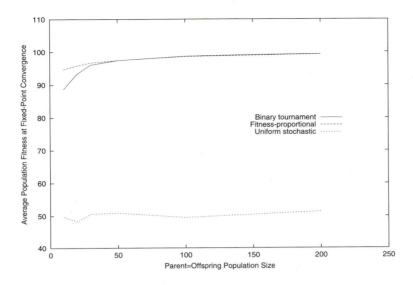

Figure 6.11: Average fixed-point fitness for various parent selection methods in a non-overlapping-generation EA with $m = n$ and no reproductive variation.

offspring that will survive to be parents in the next generation. As before, it is best to start with the simplest case involving neutral (uniform) selection.

For infinite-population models, it should be clear that applying uniform selection twice in every generation has no additional effect. It should also be clear that, for finite population models, applying *stochastic*-uniform selection twice in every generation will increase the drift effects we saw earlier. This can be alleviated by using *deterministic*-uniform parent selection, in which each parent produces exactly b offspring, implying an offspring population size of $n = b * m$. There are a variety of EAs that use this approach for parent selection, and b is often referred to as the "brood size". In this case, since the offspring population now consists of b replications of the parent population, applying stochastic sampling to the offspring population to select the m next generation parents should exhibit the same effects as the previous case with $m = n$. In particular, increasing n should have no effect on generational convergence times and $fixed(m, n) = fixed(m)$.

The same experimental setup can be used to confirm these intuitions. Figure 6.12 illustrates this for the case of $m = 50$ with both deterministic-uniform and stochastic-uniform parent selection. Note that, for the special case of $m = n$, no additional survival selection is required. So, deterministic-uniform parent selection produces an immediate population fixed point, and stochastic-uniform parent selection results in normal drift effects. However, for $n > m$ we see exactly what was expected. In the case of deterministic-uniform parent selection, we have $fixed(m, n) = fixed(m) \simeq 2m$ as before. However, for stochastic-uniform parent selection, we see a significant increase in drift effects characterized by $fixed(m, n) = fixed(m) \simeq 1.5m$.

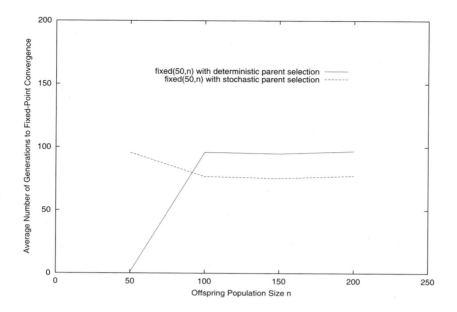

Figure 6.12: Average fixed-point convergence times due to drift in a non-overlapping-generation EA with $m = 50$ and $n > m$.

If we now consider the case of fitness-biased selection, it should be clear that applying fitness-biased selection twice in every generation will significantly increase the overall selection pressure beyond that produced in the $m = n$ case. This is generally too strong in practice and the usual case is to have deterministic-uniform parent selection together with some form of fitness-biased survival selection. In such cases the convergence dynamics are identical to analyses of the $m = n$ case.

In particular, recall that the convergence times of truncation selection depend on both m and n, and is of order $(log\ m)/(log(n/m))$. Hence, with truncation selection the convergence time can be driven down to a single generation by increasing n. By contrast, the convergence of the other selection methods depended only on m.

Figure 6.13 illustrates this for binary-tournament selection. The baseline case is $m = n$ for which $fixed(m) = log(m)$. If we then fix a particular value for m and allow n to increase as $b*m$, we see that increasing the offspring population size has no effect on generational convergence time, i.e., $fixed(m, n) = fixed(m)$.

6.3.2   Overlapping-Generation Models

As we saw in the earlier chapters, many EAs use an overlapping-generation model in which both parents and offspring compete for survival. We saw one strong motivation for this in the previous section, namely, that with stochastic selection in non-overlapping-generation EAs it is quite possible to lose some of the most fit individuals from the population. Intuitively,

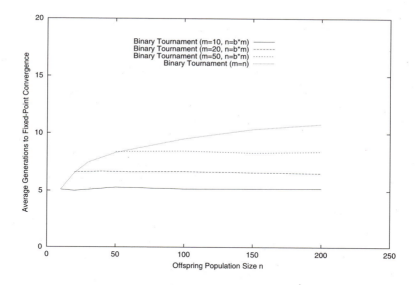

Figure 6.13: Average fixed-point convergence times for a non-overlapping-generation EA with $m = \{10, 20, 50\}$, $n = b * m$, uniform parent selection, and binary tournament survival selection.

one would expect that the effects of drift would be reduced by going to an overlapping generation EA. As before, we analyze the simpler case of uniform selection first, and then look at fitness-biased selection.

6.3.2.1 Uniform (Neutral) Selection

For infinite population models the switch from a non-overlapping-generation to an overlapping-generation model has no effect on convergence times in the case of uniform selection, since both the parent and offspring population have the same genome makeup, as does their union. However, for finite population models with overlapping generations, we need to specify the survival selection procedure used to reduce the population size from $m + n$ to m. If we want to maintain neutral selection, the only option is to set survival selection to be stochastic-uniform. However, we still have the possibility of parent selection being either deterministic-uniform or stochastic-uniform.

As noted in the previous section, in the case of deterministic-uniform parent selection, it only makes sense for n to be specified in terms of integer multiples b of m. However, in the case of stochastic-uniform parent selection, no such restriction applies, and of particular interest is the case when $n = 1$, often referred to in the literature as incremental or "steady state" EAs.

Figure 6.14 presents the results of using the empirical methodology to compare how stochastic parent selection and deterministic parent selection affect drift for $m = 50$. If we compare these results with the previous non-overlapping-generation results (figure 6.12), we

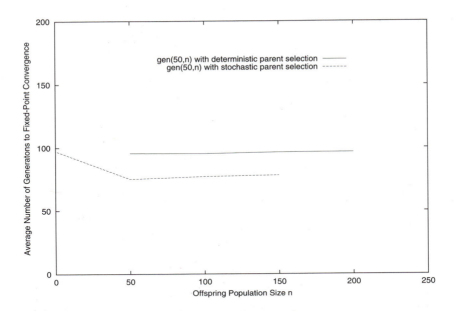

Figure 6.14: Average fixed-point convergence times due to drift for both deterministic and stochastic parent selection in overlapping-generation EAs with $m = 50$ and varying n.

note first that the drift effects are identical for $b > 1$. While surprising at first, this can be understood by noting that the non-overlapping offspring population already consists of b replications of the parent population. So, switching to overlapping simply adds another copy of the parent population to the survival selection pool. This has no additional effect on the stochastic survival selection process, and hence no effect on drift. Similarly, having stochastic selection for both parents and survival increases drift as before. So, just as in the non-overlapping case, $fixed(m, n) = fixed(m)$ for $b > 1$.

The second important thing to note in figure 6.14 is that, for stochastic parent selection, the drift effects on fixed-point convergence times are reduced linearly as n is varied from m down to 1, at which point they are nearly the same as in the deterministic case. To understand why, note that, for $n \leq M$, a total of $2n$ stochastic samples are taken each generation, and hence that total (and the related drift effect) decreases linearly with n.

6.3.2.2 Fitness-Biased Selection

Switching to an overlapping-generation model has the same drift reduction effect on EAs that use some form of fitness-biased selection. This is rather easy to verify using our experimental methodology by simply modifying any one of the non-overlapping-generation models from section 6.3.1.2 to an overlapping-generation EA and analyzing the effects. Figure 6.15 illustrates this for the case of binary-tournament selection.

As we saw in section 6.3.1.2, stochastic binary-tournament selection has associated drift

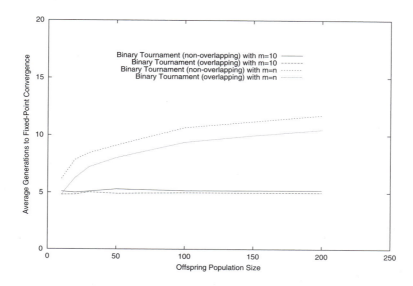

Figure 6.15: Average fixed-point convergence times for binary-tournament selection in both an overlapping and non-overlapping-generation EA with no reproductive variation.

effects. These effects are reduced by switching from non-overlapping to overlapping generations, since all parents are now guaranteed to be included in the survival selection pool.

6.3.3   Selection in Standard EAs

As we saw in the previous chapters, EA practitioners have made quite different choices when designing their EAs, including the selection methods that they used. We are now in a position to use our empirical analysis methodology to compare how some of the commonly used EAs differ with respect to selection pressure. Recall that a canonical GA uses a non-overlapping-generation model, with a parent selection method of fitness-proportional selection, and $m = n$. A common GA variant involves replacing fitness-proportional selection with binary-tournament selection. EP uses an overlapping-generation model, with deterministic-uniform parent selection, $m = n$, and truncation survival selection. A $(\mu + \lambda)$-ES uses an overlapping-generation model, with stochastic-uniform parent selection, $m < n$, and truncation survival selection. A (μ, λ)-ES is the same except that its generations do not overlap. For ESs the ratio n/m controls the truncation selection pressure. Ratios of approximately 5:1 are often used in practice.

Since the experimental methodology involves initializing the parent population in a particular way and then running it until the parent population reaches a fixed point, the most reasonable way to do a comparison is by using identical parent population sizes, and then setting the offspring population size appropriately for each EA. So, for example, a parent population size of $m = 20$ implies $n = 20$ for both GAs and EP, but $n = 20 * 5$ for an ES with a 5:1 ratio.

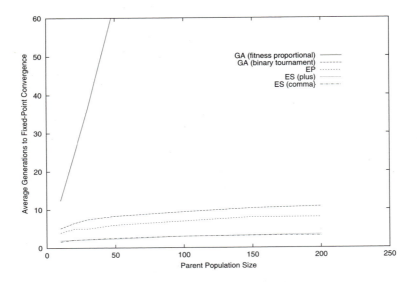

Figure 6.16: Average fixed-point convergence times for various standard EAs with no reproductive variation.

Figure 6.16 illustrates the fixed-point convergence times (averaged over 400 runs) for each of these EAs as a function of increasing parent population size. First, note that ranking the EAs by convergence times corresponds directly to the ranking of the underlying selection algorithms they use, i.e., the choice of the selection methods determines convergence behavior. Second, note the wide range of convergence pressure exhibited by these EAs, all of which have been found to be useful. So we should not expect a single "best" selection method.

As noted earlier, convergence times provide only a partial understanding of these EA differences. Using the same data set as figure 6.16, figure 6.17 plots the average fixed-point fitness for each of these standard EAs. It illustrates that stronger selection pressure by itself does not imply better fixed-point fitness values. Rather, since there is no reproductive variation, it is the combination of strong selection pressure and the reduced drift of the overlapping-generation EAs that increases the probability of not losing the best individuals from the initial population, and thus increases the probability of converging to high-fitness fixed points.

6.3.4   Reducing Selection Sampling Variance

It should be clear by now that an important EA design goal is to minimize the effects of drift, and we have seen a number on strategies for doing so. One approach is to increase population sizes, but used alone this leads to practical concerns about the running time of large-population EAs. A second approach is to use EAs with overlapping generations which, as we have seen, can be quite effective when combined with the appropriate selec-

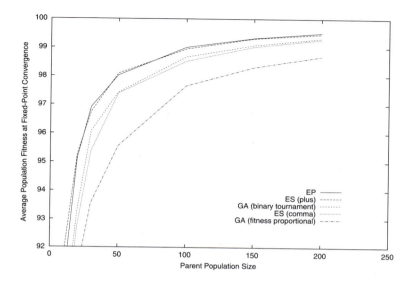

Figure 6.17: Average fixed-point fitness for various standard EAs with no reproductive variation.

tion pressure. A third approach is to use selection techniques that have smaller stochastic sampling variances. Clearly, deterministic selection methods have zero variance, but are not always appropriate. However, even in the case of stochastic selection, it is often possible to minimize sampling variance by using surprisingly simple implementation techniques.

Since EA selection pools consist of a finite number of m individuals, the requirement in general is to construct a discrete probability distribution over this set of individuals. Since the makeup of the selection pools is determined dynamically, the discrete probability distributions must be constructed dynamically as well. Conceptually, we can envision such a distribution as a "wheel of fortune" consisting of a pie chart with m pie-shaped wedges, the sizes of which correspond to the probabilities assigned to each individual. This distribution is then sampled by spinning the wheel of fortune and seeing where it stops.

If we spin the wheel k times to select k individuals, we have implemented a selection method with the standard amount of sample variance. However, this can be improved upon by using the SUS technique developed by Baker (1987) which he was able to show was an unbiased sampling technique with minimum variance. Although developed initially for fitness-proportional selection, the technique can be used to reduce the variance of any stochastic selection method that uses this wheel-of-fortune approach. The basic idea is that, if we need to make k selections, we place k evenly spaced selection points around the circumference of the wheel. Then, one spin of the wheel selects k individuals rather than just one. By simultaneously selecting all k individuals, selection variance is minimized.

As noted earlier, the pie chart is dynamically computed based on the fitnesses of the current members of the selection pool and the particular selection algorithm being used. A uniform selection method would result in a pie chart of equal-sized wedges, whereas

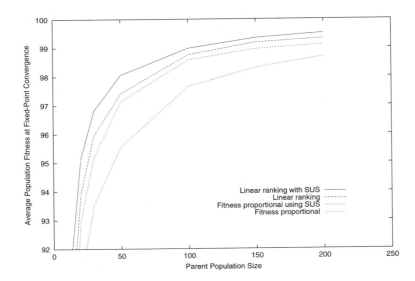

Figure 6.18: Average fixed-point fitness for ranking and fitness-proportional selection with and without SUS.

fitness-proportional, ranking and truncation selection all produce non-uniform wedges. An interesting thing to note is that tournament selection does not fit into this wheel-of-fortune model since the size of the wedges are not precomputed but inferred as part of the selection process. However, if drift is a concern in this case, we are now in a position to propose an immediate solution. As we saw earlier, binary-tournament selection and linear ranking induced the same average selection pressure. So, replacing a binary-tournament selection method with an SUS version of linear ranking should result in the same selection pressure with much lower levels of drift.

How significant are the effects of switching to SUS? Figure 6.18 shows the average fixed-point fitness for the standard linear rank-proportional selection and fitness-proportional selection methods (and, implicitly, binary-tournament selection since it is equivalent to linear ranking), and contrasts that with the equivalent SUS implementations. As can be seen, switching to SUS significantly improves fixed-point fitness for both selection methods.

6.3.5 Selection Summary

It is obvious that selection plays an important role in the behavior of EAs in general. In this section we have seen that, for finite-population EAs, its role is even more critical because selection methods are a potential source of drift, which can result in a loss of population diversity due to sampling variance in addition to the normal fitness-related loss of diversity. Fortunately, these effects can be controlled by increasing population size, by using overlapping-generation models, and with improved sampling techniques.

These results provide important insights into the interplay between population size and selection in EAs. In particular, it is clear that there is no single best combination of population size and selection method. Rather, the particular choices will depend on the choices for reproductive operators and the characteristics of the fitness landscape. These issues are explored in detail in the following sections.

6.4   Reproduction-Only Models

Section 6.3 focused on the analysis selection-only EAs. While this has helped us understand the interacting effects of population size, selection and drift, reproductive variation must be included if we are to have any hope of understanding real EAs. At the same time, the mechanisms responsible for this variation have historically been the most difficult to analyze and have engendered considerable debate. The challenge for the EC community is to design and implement *effective* computational mechanisms of inheritance, i.e., the ability to create *viable* offspring that are similar to their parents but not identical. If we take a hint from nature, we see two general strategies for accomplishing this:

- **Asexual Reproduction**: in which a single parent is cloned, and the cloned copy is perturbed (mutated) to introduce some variation.

- **Sexual Reproduction**: in which cloned (and possibly perturbed) segments from multiple parents are used to create hybrid offspring.

The form that such reproductive operators take depends, of course, on the way in which individuals are represented. However, the role they play is the same: one of diversity-increasing *exploration*, a counterbalance to the diversity-decreasing *exploitation* pressure of selection. A well-designed EA maintains a proper balance between these opposing forces. However, diversity management, while necessary, is not sufficient for good EA performance. Reproductive operators must have the ability to create *useful* variation, i.e., both *diversity* and *improvements in fitness*. Since the mechanisms of selection and reproduction interact in complex nonlinear ways, the analysis strategy will be to study reproduction in isolation first, and then analyze its interactions with selection.

Recall that our general model of EA population dynamics is of the form:

$$P(t + 1) = evolve(P(t)) = survival\_selection(reproduction(parent\_selection(P(t))))$$

where a population P at time t represents a point in an $r - 1$-dimensional simplex:

$$P(t) = < c_1(t), c_2(t), ..., c_r(t) >$$

As before, the analysis can be simplified initially by assuming a non-overlapping-generation model.

6.4.1   Non-overlapping-Generation Models

With non-overlapping-generation EAs, there is no survival selection component. Hence, our model simplifies to:

$$P(t+1) = evolve(P(t)) = reproduction(parent\_selection(P(t)))$$

We can further isolate the effects of reproductive variation by assuming uniform (neutral) selection; i.e., the probability of selecting a particular genotype to be a parent depends only on its frequency in the population:

$$P(t+1) = evolve(P(t)) = reproduction(uniform\_selection(P(t)))$$

As before, this can viewed as comprising $r - 1$ equations of the form:

$$c_i(t+1) = reproduce_i(uniform\_selection(P(t)))$$

each of which specifies the number of genotypes of type i that will be generated by the reproductive operators. For single parent (i.e., asexual) reproductive operators, this corresponds to equations of the form:

$$c_i(t+1) = \sum_{j=1}^{r} reproduce_{ij}(t)(select_j(t))$$

in which $select_j(t)$ represents the number of times genotype j is selected to be a parent at time t, and $reproduce_{ij}(t)$, the number of times an asexual reproductive process converts genotype j into genotype i. If $reproduce_{ij}(t)$ is independent of time, this simplifies further to:

$$c_i(t+1) = \sum_{j=1}^{r} reproduce_{ij}(select_j(t))$$

If parent selection is assumed to be deterministic and uniform, then $select_j(t) = c_j(t)$, and

$$c_i(t+1) = \sum_{j=1}^{r} reproduce_{ij}(c_j(t))$$

Multi-parent (sexual) reproductive operators are handled in a similar fashion. For example, two-parent reproduction is given by:

$$c_i(t+1) = \sum_{j=1}^{r} \sum_{k=1}^{r} reproduce_{ijk}(t)(select_j(t), select_k(t))$$

which again simplifies to:

$$c_i(t+1) = \sum_{j=1}^{r} \sum_{k=1}^{r} reproduce_{ijk}(select_j(t), select_k(t))$$

when $reproduce_{ijk}$ is independent of time, and further to

$$c_i(t+1) = \sum_{j=1}^{r} \sum_{k=1}^{r} reproduce_{ijk}(c_j(t), c_k(t))$$

with deterministic-uniform parent selection.

Clearly, the required *reproduce* elements of these models will be highly dependent on the genome representation and the particular choices of reproductive operators. These dependencies are explored in the following subsections.

6.4.1.1 Reproduction for Fixed-Length Discrete Linear Genomes

Recall that all of the models developed so far in this chapter have assumed a finite set of r genotypes. A standard additional assumption is that the genomes are linear structures consisting of a fixed number of L genes, each of which can take on only a finite set of values (alleles). This assumption does not significantly widen the gap between theory and practice, since many EAs use fixed-length linear representations. Making this assumption allows for an additional analytical perspective, in which one can focus on a particular gene position (locus) j and study the distribution of its k_j allele values $a_{j1}...a_{jk_j}$ in the population. Of particular interest is how the frequency $f(a_{ji})$ of allele a_{ji} in the population changes over time, which provides additional insight into the effects of reproductive variation.

Traditional Two-Parent Crossover

The traditional two-parent crossover operator produces genetic variation in the offspring by choosing for each locus i in the offspring's genome whether the allele value at locus i will be inherited from the first parent or from the second one. We can characterize the result of this process as a binary string of length L, in which a value of 0 at position i indicates that the offspring inherited allele i from the first parent, and a value of 1 at position i indicates that the allele value was inherited from the second parent. If we imagine this assignment process as proceeding across the parents' genomes from left to right, then the string 0000111 represents the case in which this reproductive process assigned to the offspring the first 4 alleles from parent one, and then "crossed over" and assigned the remaining three alleles from parent two. Patterns of this sort, in which offspring inherit an initial allele segment from one parent and a final allele segment from the other parent, are generated by the familiar 1-point crossover operator used in canonical GAs. Similarly, a 2-point crossover operator generates patterns of the form 00011100, and an (L-1)-point crossover operator simply alternates allele assignments. An interesting alternative to n-point crossover is the "uniform" crossover operator (Syswerda, 1989), in which alleles are inherited by flipping an unbiased coin at each locus to determine which parent's allele gets inherited, thus uniformly generating all possible crossover patterns.

Recall from the analysis in section 6.3 that selection-only EAs using uniform (neutral) selection converge to a fixed point. With infinite-population models, that fixed point is the initial population $P(0)$. So, what happens if we add a two-parent crossover operator to these uniform selection models? Clearly, every two-parent crossover operator has the ability to introduce new genomes into the population that were not present in the initial population $P(0)$. However, since the offspring produced can only consist of genetic material inherited from their parents on a gene-by-gene basis, no new gene values (alleles) can be introduced into the population. Hence, any new genomes must consist of recombinations of the alleles present in $P(0)$, and all population trajectories are restricted to points in the simplex representing those populations whose alleles are present in $P(0)$. Thus, infinite population EAs with neutral selection and two-parent crossover no longer have $P(0)$ as their fixed point. Rather, they converge to a rather famous fixed point called the "Robbins equilibrium" (Geiringer, 1944). To express this more precisely, let L be the length of a fixed-length genotype, and let a_{ij} represent the allele value of the jth gene of genotype i. Then, the population fixed point is given by:

$$c_i(fixed\_point) \;=\; \prod_{j=1}^{L} f_{a_{ij}}(0)$$

where $f_{a_{ij}}(0)$ is the frequency with which allele a_{ij} occurs in the initial population $P(0)$. Stated another way, at the fixed point, the population is in "linkage equilibrium" in the sense that any correlations (linkages) between allele values on different loci that were present in $P(0)$ no longer exist.

This rather elegant and mathematically useful result must, however, be applied with some care. Suppose, for example, $P(0)$ consists of only a single genotype. Then, every off-spring produced by two-parent crossover will be identical to the parents, and $P(0)$ is a fixed point in this case. In general, in order to reach a Robbins equilibrium, every possible genotype must be able to be generated from the genotypes in $P(0)$ using two-parent crossover. Stated another way, the *closure* of $P(0)$ under 2-point crossover must be G, the set of all possible genotypes. If not, the convergence is to a Robbins equilibrium with respect to the genomes G' in the closure of $P(0)$.

To get a sense of this, imagine an infinite population $P(0)$ consisting of an equal number of two genotypes of length 5, one represented by the string AAAAA and the other by BBBBB. At each of the 5 loci there is a 50-50 split between the A and B alleles. Using uniform selection and *any* form of two-parent crossover, the fixed point will be a population of a distinct set of genotypes in equal proportions. Whether that set will consist of all the 2^5 possible genotypes G will depend on whether G is the closure of $P(0)$ under a particular form of two-parent crossover.

It is instructive to explore the extent to which these results carry over to finite-population EA models. First, as we saw in section 6.3, to avoid losing genotypes due to drift effects we need to focus on finite-population EAs that use *deterministic*-uniform parent selection. In addition, recall that all finite-population EAs are restricted to visiting points in the simplex corresponding to gene frequencies expressed as multiples of $1/m$, where m is the population size. If we imagine the set of such points in a nearby neighborhood of the corresponding Robbins equilibrium point for the finite population model, then finite-population trajectories converge in a probabilistic sense to this neighborhood. That is, as evolution proceeds, the probability of a finite-population selection-only EA being in this neighborhood increases to a value close to 1.0. Notice that it will never be exactly 1.0 since there is always a small, but nonzero probability of leaving the neighborhood, since all the original allele values are still in every $P(t)$.

The proof that these finite-population selection-only EAs converge in probability to a neighborhood of a Robbins equilibrium point requires a Markov chain analysis that is beyond the scope of this book. However, it is rather easy to illustrate using our experimental framework. Suppose we let G be the set of all genomes of length 5 constructed from genes that have only two allele values (A or B). Then, the cardinality of G is $2^5 = 32$ and, for any initial $P(0)$ containing uniform allele frequencies, the infinite population model would converge to the Robbins equilibrium point consisting of uniform genotype frequencies c_j for all genotypes in the closure of $P(0)$. If the closure of $P(0)$ is G, then $c_j = 1/32$. Suppose we measure the distance that a particular finite population is from this point in the simplex using the standard root-mean-square error measure:

$$rms(P(t)) \;=\; \sqrt{\sum_{j=1}^{L}(c_j(t) - 1/|G|)^2}$$

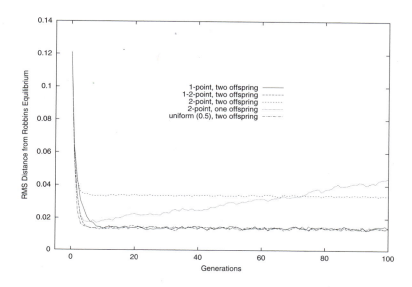

Figure 6.19: Average rms distance from Robbins equilibrium for several two-parent crossover operators.

Figure 6.19 plots this measure over time for a finite population EA of size 128 in which the initial population $P(0)$ consists of an equal number of two genotypes, AAAAA and BBBBB. The plots represent the *rms* value for five different crossover operators averaged over 10 independent runs for each operator.

Notice that, for three of the crossover operators, the populations quickly reach statistical equilibrium states near the Robbins equilibrium point. For one operator the equilibrium state was much farther away, and for one operator no equilibrium state was achieved. The labels on the graphs provide a hint as to why we observe different population dynamics. An empirical observation that has been known for many years in the GA community is that problem-solving performance is often improved by defining two-parent crossover to produce two offspring rather than just one, the first one corresponding to the result of starting the copy operation with the first parent, and the second offspring the result of starting the copy operation with the second parent. So, for example, a 2-point crossover operator defined by the pattern 01110 when applied to parents AAAAA and BBBBB would produce a complementary pair of offspring ABBBA and BAAAB. This results in sets of offspring that have the same allele frequencies as their parents. Combining this with deterministic-uniform selection results in no change in population allele frequencies from generation to generation, and is the basis for Culberson's GIGA EA (Culberson, 1994). However, if only one offspring is produced, a new source of drift is introduced, in that the number of times a member of the current population is chosen to be the *first* crossover parent can vary widely from the expected value of 2.

The second peculiarity in figure 6.19 is the result of a fairly obscure, but important, detail regarding the way in which 2-point crossover is implemented. Implementations generally pick two distinct crossover points from a uniform distribution over K possible crossover points. If K=L (the length of the genome), the crossover patterns produced include those produced by 1-point crossover as well. If K=L-1 (a frequent choice), 1-point crossover patterns are excluded. Notice that the latter case resulted in an equilibrium state much farther from Robbins equilibrium than the former. A brief glance at the equilibrium population provides the explanation. With K=L-1, the closure of $P(0)$ includes only 1/2 of the 2^5 alleles in G. For that subset of G, the population is near Robbins equilibrium. By contrast, when K=L, G is the closure of $P(0)$. An interesting question for the reader to consider is whether this is true for arbitrary initial populations $P(0)$.

The final thing to note in figure 6.19 is that when we compare the results of the three crossover operators that produce two offspring *and* produce G as the closure of $P(0)$, they all achieve similar statistical proximity to the Robbins equilibrium point. Although it is a bit difficult to see, it is also the case that proximity is achieved more rapidly as the number of crossover points is increased.

Recall that the results in figure 6.19 were obtained under the assumption of *deterministic*-uniform parent selection. As we saw in the previous section, if selection is *stochastic*, additional "genetic drift" is introduced, resulting in a steady loss of population diversity over time. If we combine this with the reproductive variation provided by two-parent crossover, we obtain interesting overall population dynamics. Figure 6.20 plots the results of rerunning the experiments in figure 6.19 for the three crossover operators that had achieved a Robbins equilibrium under deterministic-uniform parent selection. In each case the initial population $P(0)$ is positioned on the edge of the simplex halfway between the vertex representing a uniform population of all AAAAAs and the vertex representing a population of all BBBBBs. Under two-parent crossover the population moves fairly quickly toward the interior Robbins equilibrium point. However, as the population approaches it, the effects of genetic drift begin to dominate and the population begins to drift steadily away. Since two-parent crossover cannot introduce new alleles into the population, the population trajectories ultimately terminate at one of the vertices of the simplex, just as we saw in the earlier section on genetic drift.

K-Parent Crossover

Although there are not many examples in nature, one can easily generalize two-parent crossover to K-parent crossover ($K \geq 2$). For example, the offspring produced by a 1-point crossover operator applied to three parents would inherit an initial segment of alleles from one parent, an intermediate segment from a second parent, and a final segment from a third parent. For uniform K-parent crossover, a K-sided coin would be flipped at each gene position to determine which parent's allele value is inherited. Such left-to-right "scanning" crossover operators have been studied empirically in Eiben et al. (1994) and elsewhere.

With infinite population models the effects of increasing K in this manner are clear: namely, a speedup in the rate of convergence to a Robbins equilibrium. If we allow K to be the entire population, then for infinite population models a Robbins equilibrium is reached in one generation! For finite population models the story is more complicated. Recall from the previous section that even when parent selection is deterministic and uniform, unless two-parent crossover produced two complementary offspring, there is steady genetic drift

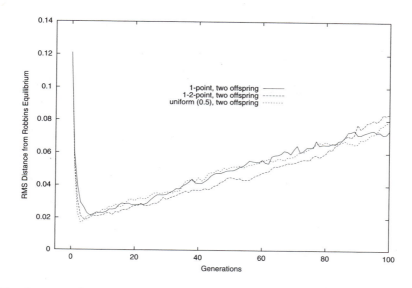

Figure 6.20: Average distance from Robbins equilibrium for several two-parent crossover operators in the presence of genetic drift.

because parents do not in general participate exactly the same number of times as both the first and the second parent. A similar effect applies to the K-parent case. However, it should be clear that eliminating that source of drift is more challenging in the K-parent case. For example, with 3-parent 1-point crossover, there are 6 members in the complementary offspring set. If all of them are included in the offspring population, its size is now double that of the parent population and some form of survival selection is required. For most EA implementations this is not done; rather, the drift effects are tolerated.

The particular case in which parent selection is deterministic uniform and uniform K-parent crossover is used with $K = M$ (the population size) deserves special attention. In this case, M offspring are produced by sampling the allele frequency distributions at each of the L loci of the current population P(t), i.e., its Robbins equilibrium point. Hence, for reproductive purposes, the entire population can be dispensed with and replaced with a set of L discrete probability distributions that get updated each generation. As a consequence, a variety of "population-less" EAs have been studied (see, for example, Baluja and Caruana (1995)). The theoretical implications of EA populations evolving near (or at) Robbins equilibrium points is clear – it makes the mathematical analysis much simpler, and that alone has been used as an argument for preferring EAs of this type (e.g., Mühlenbein (1997)). However, the implications on EA performance are much more subtle and complex, and involve the interaction of fitness-biased selection with reproduction. These issues will be addressed in section 6.5.

Traditional Discrete Mutation

In this section the focus is on the effect that mutation has on population dynamics. Just as with recombination, these effects are first analyzed in isolation by assuming a non-overlapping-generation model with uniform (neutral) parent selection. For fixed-length linear genomes with discrete allele values, traditional reproductive mutation operators are defined as a two-stage process in which a parent genome is first cloned, and then individual gene positions on the cloned genome are probabilistically selected to undergo a mutation. One mechanism for doing so is to flip a coin at each locus, the result of which is a binary string pattern like 0010...101 in which the 1s represent the loci to be mutated. By changing the bias of the coin, the expected number of mutations per genome can be increased or decreased. Alternatively, one might define a k-loci mutation operator in which *exactly k* loci are mutated, but the choice of the k loci is stochastic with uniform probability.

For each of the selected loci, mutation consists of stochastically selecting an alternate allele value with uniform probability from the set of allele values defined for that gene. In the case of binary-valued genomes, this corresponds to the familiar "bit-flip" mutation operator.

As before, G represents the set of all possible genomes. For mutation operators that stochastically select the number of loci to be mutated, it is possible for any member of G to be produced as the offspring of any other member of G in one reproductive step if the mutation rate is nonzero. To see this, let the 1s in a binary string of length L indicate where two members of G differ in their allele values. Then the probability of this reproductive event is the product of the probability of that particular binary string pattern being generated, and the product of the probabilities that each individual mutation will change each of the genes to matching allele values. Since each of these probabilities is nonzero, so is their product. Moreover, the probabilities are symmetric, i.e., $p\_mut(i,j) = p\_mut(j,i)$ for all genotypes $i, j \in G$.

For infinite population models, the implications of this for the dynamics are quite clear. Regardless of the makeup of $P(0)$, every trajectory in the simplex converges to the fixed point in which every genotype in G is present in identical proportions, i.e., $c_i = 1/|G|$ for all genotypes $i \in G$. To see this, note that the transition from $P(t)$ to $P(t+1)$ is given by:

$$c_i(t+1) = c_i(t) - \left(\sum_{j=1}^{r} c_i(t) * p\_mut(i,j)\right) + \left(\sum_{j=1}^{r} c_j(t) * p\_mut(j,i)\right)$$

for all genotypes $i \in G$. Since $p\_mut(i,i) = p\_mut(j,i)$, $c_i(t+1) = c_i(t)$ when all c_j are equal. This fixed point is both reachable and stable, since, if $c_i(t) < c_j(t)$, there will be fewer mutations from genotype i to genotype j than the reverse, thus decreasing the difference between c_i and c_j.

For finite population models that use deterministic-uniform parent selection, the dynamics are similar, but restricted to those points in the simplex that can be represented by populations of size m. Regardless of the makeup of the initial population $P(0)$, finite-population mutation-only EAs probabilistically converge to a neighborhood of the *uniform* Robbins equilibrium point determined by G.

The proof of this requires a Markov chain analysis that is beyond the scope of this book. However, it can be demonstrated easily with our empirical analysis methodology. Suppose we start with an initial population $P(0)$ as far away as possible from the equilibrium

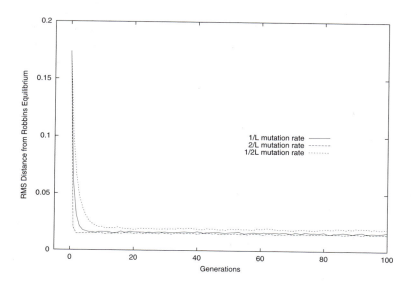

Figure 6.21: RMS distance to a uniform Robbins equilibrium for several mutation rates.

point, namely an initial population positioned on a vertex of the simplex (i.e., a uniform population) and measure as before the *rms* distance that $P(t)$ is from the equilibrium point (the center point in the simplex defined by $c_i = 1/|G|$). Figure 6.21 shows this effect for genomes of length 5 (i.e, $|G| = 32$) and a population size of 128. Notice that increasing the mutation rate decreases the average time it takes a population to travel from a simplex vertex to a point near the uniform Robbins equilibrium.

As before, if we switch to *stochastic*-uniform parent selection, we introduce a source of genetic drift. However, in this case, mutation has the capability to reintroduce into the population alleles that were lost due to genetic drift. Hence, one possible use of mutation is to counteract drift effects by introducing new genomes into the population often enough to maintain a constant level of diversity. Since mutation operates on individual genes, it is rather complex calculation to determine precisely what the mutation rate should be to achieve this balance. However, it has been shown empirically to be well-approximated by a mutation rate of $1/L$, i.e., one mutation per offspring on average.

This is easy to illustrate with the empirical analysis framework. Suppose we look at populations of binary-valued genomes of length 40. If we use the average Hamming distance between all pairs of individuals in the population as a measure of diversity, then a randomly generated initial population $P(0)$ will have an average diversity measure of approximately 20.0. If we monitor this diversity over time, we can see the effects of various mutation rates. Figure 6.22 plots the results obtained from the average of 50 independent runs for four different mutation rates.

If our goal is to maintain maximal diversity, then a mutation rate of $L/2$ is required. However, if our goal is simply to maintain steady-state diversity, then a mutation rate of

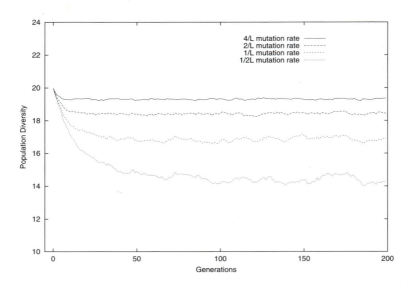

Figure 6.22: Population diversity for several mutation rates.

$1/L$ is generally sufficient. This observation provides the EA practitioner with a useful EA design heuristic: choose a mutation rate at least high enough to counterbalance the steady-state effects of genetic drift.

Crossover and Mutation Interactions

Since many EAs use both crossover and mutation, it is instructive to analyze their combined effects on population dynamics. In this section this is done under the assumption of uniform (neutral) parent selection. In section 6.5 the additional effects due to fitness-biased selection are analyzed.

Recall that infinite population models with uniform parent selection and only crossover converged to a Robbins equilibrium point in the simplex determined by the genetic makeup of $P(0)$. By contrast, we saw that these same infinite population models, using only mutation, converged to the center point in the simplex, the uniform Robbins equilibrium point *regardless* of the makeup of $P(0)$. If both reproductive operators are simultaneously active, the results are precisely what one might expect: convergence to the uniform Robbins equilibrium point regardless of the makeup of $P(0)$.

Crossover's contribution is to speed up the rate at which a population approaches the uniform Robbins equilibrium point by means of its ability to produce with high probability genotypes which, under the same conditions, would be produced with low probability using mutation. For example, given two parents of length L, a 1-point crossover operator would with probability $1/(L-1)$ produce an offspring that inherits $1/2$ of its alleles from each parent, while a mutation operator with a rate of $1/L$ would do so with probability:

$$(1 - \tfrac{1}{L})^{\frac{L}{2}} * (\tfrac{1}{L})^{\frac{L}{2}}$$

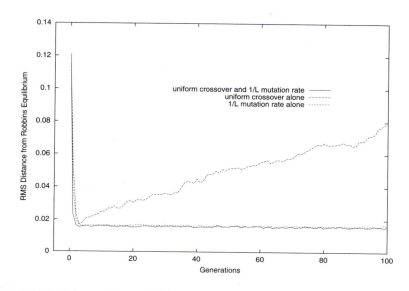

Figure 6.23: RMS distance from Robbins equilibrium for various choices of reproductive operators.

Even for small genome lengths the difference in probabilities is quite large. For example, if $L = 10$, $1/(L-1) \cong 0.111$ and $((1-1/10)^5 * (1/10)^5)^2 \cong .35 \times 10^{-7}$. If crossover is defined to produce both complementary offspring, then one obtains a second individual with the same property at no additional probability cost, while the probability of doing so under mutation is independent of the event that produced the first offspring and has the same probability. Hence, the probability of producing two offspring with this property is just the square of doing it once:

$$((1 - \tfrac{1}{L})^{\frac{L}{2}} * (\tfrac{1}{L})^{\frac{L}{2}})^2$$

These same observations carry over to the finite population case. With *deterministic*-uniform parent selection, EA populations converge probabilistically to a neighborhood of the uniform Robbins equilibrium point. With *stochastic*-uniform parent selection the same is true if the mutation rate is sufficiently high to compensate for genetic drift. These effects are easily demonstrated using the empirical analysis methodology. Figure 6.23 provides an example of the combined effect of crossover and mutation by contrasting it with its mutation-only and crossover-only counterparts. With only crossover, EA populations using stochastic-uniform parent selection initially approach a Robbins equilibrium point, and then drift away to one of the vertices of the simplex. With only mutation, these same populations converge in probability to a neighborhood of the uniform Robbins equilibrium point. When both crossover and mutation are present, populations also converge in probability to the uniform Robbins equilibrium point, but at a faster rate.

In addition to characterizing the effects that reproductive operators have on population

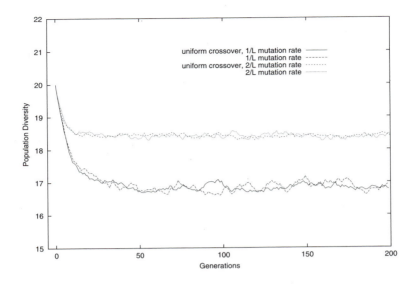

Figure 6.24: Population diversity for several choices of reproductive operators.

trajectories and fixed points in the simplex, it is helpful to understand their effects on population diversity. Based on the earlier discussion, one would expect that mutation would play a dominant role in determining the level of diversity, while crossover provides a pressure toward uniform-frequency diversity. This can be easily illustrated using the empirical methodology. Figure 6.24 shows how the diversity of a finite population changes over time for various combinations of reproductive operators, illustrating the primary role that mutation plays in maintaining the level of genetic diversity.

6.4.1.2   Reproduction for Other Genome Types

The analyses in the preceding sections were based on the assumption that the genome was a fixed-length linear structure consisting of L discrete-valued genes, and that the cardinality of the set G of possible genomes was finite. These assumptions are not unreasonable in the sense that many EAs used in practice satisfy them, and these are assumptions frequently made in the biological literature, allowing us to apply important theoretical results (such as Robbins equilibrium) directly from that literature. However, the EC community has developed a variety of EAs that are frequently used in practice, but fail to satisfy these assumptions. The theoretical implications of relaxing these assumptions is explored in this section.

Fixed-Length Continuous-Valued Linear Genomes

Perhaps the most pervasive "other" fixed-length genome type is one in which the gene values are continuous rather than discrete. The typical situation in which this occurs is when the problem to be solved using an EA is a real-valued parameter-optimization problem, and so a natural choice for the internal genome representation is a linear vector of the parameters to be optimized. As discussed in chapter 3, this was the representation chosen by the original developers of the ES family of EAs, and continues to be the preferred representation of the ES community today.

If we look at things from a slightly broader perspective, real-valued vector representations are an example of a phenotypic representation, in that there is no difference between the internal genotype representation and the external phenotype on which the notion of fitness is defined. As discussed earlier in chapter 5, an advantage of using a phenotypic representation is that it provides the possibility of improving on the performance of *domain-independent* reproductive operators by introducing new ones that take advantage of *domain-specific* properties. For real-valued parameter-optimization problems, the large body of knowledge about smoothness, continuity, and the properties of functions defined over R^L is a rich source of domain-specific ideas.

From a theoretical perspective, the switch from discrete-valued to continuous-valued genes is a significant one. The entire mathematical framework developed in this chapter so far has been based on the assumption that the set G of possible genomes is finite. With continuous-valued genes this is no longer true and, as a consequence, the analyses built on this assumption (the notion of a simplex, population trajectories through a simplex, convergence in a simplex, etc.) do not apply. Rather, the analysis framework is based on well-developed techniques from real-valued, multi-variate functional analysis. In addition, since real-valued vector representations have been so tightly coupled with real-valued parameter-optimization problems, most of the theoretical analysis is focused on optimization-related issues. A discussion of optimization-oriented analysis will be deferred until section 6.9.1. In this section the focus will be on application-independent issues.

To do so, it is best to adopt the "natural" perspective in which genomes represent vectors in R^L and EAs that evolve a population of such vectors over time. For infinite population models that have only uniform (neutral) parent selection and no reproductive variation, it should be clear that just as with the discrete case, $P(0)$ is a fixed point. The same is true for finite population models that use *deterministic*-uniform parent selection. Switching to *stochastic*-uniform parent selection introduces the same drift effects as the discrete case, resulting in convergence to a fixed point consisting of a uniform population of individuals, the genome of which was in $P(0)$. Every genome in $P(0)$ has equal probability of being associated with a fixed point.

So, at this level of abstraction, things are much the same as in the discrete case. The differences become apparent, however, when we look at the effects of reproductive variation.

Traditional Real-Valued Mutation

If we think figuratively of a mutation as a perturbation, the notion of a Gaussian mutation operator with a mean of 0.0 and a standard deviation of σ seems intuitively to have the right properties for real-valued genes. If we think of real-valued genomes as vectors in R^L, the notion of one or more Gaussian mutations per genome as a perturbation of these vectors also seems intuitively useful. If we imagine a population of such vectors in R^L, then the natural question to ask is how that population of vectors evolves over time with such a reproductive operator. As before, it is helpful to study the effects first in isolation by assuming uniform (neutral) parent selection.

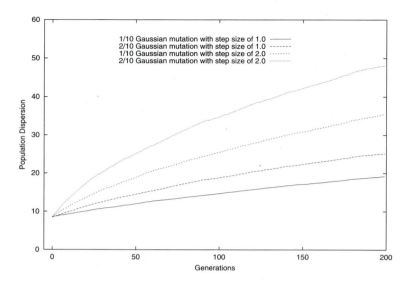

Figure 6.25: Population dispersion for several choices of Gaussian mutation operators.

Since we are dealing with a population of real-valued vectors, there is a well-defined notion of Euclidean distance between two members of the population, and a well-defined notion of population dispersion, namely, the average distance of population members from the centroid of the population. It is quite normal for EAs using real-valued genomes to generate the initial population $P(0)$ (uniform) randomly in a bounded region of R^L (typically a hyper-rectangle representing the upper and lower bounds of the gene values), but not restrict subsequent population members to this region. In this case the dispersion of $P(0)$ is finite, and of interest is how this dispersion changes over time with a Gaussian mutation operator $GM(0, \sigma)$ present.

Intuitively, one would expect that the effect of repeated Gaussian mutations (with neutral selection) would be a steady increase in the dispersion of the population. This intuition is easy to confirm with our empirical analysis framework in which we generate a finite population $P(0)$ in a bounded region of R^L, and then use *deterministic* parent selection and $GM(0, \sigma)$ to evolve the population over time. Figure 6.25 illustrates this for several different variations of Gaussian mutation operators applied to populations of real-valued genomes of length 10.

As one might expect, the dispersion of the population increases as a function of both the number of genes mutated and the average size of the individual mutations. So, for both infinite population models and finite population models with *deterministic*-uniform parent selection and $GM(0, \sigma)$, the steady state is one of maximal dispersion.

However, *stochastic*-uniform parent selection introduces drift effects that are in opposition to this dispersion pressure. Figure 6.26 illustrates this for several different variations of Gaussian mutation operators. In the presence of drift, the population dispersion settles

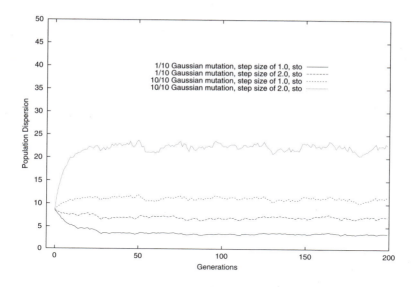

Figure 6.26: Population dispersion with drift for several choices of Gaussian mutation operators.

into a dynamic steady state, the value of which is a function of both the number of genes mutated and the average size of the individual mutations.

Notice that these population dynamics are analogous to the dynamics we observed for discrete-valued genes in section 6.4.1.1. In that case, with no drift the populations converged to the uniform Robbins equilibrium point, and with drift present they settled into a dynamic equilibrium some distance away from the uniform Robbins equilibrium point.

Recombination for Real-Valued Genomes

The most straightforward recombination operator for real-valued genomes is the crossover operator that is directly analogous to the discrete case, in which offspring probabilistically inherit genes from two (or more) parents. Since this form of crossover cannot introduce any new alleles into the population, the effects of crossover alone on population dynamics are identical to the discrete case, namely, converging to the Robbins equilibrium point defined by $P(0)$ in the absence of drift, and converging to a single genome population when drift is present.

The geometric properties of this form of crossover are easily seen by considering the case of two parents of length 2. In this case, the parents represent two of the four vertices of the rectangular region defined by the values of the parents' genes. The offspring produced by 1-point crossover correspond to the remaining two verticies. This geometric perspective suggests some alternative (phenotypic) forms of recombination. A popular variation is to have offspring inherit some linear combination of their parents' alleles, removing the restriction that offspring correspond only to verticies, and allowing them to correspond to locations in the hyper-rectangle defined by two parents (Schwefel, 1995). Alternatively,

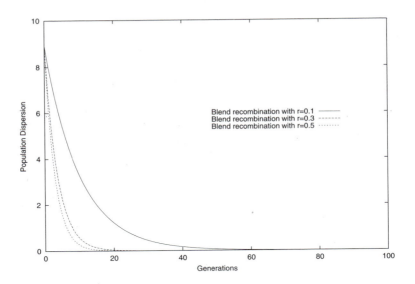

Figure 6.27: Population dispersion for simple 2-parent blending recombination.

one might consider the centroid of the population as the (phenotypic) version of M-parent recombination (Beyer, 1995).

From a population-dynamics point of view, these "blending" recombination operators behave like mutation operators in the sense that they are a constant source of new gene values. However, they differ from Gaussian mutation in that the offspring are not simply random perturbations of their parents. Rather, they lie geometrically in between their parents. The effect is to introduce genotypic variation that results in a reduction in phenotypic dispersion. Figure 6.27 illustrates this for a simple 2-parent blending recombination operator that assigns to each gene i in the offspring the values of the corresponding parent genes blended as $r * a_{1i} + (1 - r) * a_{2i}$. As the blending ratio r varies from 0.0 to 0.5 (or from 1.0 to 0.5), the rate of coalescing increases.

To be useful in practice, this pressure to coalesce must be balanced by a mutation operator. If we combine the Gaussian mutation operator analyzed in the previous section with this blending recombination operator, we observe the behavior illustrated in figure 6.28. In practice, the blending ratio frequently defaults to 0.5 (averaging). To compensate for the corresponding pressure to coalesce, fairly strong mutation pressure is required. This particular figure was generated using the same experimental setup that was used in figure 6.25. With both recombination and mutation active, population dispersion fairly quickly reaches a dynamic steady state, the level of which depends on the mutation pressure. Notice that a fairly aggressive mutation operator is required in order to maintain or exceed initial diversity levels. This provides some insight into why, in practice, much stronger mutation pressure is required when used with blending recombination than is required when used with discrete recombination.

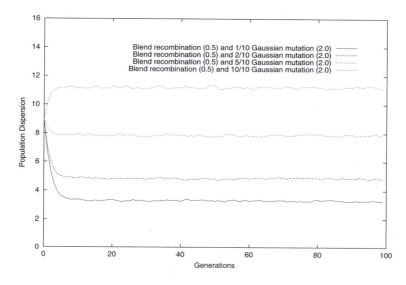

Figure 6.28: Population dispersion for simple 2-parent blending recombination and Gaussian mutation.

A more detailed analysis of these real-valued mutation and recombination operators has traditionally been done in the context of function optimization. As a consequence, this more detailed analyses is presented later in this chapter in section 6.9.1.

Fixed-Length Integer-Valued Linear Genomes

Integer-valued genes can be conveniently viewed as a special case of discrete-valued genes if they are restricted to a finite set of values, or as a special case of real-valued genes if they can take on an infinite number of values. As such, most of the population-dynamics analysis of discrete and real-valued representations is easily extended to the integer-valued case. For example, it is not hard to imagine a discrete (binomial) analog to Gaussian mutation, or blending recombination operators restricted to integer values. Consequently, there is little additional analysis that is required at the application-independent level.

Fixed-Size Nonlinear Genomes

There are many application domains in which the natural phenotypic representation of the objects to be evolved is a nonlinear fixed-size structure. Examples include matrices describing solutions to transportation problems, and graph structures with a fixed number of nodes representing finite-state machines or artificial neural networks. Since each such structure can be "linearized", it is generally quite straightforward to map these problem domains onto an internal fixed-length linear genome, and then use the corresponding mutation and recombination operators. This has the advantage of being able to reuse a significant portion of existing mature software, but also raises some issues for the EA practitioner. For example, there is often more than one way to linearize a structure. In the case of matrices, one could do so by row or by column. From an EC point of view, is one better than the other? How one might answer such questions is explored in more detail in section 6.6.

Variable-Length Genomes

There are important application domains in which the natural phenotypic representation for the objects to be evolved is a structure of variable length. Examples include job-shop scheduling problems and evolving programs. In these cases, mutation and recombination operators are frequently defined in such a way that the size of the offspring can differ from their parents. This introduces an interesting dynamic that is not present in the fixed-length case: namely, how a population's average genome size changes over time. With neutral selection, this dynamic is completely determined by the choice of and frequency with which size-altering reproduction operators are applied.

A common phenomenon observed when evolving programs is a steady increase in program size without significant increases in fitness (Kinnear, 1994; Ramsey et al., 1998), and has been dubbed the "bloat" problem. It is caused by an imbalance between the reproductive operators that increase genome size and those that reduce it. This is motivated by the need to explore variable-length genome spaces in a practical manner, by starting with small genomes and then increasing their size over time. The difficulty with program spaces is that in general their fitness landscapes are quite flat, with only sparsely located regions of high fitness. The result is primarily neutral selection and significant bloat. This can be addressed in a variety of domain-dependent ways. The usual domain-independent strategy is to modify the fitness function to reward parsimony, i.e., assign higher fitness to programs that have identical behavioral fitness but are smaller in size (Ramsey et al., 1998).

6.4.2   Overlapping-Generation Models

So far the analysis of reproduction-only EAs has focused on for non-overlapping-generation models. We are now in a position to characterize the effect on population dynamics caused by switching to an overlapping-generation model. Just as we saw in the analysis of selection-only EAs (section 6.3.2), such a switch has no effect on infinite population models, but does have implications for finite population models, since we must now specify a survival section procedure to reduce the combined parent and offspring population size of $m + n$ to a population of size m. Recall that a simplifying assumption made in analyzing reproduction-only EAs was to consider initially the case of uniform (neural) selection. If we are to maintain that assumption, then our only choice for survival selection is stochastic-uniform selection. For parent selection we still have the choice of either deterministic- or stochastic-uniform selection. If we think of the non-overlapping case as implementing deterministic survival selection, then there are four cases to consider:

- Non-overlapping with deterministic parent selection and deterministic survival selection,

- Non-overlapping with stochastic parent selection and deterministic survival selection,

- Overlapping with deterministic parent selection and stochastic survival selection, and

- Overlapping with stochastic parent selection and stochastic survival selection.

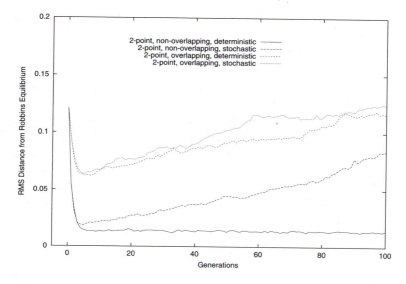

Figure 6.29: Average distance from Robbins equilibrium for 2-point, 2-offspring crossover for various population models.

Intuitively, one would expect to see drift effects increase as the number of stochastic selection methods increases. One way to see that this is indeed the case is to recall the analysis of traditional 2-parent crossover operators with respect to convergence to Robbins equilibrium points for non-overlapping-generation EAs (figures 6.19 and 6.20). Figure 6.29 illustrates the effect of switching to an overlapping-generation model with stochastic survival selection for the specific case of 2-point 2-offspring crossover.

Figures 6.19 and 6.20 clearly illustrated the drift effects due to stochastic-uniform parent selection for the non-overlapping-generation case involving crossover operators. Figure 6.29 illustrates the effect of adding stochastic survival selection to these models.

Clearly, as we increase the number of stochastic selection methods, there is a significant decrease in diversity as indicated by the drifting away from Robbins equilibrium. The interesting thing to note in figure 6.29 is the difference between the two EA models that have the same number of stochastic selection methods (one), but differ in when it is used (parent selection vs. survival selection). The 2-point crossover operator used here is the one that produces two complementary offspring and, as we saw in figure 6.19, reduces the drift away from Robbins equilibrium. However, when stochastic selection is used for survival selection rather than for parent selection, these complementary pairs are much less likely to survive as a pair, resulting in a higher drift rate away from Robbins equilibrium.

6.4.3 Reproduction Summary

In this section the focus has been on analyzing reproduction-only EAs in order to better understand the effects that reproductive operators have on population dynamics. In contrast to earlier observations that selection-only EAs converged to uniform-population fixed points, the steady-states of reproduction-only EAs are characterized by populations with maximal genotype diversity. If the genome space G is finite, then steady-state is a Robbins equilibrium. Both the equilibrium point itself and the rate at which this equilibrium point is reached depend on the particular reproductive operators that are used and the frequency with which they are applied.

In the case of real-valued representations, additional insight was obtained by looking at phenotype diversity. With a blending recombination operator alone, populations coalesce to a single phenotype. With Gaussian mutation alone, populations continue to disperse phenotypically indefinitely. When blending recombination and Gaussian mutation are both present, populations reach a steady-state of phenotypic diversity.

These insights provide for a more principled approach to "diversity management" in that they help us better understand the effects of increasing the mutation rate or modifying a crossover operator. But diversity management involves more than just reproduction. It requires an understanding of the interacting effects of selection and reproduction, which is explored in detail in the next section.

6.5   Selection and Reproduction Interactions

Now that we have a fairly clear picture of the population dynamics of selection-only and reproduction-only EAs, we are in a position to understand how these two forces interact. At a high level, we see selection as generating pressure to reduce population diversity by favoring genomes with higher fitness. By contrast, we see reproductive operators as providing additional diversity in the form of offspring whose genomes are similar but not identical to their parents. If our goal is to design EAs that are capable of producing new genomes with increasing fitness, selection and reproduction must interact in constructive ways. The precise form of this interaction will depend on the specific algorithmic details. However, it is possible to get a sense of this interaction at a higher level of abstraction. We explore this possibility first before diving into algorithmic details.

6.5.1   Evolvability and Price's Theorem

Intuitively, evolvability captures the notion that a population is able to make progress over time with respect to some measure of quality, such as the average fitness of the population. In order to achieve this, selection and reproduction must work together to produce "useful" population diversity that is likely to result in increases of a particular measure of quality. For example, if we focus on average fitness of the population, then evolvability is enhanced by choosing reproductive operators that result in a high degree of correlation between the fitness of parents and their offspring.

This can be more difficult to achieve than one might expect, since fitness is generally expressed in terms of the phenotypic properties of individuals. Hence, it is quite possible for reproductive operators to exhibit high degrees of genetic heritability and yet produce offspring whose phenotypic fitness varies significantly from that of the parents.

These observations concerning the interaction of selection and reproductive variation are not new. In 1970, George Price published a paper in which he presented an equation that has proved to be a major contribution to the field of evolutionary genetics (Price, 1970; Frank, 1995). The equation describes the existence of a covariance relationship between the number of successful offspring that an individual produces and the frequency of any given gene in that individual.

Although Price focused on gene frequency, his equation is more general and can be used to estimate the change in any measurable attribute Q from the parent population to the child population (see, for example, Altenberg (1994)). More importantly, the equation separates the change in Q attributable to selection from the change attributable to the reproductive operators. Specifically, Price showed that the overall change in some measure of population quality Q from one generation to the next is given by:

$$\Delta Q = \frac{Cov(z,q)}{\bar{z}} + \frac{\sum z_i \Delta q_i}{N\bar{z}}$$

where q_i is the measured quality of parent i, z_i is the number of children to which parent i contributed genetic material, $\bar{z}$ is the average number of children produced by each parent, N is the number of parents, and Δq_i is the difference between the average q value of the children of i and the q value of parent i.

So, for example, if we are interested in the change in average fitness from one generation to the next, the covariance term represents the contribution made by selection: namely, how strongly parent selection correlates with fitness. The second term represents the contribution made by the reproductive operators, measured by the difference in fitness between the parents and their offspring. Together, these two terms characterize the balance that must be struck between too much exploitation (selection) and too much exploration (reproductive variation).

As such, Price's theorem provides a high-level heuristic guideline for the EA designer. It does not specify the particular algorithmic details for achieving evolvability. Rather, it provides a "litmus test" for particular design choices by emphasizing the importance of balancing these two forces (see, for example, Langdon and Poli (2001)). In addition, it helps explain how EAs with strong selection pressure and aggressive reproductive variation can exhibit a level of evolvability similar to other EAs with weaker selection pressure and less aggressive reproductive variation.

As originally stated, Price's Equation combined the effects of all the reproductive operators into a single term. Since the EA designer can also choose to include more than one type of reproductive operator, it is helpful to separate their individual effects. For example, Potter et al. (2003) extended the equation as follows:

$$\Delta Q = \frac{Cov(z,q)}{\bar{z}} + \sum_{j=1}^{P} \frac{\sum z_i \Delta q_{ij}}{N\bar{z}}$$

where P is the number of reproductive operators and Δq_{ij} is the difference between the average q value of the children of i measured before and after the application of operator j.

Adopting Price's perspective allows us to focus on how specific combinations of selection and reproduction interact with respect to overall EA evolvability. This will be accomplished using, for the most part, the experimental analysis methodology in the following manner: two specific selection pressures of different strengths (first term in Price's equation) will be chosen, and then the interacting effects of various reproductive operators will be analyzed. In particular, a GA-like EA-1 will be used that is a non-overlapping-generation EA with

$m = n$ and binary tournament for parental selection, and compared with an EP-like EA-2 that is an overlapping-generation EA with $m = n$ with stochastic-uniform parental selection and truncation survival selection. The analysis in section 6.3 makes it clear that EA-2 exhibits a much stronger selection pressure than EA-1.

In the same spirit as section 6.4, the initial focus is on on fixed-length genomes containing genes that take on only a finite number of discrete values, and then later these assumptions are relaxed. In this context, in order to see the interacting effects of selection and repro-duction on fitness, we will need landscapes that are sufficiently complex and yet easy to analyze. For this analysis we use $f(x_i) = \sum_{i=1}^{2} x_i^2$, $-3 \leq x_i \leq 4$ which is asymmetric and multi-peaked with a single global at $< 4.0, 4.0 >$. To keep things simple, we use a standard binary representation for both EAs.

6.5.2   Selection and Discrete Recombination

If we think of genes as the arguments to a function that creates a phenotype with an associated fitness, it is quite likely that certain combinations of gene values (alleles) are correlated with high fitness. In general, those linkages are not known *a priori*. Rather they need to be discovered and preserved as part of the evolutionary process. With fitness-biased parent selection, individuals in the population with these alleles are likely to be selected as parents. We are interested in the fitness of the offspring produced by such parents using discrete recombination.

6.5.2.1   Discrete Recombination from a Schema Perspective

One traditional way of analyzing these effects for two-parent crossover operators is via "Schema Theory" (Holland, 1975). Here a schema is a notational device for representing arbitrary linkages associated with fixed-length genomes of length L. As such, a schema is a string of length L in which a * in position i represents a "don't care" symbol, and a specific allele value a_{jk} specifies a linked allelle of interest. So, for example, the string A*****B represents a particular two-allele linkage (and order-two linkage), while **ABA** represents a third order linkage. This notation provides us with a means of characterizing how likely it is that a kth-order schema will be preserved (inherited) using two-parent crossover.

This analysis is easiest to understand using 1-point crossover. With no loss of generality, we assume that the first parent contains the kth-order schema of interest. The situation in which that schema is *least likely* to be inherited is when the second parent has none of the alleles specified by that schema. If the first allele of the schema occurs at locus i and the last allele occurs at locus j, then the schema will only be inherited if the crossover point occurs before i or after j. Since crossover points are selected uniformly at random, the probability of inheritance is simply $((L - 1) - (j - i))/(L - 1)$. This result immediately highlights an important property of 1-point crossover: the probability that a set of linked genes will be inherited is a function of how close they are to each other on the genome. If we let $d = j - i$ represent the length of a kth-order schema, then maximally compact schemata ($d = k$) have the highest probability of being inherited, while maximally dispersed schemata ($d = L$) have the lowest probability.

It is also straightforward to analyze the case in which the second parent shares some of the alleles of the schema of interest. In such cases, these alleles are guaranteed to be inherited regardless of where the crossover points fall. This means that those allele positions are logically equivalent to "don't cares", and the probabilities are exactly the same as the corresponding $(k - s)$-order schema derived from the original one by replacing the shared alleles with '*'s. If the length d' of the new schema is less than the length d of the original one, then the probability of inheritance is correspondingly increased.

This same approach can be generalized to n-point crossover as well (see, for example, De Jong and Spears (1992)), and clearly shows that, as n increases, the probability of inheriting a kth-order schema decreases. It also shows that all n-point crossover operators exhibit this distance bias, in which compact schemata of order k are more likely to be inherited than disperse ones.

By contrast, uniform crossover exhibits no such compactness bias. It is easy to see that for uniform crossover the worst-case probability of inheriting a kth-order schema is simply 0.5^k *regardless* of its (lack of) compactness. If the second parent shares s of the schema alleles, the probability of inheritance increases to $0.5^{(k-s)}$.

This feature of uniform crossover, that it does not exhibit the compactness bias that n-point crossover does, is dampened by the fact that the probability of inheritance falls off rapidly as the order k of the schema increases. However, this can be ameliorated by parameterizing the bias of the coin being flipped. If we let p_h represent the bias of the coin (the probability of heads), we can vary it from 0.0 to 0.5 (or equivalently from 1.0 to 0.5). This generalized uniform crossover operator has been dubbed "parameterized uniform crossover" (Spears and De Jong, 1991), and allows one to directly control the probability $(p_h)^k$ of inheriting a kth-order schema.

By varying p_h we can obtain significant insights into the amount of crossover-induced diversity as well as its ability to produce fitness improvements as described in the following sections.

6.5.2.2   Crossover-Induced Diversity

A common measure of genetic diversity in a population of m individuals with fixed-length binary genomes is to compute the average Hamming distance between each unique pair of individuals in the population:

$$pop\_diversity = \frac{1}{\frac{m^2 - m}{2}} \left(\sum_{i=1}^{m-1} \sum_{j=i+1}^{m} hamming\_distance(i, j) \right)$$

While this measure of population diversity can be improved in a variety of ways (see, for example, Morrison and De Jong (2002)), it is sufficient for our purposes to understand how increasing p_h affects the population diversity in EA-1 and EA-2. Figures 6.30 and 6.31 illustrate these effects with parent and offspring population sizes of $m = n = 50$. As before, the plotted data points represent the averages of 400 independent runs.

In this particular case, a standard binary representation was used, involving 17 bits for each landscape variable, resulting in a total genome length of 34. Hence, the expected Hamming distance between two randomly generated individuals is 17. The baseline case is no crossover, representing the underlying pressure to converge due to selection and drift. As expected, increasing p_h from 0.0 to 0.5 increases population diversity and, as a consequence, increases the time required for both EAs to converge to a uniform-population fixed point.

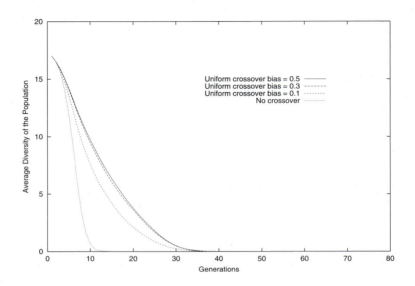

Figure 6.30: Average population diversity for EA-1 with parameterized uniform crossover.

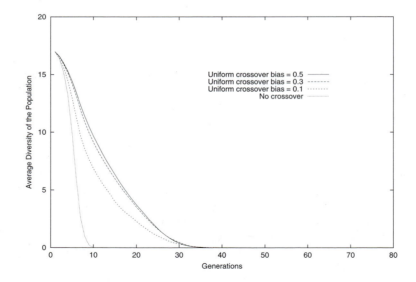

Figure 6.31: Average population diversity for EA-2 with parameterized uniform crossover.

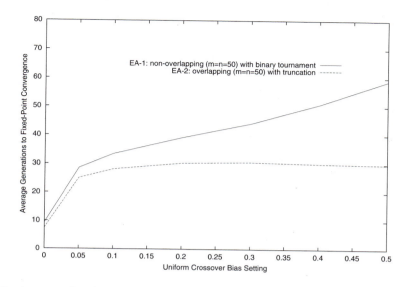

Figure 6.32: Average fixed-point convergence times for EA-1 and EA-2 with parameterized uniform crossover as a function of p_h.

Although figures 6.30 and 6.31 appear quite similar visually, there is a subtle and important difference in the way in which increasing p_h increases diversity and convergence times between EA-1 and EA-2. This difference can be seen more easily in figure 6.32 in which the average convergence times of both EAs are plotted as a function of increasing p_h.

Notice that for EA-1, as we increase p_h from 0.0 to 0.5 (i.e., decrease heritability), we see a steady increase in the time required to converge to a population fixed point. However, for EA-2, this is clearly not the case. To understand why, it is important to note that, regardless of the setting of p_h, the ability of crossover to produce diversity decreases over time as the population becomes more homogeneous, since both parents share an increasing number of common alleles. In general, crossover has the interesting property that it requires population diversity in order to produce diversity! Recall that EA-2 is using truncation selection, which produces much stronger selection pressure than that produced using binary-tournament selection in EA-1. In this particular case, truncation selection reduced diversity so rapidly that increasing p_h had almost no effect on convergence times.

Additional insight is obtained if we look at the average fitness of the population fixed points reached in figures 6.30 and 6.31. This is displayed in figure 6.33. Here we see the first indication of the need for a balance between crossover-induced exploration and selection-induced exploitation. For EA-1 notice how the average fixed-point fitness increases until p_h reaches about 0.2, and then begins to decrease, indicating that the higher rates of crossover result in too much exploration for the given selection pressure. Stated another way, as p_h increases diversity, there comes a point after which EA-1 is losing good parents faster than it is able to produce offspring with higher fitness.

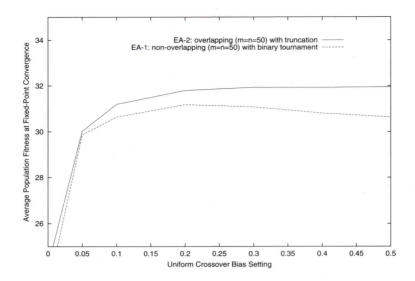

Figure 6.33: Average fixed-point fitness for two EAs with different selection pressure and parameterized uniform crossover.

However, for EA-2, no such balance is achieved. The fixed-point fitness continues to increase as p_h increases. This example makes it clear that there is no single "optimal" setting for p_h. Rather, it depends to a large extent on the strength of the selection pressure being used.

6.5.2.3   Crossover-Induced Fitness Improvements

As we noted earlier, maintaining diversity is a necessary but not a sufficient condition for good EA performance. In addition, the reproductive operators must produce "useful" diversity. There are many ways one might quantify operator usefulness. A simple starting point is to measure the frequency with which reproductive operators produce offspring that have higher fitness than their parents. This has been called the "success rate" in the ES community and is used as the basis for their adaptive mutation operator.

For crossover, it is a bit more difficult to define success since there are two parents involved. A weak definition of success would require an offspring to have higher fitness than at least one of its parents. A stronger requirement would be to have the offspring fitness exceed both of the parents. A middle ground position that makes the definition more comparable to mutation is that the fitness of the offspring must be greater than the fitness of the *first* parent chosen. This is the definition used in this book.

If we calculate operator success rates on a generational basis, one would expect the success rate of any non-adaptive reproductive operator to decline over time as the average fitness of the parent population increases and the opportunities for further fitness improvements become increasingly sparse. We can use the empirical analysis methodology to gain

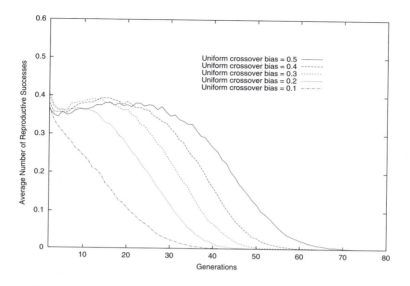

Figure 6.34: Success rates for uniform crossover using EA-1.

further insights. Figure 6.34 illustrates the success rate of parameterized uniform crossover for various values of p_h using EA-1.

Somewhat surprisingly, figure 6.34 shows a steady increase in the success rate as p_h increases even though in figure 6.33 we saw fixed-point fitness steadily decline when p_h increased beyond 0.2. The reason becomes immediately evident if we look at the average change in parent-offspring fitness for *all* crossover events (not just the successful ones), as illustrated in figure 6.35. When the actual values of the crossover-induced fitness changes are taken into account, the average change in fitness is negative (exploration) and increases in negativity as p_h increases.

So, selection is producing increases in average fitness and crossover is decreasing average fitness, and as figure 6.36 illustrates, the best EA performance is obtained when these two opposing forces are properly balanced. When there is too much exploration, the rate at which average population fitness increases is reduced and, as we noted earlier, it is easier for a reproductive operator to be successful when average population fitness is lower. Hence, in this case uniform crossover with $p_h = 0.5$ has the highest success rate, precisely because it is retarding the increase in average population fitness the most!

Additional insights can be obtained by comparing these observations with the equivalent ones exhibited by EA-2. Figure 6.37 plots the success rates of uniform crossover using EA-2. If we compare that with EA-1 (figure 6.34), we see several things of note. Just as with EA-1, increasing p_h in EA-2 increases the success rate of uniform crossover. However, note that the initial success rates under EA-2 are significantly higher than under EA-1. This can be understood by recalling that EA-1 and EA-2 use different parent-selection procedures (binary tournament and stochastic-uniform). Hence, the unbiased selection in EA-2 is likely

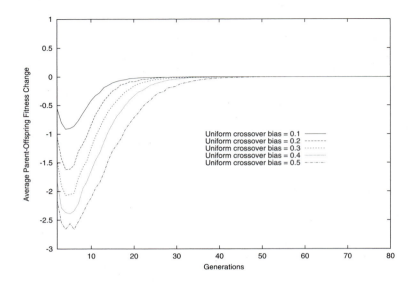

Figure 6.35: Average change in parent-offspring fitness for uniform crossover using EA-1.

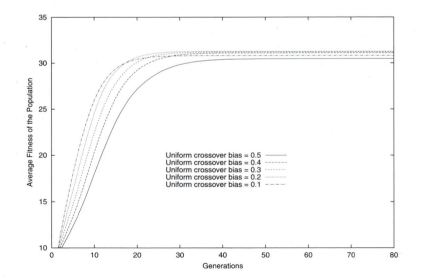

Figure 6.36: Average population fitness for uniform crossover using EA-1.

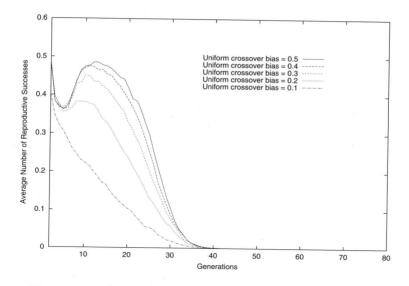

Figure 6.37: Success rates for uniform crossover using EA-2.

to produce a mating pool with lower average fitness than in EA-1, thus making it easier for crossover to be successful.

If, in addition, we compare the average change in fitness from parent to offspring (figure 6.35 vs. figure 6.38) and the average fitness of the population (figure 6.36 vs. figure 6.39), we can clearly see how the effect of the increased selection pressure more severely restricts the ability of uniform crossover to provide reproductive diversity. Hence, unlike EA-1, increasing p_h all the way to 0.5 continues to provide modest improvements in performance, indicating again that there is no single best value for p_h.

6.5.3 Selection and Other Recombination Operators

To keep things simple initially, the focus has been on one of the simplest and most widely used classes of sexual reproduction operators: crossover operators that are designed to produce offspring from two parents with fixed-length discrete-valued genomes. However, this analysis can be extended fairly easily as these assumptions are relaxed. For example, we saw in section 6.4 that increasing the number of parents involved in a single reproductive event increases the amount of diversity produced. From a schema perspective, increasing the number of parents reduces heritability. This increase in exploration results in longer fixed-point convergence times. For EA-1 additional increases in exploration result in lower fixed-point fitness, while just the opposite is true for EA-2. If we focus on improving average population fitness, an increase in exploration will require a corresponding change in selection pressure in order to maintain a balance.

So far, the analysis in this section was done using an internal binary representation of the fitness landscape. The same results carry over to real-valued representations using discrete

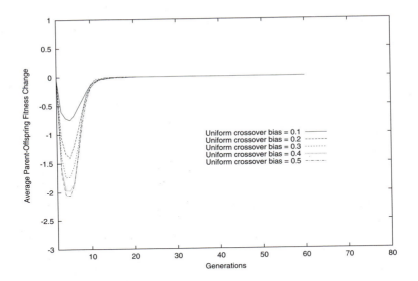

Figure 6.38: Average change in parent-offspring fitness for uniform crossover using EA-2.

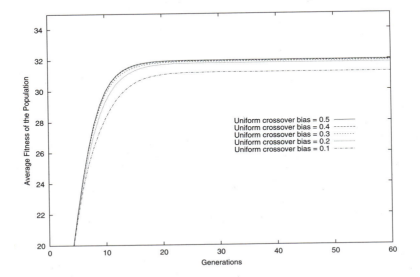

Figure 6.39: Average population fitness for uniform crossover using EA-2.

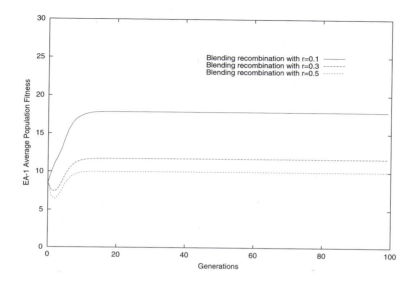

Figure 6.40: Average population fitness with blending recombination using EA-1.

recombination, since no new allele values can be introduced into the population. However, as we saw in section 6.4, the results are quite different for real-valued representations that use a blending recombination operator. Recall that the example fitness landscape used for the analyses in this section was $f(x_i) = \sum_{i=1}^{2} x_i^2$, $-3 \le x_i \le 4$. If we replace the binary representation used in EA-1 and EA-2 with a two-gene real-valued representation, and use blending recombination rather that discrete recombination, we observe the behavior illustrated in figures 6.40 and 6.41.

Recall from the analysis in section 6.4 that increasing the blending ratio from 0.0 to 0.5 increases the pressure for phenotypic convergence. Hence, for a fixed amount of selection pressure, smaller values of r allow for more exploration and higher converged fitness values. Switching from EA-1 to EA-2 increases selection pressure (truncation vs. binary tournament). This increase provides a better counterbalancing exploitation force. Finally, recall that EA-2 is an overlapping-generation model with truncation survival selection. Hence, average population fitness is monotonically non-decreasing over time.

6.5.4 Selection and Mutation

Asexual reproduction operators can take many forms as well. To keep things simple initially, the focus will be on a standard class of mutation operators for fixed-length genomes that first make a clone of the parent and then modify, on average, j of L cloned genes. In this case increasing j decreases heritability and increases reproductive variation. Of interest, then, is how to choose an appropriate level of heritability.

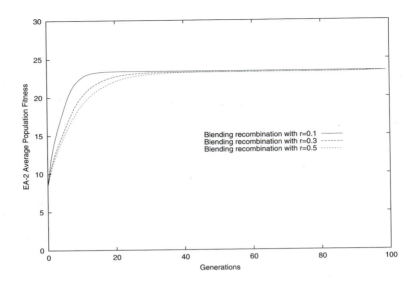

Figure 6.41: Average population fitness with blending recombination using EA-2.

6.5.4.1   Mutation from a Schema Perspective

Just as we saw for crossover, Holland's Schema Theory also provides a useful perspective on the role of mutation. If we think of a kth-order schema as defining a set of k gene values (alleles) that are associated with high fitness (and thus likely to be selected as a parent), we are interested in the fitness of the offspring produced via mutation. Schema theory quantifies how increasing the mutation rate decreases the probability of inheriting a kth-order schema (i.e., mutation becomes increasingly disruptive). Specifically, if p_m is the probability that a gene will be mutated, then the probability p_{inh} that an offspring inherits a kth-order schema is simply:

$$p_{inh}(k) = (1 - p_m)^k$$

So, unlike crossover, a mutation operator applied at a fixed rate p_m maintains a fixed level of heritability throughout an entire evolutionary run. This means that, as higher order schemata are formed, they incur a higher mutation load and are less likely to be inherited unmodified. On the other hand, reducing p_m improves heritability at the expense of diversity. Finding a balance between diversity and heritability is a key issue for the EA designer, and is explored in the following subsections.

6.5.4.2   Mutation-Induced Diversity

From a diversity management point of view, it is important to understand more clearly how increasing the mutation rate affects population diversity, and what differences there are (if any) from crossover-induced diversity. This will be accomplished by using the same

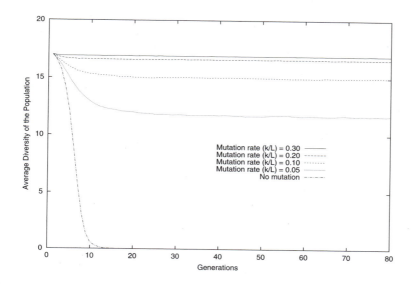

Figure 6.42: Average population diversity for EA-1: a non-overlapping-generation EA with $m = n = 50$, binary-tournament selection and bit-flip mutation.

empirical setup that was used to study the effects of crossover, namely by using EA-1 and EA-2 on the same fitness landscape with the same binary representation. The only difference is that the uniform crossover operator has been replaced by a bit-flip mutation operator as the source of reproductive variation.

Figures 6.42 and 6.43 provide our first insights by showing how population diversity is affected by increasing the mutation rate k/L. In each figure the baseline case of no mutation illustrates the rate at which diversity is lost due to selection and drift. If we compare these figures with the corresponding ones for crossover (figures 6.30 and 6.31), we see rather striking differences in mutation-induced diversity. First, note how much larger the diversity increase is as k/L increases. Second, note that much higher levels of diversity can be reached and maintained. In this particular case for EA-1, a mutation rate of $k/L = 0.3$ is sufficient to maintain maximum population diversity indefinitely!

Additional insights can be obtained by studying the effect that various mutation rates have on average population fitness over time. Figures 6.44 and 6.45 illustrate this for the same data sets used in the two previous figures.

Figure 6.44 shows how sensitive non-overlapping-generation EAs are to aggressive exploration. Again, the baseline case of no mutation indicates the changes in population fitness due solely to selection and drift. For EA-1 maximum improvements in performance are only obtained with very low mutation rates (e.g., $k/L = 1\%$). Performance degrades rather quickly after that, a familiar theme in the GA community.

By contrast figure 6.45 shows how EA-2, a strong elitist EA, *requires* a more aggressive exploration operator in order to maintain a proper balance, which is a familiar theme in

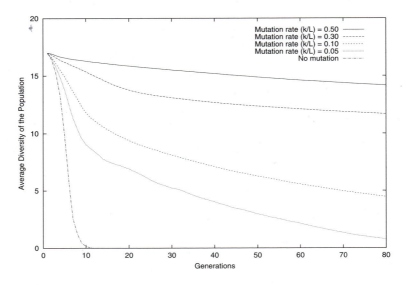

Figure 6.43: Average population diversity for EA-2: an overlapping-generation EA with $m = n = 50$, truncation selection and bit-flip mutation.

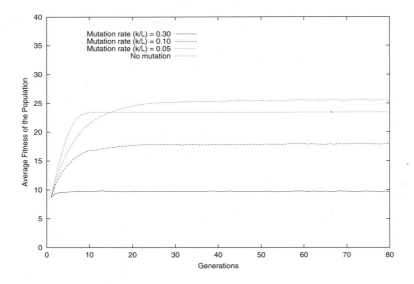

Figure 6.44: Average population fitness for EA-1 with bit-flip mutation.

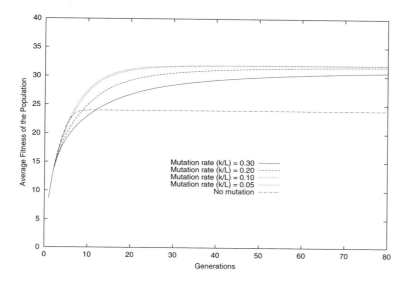

Figure 6.45: Average population fitness for EA-2 with bit-flip mutation.

the ES and EP communities. Also notice that, unlike the crossover analysis of the previous section, the mutation rate *can* be increased sufficiently to counterbalance the strong selection pressure of EA-2. In this particular case we observe increases in average fitness until k/L is approximately 0.20, and then average fitness decreases as mutation becomes too explorative.

So, just as we saw with crossover, there is no single best setting for the mutation rate. Rather, it depends on the strength of the (counterbalancing) selection pressure being used.

6.5.4.3 Mutation-Induced Fitness Improvements

It is also important to understand the degree to which mutation produces *useful* diversity. If we use the same "success rate" measure that we used for crossover, we can get a sense of how the two operators differ in this respect. Figure 6.46 illustrates the success rates of mutation for various values of k/L using EA-1, while figure 6.47 illustrates the same thing for EA-2.

Note that in this context we need to be careful about interpreting the results of the success rates of small mutation rates. Recall that for these examples the genome length was 34, so a $1/L$ mutation rate is approximately 0.03. Since the mutation operator is stochastic as we reduce the mutation rate toward $1/L$ or lower, we increase the likelihood of not making any mutations (i.e., producing a clone) and thus artificially reducing the success rate, as illustrated in figure 6.46.

Figure 6.46 also illustrates that, just as we saw with crossover, increasing k/L increases the success rate of mutation for EA-1. Surprisingly, we see just the opposite for EA-2 as shown in figure 6.47. As we increase k/L, the success rate decreases. To understand why,

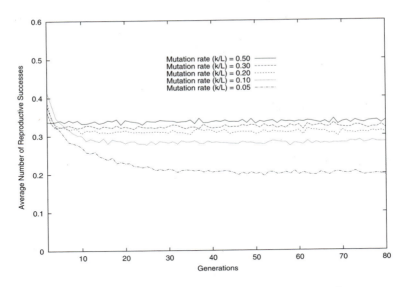

Figure 6.46: Success rates for mutation using EA-1.

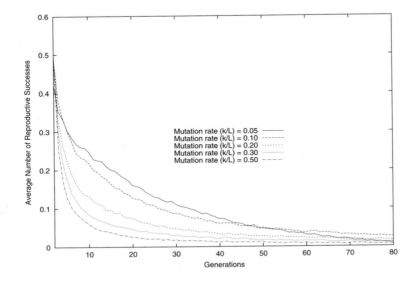

Figure 6.47: Success rates for mutation using EA-2.

recall that EA-2 uses an overlapping-generation model with truncation survival selection. As we saw earlier, this means that the average fitness of the population can never decrease, regardless of how aggressive the reproductive operators are. As a consequence, success rates cannot be increased by lowering the average fitness of the population as they can with non-overlapping-generation models like EA-1. Rather, in overlapping models like EA-2, success rates decrease as reproductive operators get more aggressive, and increase as the operators become more conservative.

Figures 6.44 and 6.45 make it clear how important the exploration/exploitation balance is in improving population fitness. They also point out the difficulty of achieving the proper balance. Both EA-1 and EA-2 exhibited mutation rate "sweet spots", but at quite different levels of mutation strength. Currently our theory is not strong enough to predict these sweet spots. Rather, they are obtained experimentally. This observation was the motivation for the ES community to develop early on an adaptive mutation operator that dynamically increased/decreased its exploratory power in an attempt to maintain a uniform success rate of approximately 20% (Schwefel, 1981).

6.5.5 Selection and Other Mutation Operators

To keep things simple initially, the focus has been on one of the simplest and most widely used family of asexual reproduction operators: mutation operators that are designed to clone a parental genome and add some genetic variability by modifying one or more gene values. Although the analysis focused on discrete mutation operators, the general results are the same for real-valued representations with Gaussian mutation, namely, the importance of finding a balance between selection and the strength of mutation.

Obviously, there are more complex asexual reproduction mechanisms that might change the genome length, make correlated changes to gene values, move genes around on the genome, etc. Since these issues are intimately related to representation issues, we will defer further discussion and revisit these issues in section 6.6.

6.5.6 Selection and Multiple Reproductive Operators

In practice most EAs have more than one reproductive operator active during an evolutionary run. This means that, in addition to understanding the properties of the individual operators, the EA designer must also understand how they work in combination with each other. In the case of the crossover and mutation operators studied in the previous sections, our understanding of how they work independently suggests that the two reproductive operators are in many ways complementary to each other and, if properly combined, could result in better EA performance improvements than by using one or the other alone. For the discrete reproductive operators, the constant level of genotype diversity produced by mutation provides a means by which crossover-generated diversity can now be maintained indefinitely (if desired). For the real-valued reproductive operators, Gaussian mutation can compensate for the loss of phenotype diversity due to blending recombination. In each case, the key is finding the balance between the exploitation of selection and the exploration of reproduction.

If we focus on the offspring population, one could imagine finding some individuals that were produced by the application of a single reproductive operator and others that were produced by the application of multiple reproductive operators. Clearly, the character of the offspring population diversity will change significantly as we vary the percentage of each type and, from a diversity management perspective, we need to understand the character of this change. We will use empirical analysis techniques to provide some useful insights based on the same EAs, EA-1 and EA-2, used in the previous sections, but now with a focus on the use of both crossover and mutation.

We begin by analyzing the case in which every offspring is produced by first applying crossover and then applying mutation. We want to contrast that with the situation in which only one operator is applied. Some thought needs to be given as to how best to do this. Simply turning on/off the two operators is not probably not sufficient, since, as we have seen, each operator has an important impact on diversity management. So, turning an operator on/off is likely to upset a particular EA's exploration/exploitation balance. A better strategy is to allow each variation to be appropriately tuned, and then analyze variational differences.

In addition, it is helpful to increase the complexity of the fitness landscape somewhat in order to amplify any differences. Recall that we have been using $f(x_i) = \sum_{i=1}^{2} x_i^2,\ -3 \leq x_i \leq 4$ as the our standard fitness landscape for the empirical analyses. Simply increasing the dimensionality from 2 to 4 adds additional complexity while remaining simple enough to visualize: an asymmetric and multi-peaked landscape with a single global maximum of 64 at $< 4.0, 4.0, 4.0, 4.0 >$. As before, we begin with an analysis of the discrete representation case, which uses a standard internal binary representation involving 17 bits per variable, and follow that with an analysis of the real-valued case.

We analyze first the effects on EA-1, the non-overlapping-generation EA that uses a binary tournament to select parents. We perform our empirical analysis on three variations: crossover only, mutation only, and crossover plus mutation. Figure 6.48 illustrates the tuned effects of these various combinations of mutation and crossover on average population fitness (averaged over 400 independent runs).

In this particular case, crossover alone produced better population averages than mutation alone, but in neither case is the population fitness converging to the global optimum of 64 by 120 generations. In the case of the crossover-only version, we know why from our earlier analyses: already by generation 40 it has converged to a uniform-population fixed point (which is on average suboptimal) and will make no further progress regardless of how long it is run. In the case of the mutation-only system, as expected, we see a slower rate of convergence but, as we saw earlier, as the average population fitness increases, it becomes increasingly difficult for a fixed-rate mutation operator to improve average population fitness.

By contrast, for the tuned version involving both crossover and mutation, we still observe a steady increase in population fitness even after 120 generations. Notice also that the tuned diversity parameters of the combined version are lower than the corresponding single-operator versions.

Figure 6.49 presents this same analysis for EA-2. In this particular case, using an overlapping-generation model with truncation selection, the average population fitness approaches the global optimum of 64 for all three variations, but the rank order is the same as

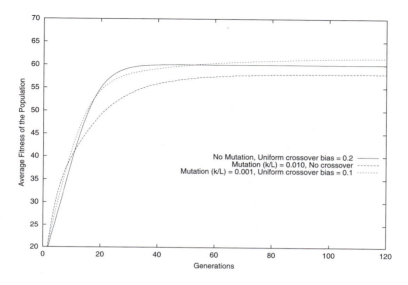

Figure 6.48: Average population fitness for EA-1 with $m = n = 50$.

with EA-1. Notice also that, as suggested by our earlier analyses, these results are obtained by using much higher levels of exploration than with EA-1.

While presented in a specific context here, these results are quite general. EA-1 was chosen as a prototype for GA-like EAs, for which there is a large body of empirical evidence that a proper exploration/exploitation balance is obtained by using crossover and mutation operators with high degrees of heritability. By contrast, EA-2 was chosen as a prototype for ES- and EP-like EAs that historically perform best with reproductive operators tuned to much lower levels of heritability. Although not displayed here, similar results are obtained when using a real-valued representation along with Gaussian mutation and blending recombination.

Of course, there are other ways of combining multiple reproductive operators in an EA. An offspring population of size m could be generated by specifying which fraction of m is to be produced by an operator. So, for example, the GA community routinely uses a "crossover rate" parameter set in the range 0.6–0.8 that specifies exactly that. By contrast, mutation is applied to each offspring but at a sufficiently low (k/L) rate that an individual may receive no mutations. The result is an offspring population with a mixture of individuals generated by crossover alone, mutation alone, crossover plus mutation, and even some parental clones. It should be clear that such reproductive strategies are less explorative than those in the case just analyzed. Such strategies are generally paired with fitness-proportional parental selection which, as we have seen, produces a weaker selection (exploitation) pressure than the binary-tournament selection used in EA-1.

So, the recurring theme here is finding an appropriate balance between exploration and exploitation. As we have seen in this chapter, exploitation pressure is a function of popu-

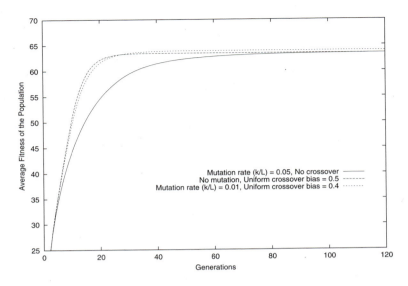

Figure 6.49: Average population fitness for EA-2 with $m = n = 50$.

lation size (drift), selection algorithms, and the type of generational model used. For each combination, a different counterbalancing exploration pressure must be provided by the reproductive operators. In some cases only mild exploration is required; in other cases rather aggressive exploration is needed.

6.5.7   Selection, Reproduction, and Population Size

The reproductive operators that we have been analyzing are themselves stochastic in the sense that if we use the same parent(s) to produce $b > 1$ offspring, each offspring is likely to be genetically different and have a different fitness. If we focus on offspring fitness and let b go to infinity, we can induce a probability distribution over the set of all possible offspring fitness values. For finite b, producing b offspring from the same parent(s) can then be viewed as taking a sample of size b from this distribution. While these distributions are difficult to characterize in general (see, for example, Grefenstette (1994)), it is clear that $b = 1$ constitutes a rather small sample! So, for example, if our goal is to produce at least one offspring whose fitness is higher than its parents, one can generally improve the likelihood of that happening by increasing b. In biological terms b corresponds to the "brood size" and, depending on the species, can vary from one or two to as many as a thousand or more.

While a formal analysis of the effects of brood size is difficult and beyond the scope of this book, we can use what we have learned so far in this chapter to obtain a fairly accurate understanding of the effects of increasing b (or more generally, n, the offspring population size).

The first thing to note is that having an offspring population size n different from the parent population size m only makes sense for finite population models. For finite population models using *deterministic* parent selection, the standard method for increasing n is by specifying an integer brood size b to be applied uniformly to all parents implying $n = b * m$. If a finite population model uses *stochastic* parent selection, n is not required to be an integer multiple of m.

A second issue to consider is how best to analyze and compare the effects of varying n. Since in this chapter we are focusing on population dynamics rather than application issues, we are studying the effects on convergence and steady-state population fitness. Clearly, if there is no cost associated with increasing n, larger values (more exploration) will produce better results. However, the running time of an EA is generally estimated in terms of a linear function of the number of fitness evaluations (which is generally the same as the number of births). So a larger n implies increased cost per generation, and suggests that there is another important exploration/exploitation tradeoff: given a fixed budget of $T = m + t * n$ births (evaluations) for an entire evolutionary run, how should m and n be chosen? Surprisingly, the answers turn out to be quite different for overlapping-generation models than for non-overlapping models.

6.5.7.1 Non-overlapping-Generation Models

For non-overlapping-generation models, if we want to maintain a constant parent population size, it only makes sense to have $n \geq m$. If $n > m$, we must now specify a survival selection method to reduce the n offspring to the m parents required for the next generation. If we want to maintain the same selection pressure as the $m = n$ case, then we need to use stochastic-uniform survival selection. But, as we saw in section 6.3, adding any stochastic-selection procedure to a non-overlapping-generation EA introduces additional drift effects. This sets up an interesting interplay between the potential advantages of increasing b (or more generally, n), and the potential negative effects of additional genetic drift. We can get a sense of this interplay by studying the tuned behavior of EA-1 on the same 4-dimensional, multi-peaked asymmetric fitness landscape as in the previous section. Figure 6.50 shows the effects that various combinations of m and n have on average population fitness.

Notice that increasing n while holding m fixed significantly degrades average population fitness. That is, any perceived advantage to increased exploration is more than offset by the genetic drift introduced by the additional stochastic survival selection. In this case, because of the asymmetric multi-peaked nature of the landscape, increases in population fitness are obtained by increasing m (the amount of parallelism).

Alternatively, one could maintain the current selection pressure of a non-overlapping-generation $m = n$ EA without additional drift effects by switching to deterministic-uniform parent selection and then using the original parent selection method for survival selection. Recall that our $m = n$ EA-1 uses binary tournament parent selection. If we modify it to be a $n > m$ EA (EA-1a) with deterministic-uniform parent selection and binary tournament survival selection, and compare it with EA-1 on the same landscape and with the same reproduction parameter settings, we see the sorts of things illustrated in figure 6.51. By not adding a second source of genetic drift, the average population fitness of EA-1a is much improved over the corresponding version of EA-1. However, the cost of increasing n still outweighs any benefits obtained from the additional exploration.

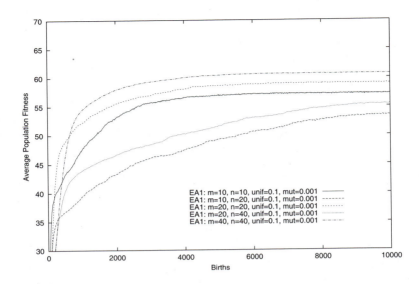

Figure 6.50: Average population fitness for EA-1 for several values of m and n.

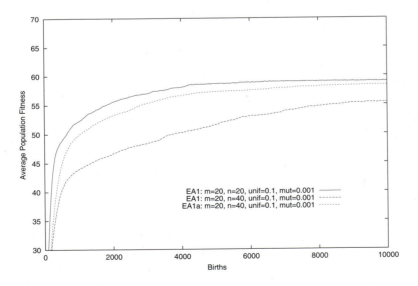

Figure 6.51: Average population fitness for EA-1 and EA-1a.

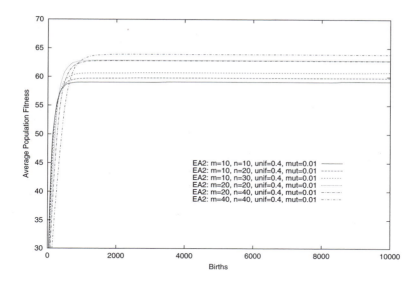

Figure 6.52: Average population fitness for EA-2 for various values of m and n.

While these results are for specific cases, they are representative of a large body of empirical evidence suggesting that there are few advantages to increasing n in non-overlapping-generation EAs.

6.5.7.2 Overlapping-Generation Models

By contrast, particularly in the ES community, there is a considerable amount of formal and empirical evidence that shows that performance can generally be improved by having b, the ratio of the offspring population size to the parent population size, be greater than one (see, for example, Jansen and De Jong (2002)). Because overlapping-generation EAs already have a survival selection procedure specified for reducing the m parents and the n offspring to the m parents of the next generation, increasing n requires no additional procedural changes. This simplifies the analysis and allows us to focus on a cost/benefit analysis of increasing n.

To get a sense of this, we observe the behavior of the tuned overlapping-generation EA-2 from the previous section on the same 4-dimensional asymmetric multi-peaked fitness landscape. Figure 6.52 depicts the results for various values of m and n.

Notice that, in contrast to the non-overlapping-generation case, increasing n does not degrade the long-term average population fitness. For the smaller parent population sizes, increasing n improves average fitness, but this effect diminishes as m increases. To understand why, recall that EA-2 uses deterministic truncation survival selection. As we saw in the previous section, this permits a much more aggressive exploration process during reproduction (as reflected in the tuned values for uniform crossover and bit-flip mutation)

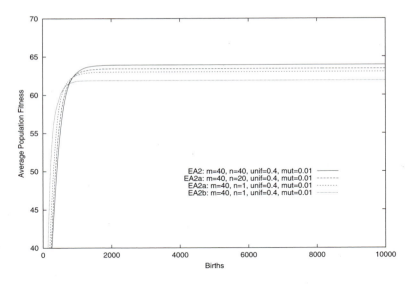

Figure 6.53: Average population fitness for EA-2 for $n < m$.

without negatively affecting average (parent) population fitness.   In order for increasing n to be cost effective, it must result in an increase in the long-term average population fitness. There is considerable theoretical and experimental evidence that, for simple fitness landscapes, EAs like EA-2 are most cost-effective when $m = n = 1$. However, as the complexity of the fitness landscape increases, larger values of m and n are required. Intuitively, to increase long-term population fitness, EAs like EA-2 must be able to find and follow trajectories to the higher fitness peaks in complex fitness landscapes. The values of m and n play interacting roles in their ability to do so. The asymmetric multi-peaked landscape used in figure 6.52 was sufficiently complex that small values of m were insufficient to find the higher peaks consistently. This is compensated to some extent by increasing n, but not as much as increasing m. As m increases, the cost-effectiveness of $n > m$ decreases.

This raises the interesting question of whether it might be cost-effective to have $n < m$ in such situations. To do so requires a procedural change to EA-2. Recall that it uses uniform *deterministic* parent selection. In order to allow $n < m$, this needs to be changed to uniform *stochastic* parent selection, and this, as we saw in section 6.3, introduces drift effects. Figure 6.53 illustrates this on the multi-peaked landscape. The curves labeled EA-2a represent EA-2 with stochastic-uniform parent selection. The reduction in long-term population fitness is due to the fact that with stochastic parent selection, decreasing n increases the likelihood that an individual will never be selected as a parent.

One might be tempted to remedy this by increasing the parent selection pressure to something like binary-tournament selection to increase the likelihood that the more fit individuals will be chosen as parents. However, increasing the selection pressure only generally helps with simple fitness landscapes. With more complex ones, it is likely to reduce the likelihood of finding the highest fitness peaks. This is illustrated by the EA-2b graph in figure 6.53 in which stochastic-uniform selection was replaced with binary-tournament selection.

6.5.8 Summary

In this section we studied the interacting effects of selection and reproduction on population dynamics. We saw the importance of finding a balance between the exploitive pressure of selection and the exploratory pressure of reproductive variation in order to achieve high steady-state population fitness. We noted that the desired balance could be obtained in different ways, such as by combining strong selection pressure with aggressive reproductive operators, or by combining weaker selection with milder levels of reproductive variation. We also saw that, in general, the sexual and asexual reproductive operators complemented each other in providing useful offspring variation.

In addition, we noted the important role that fitness landscape complexity plays. Both the balance necessary to achieve high levels of fitness and the effectiveness of the reproductive operators depend heavily on the structure of the fitness landscape. This dependency is studied in more detail in section 6.7.

6.6 Representation

One of the most important decisions that must be made when applying an EA to a new application area is how to represent internally the individuals (objects) to be evolved. Intuitively, we want to choose a representation that captures an application area at the right level of abstraction. For example, if we want to evolve new chair designs, we are much more likely to evolve interesting designs if we represent the design space in terms of materials, colors, shapes, etc., than if we model it at the atomic level. At the same time, if we model it at too high a level (e.g., a few simple parameters to be tuned), we have constrained the design space significantly and are unlikely to evolve any novel designs. Finding the right level of abstraction for a problem is an acquired skill and the results are highly problem dependent.

Having settled on an appropriate level of abstraction, we still need to decide how to map that into an internal representation. EC representation theory in its current state is not strong enough to make general predictions about which representations are best for particular applications. Most of our knowledge is derived empirically, but quite suggestive of general principles and issues to be considered when designing a new representation or choosing among existing ones.

At a high level of abstraction, a good representation has two important properties: 1) it captures the important features of the application domain that are necessary for effective problem solving, and 2) allows for the design of effective reproductive operators. How to achieve these properties is explored in the following subsections.

6.6.1 Capturing Important Application Features

Formally, a representation is a mapping between an external, application-specific space and an internal algorithmic space, i.e., $f : external\_space \rightarrow internal\_space$. At first glance, it would seem important that every point in the external space be represented by at least one point in the internal space. However, most internal spaces are discrete, while many external spaces are continuous. Hence, any mapping of a continuous space onto a discrete space must be restricted to a particular set of discrete points in continuous space. How one chooses to discretize a continuous space is important, application specific, and more of an art than a science. The primary goal is to ensure the discretization is sufficiently fine-grained to make sure that potentially interesting parts of the external space are represented internally without creating an internal space that is computationally infeasible to search.

A second desirable property is that representation mappings preserve external constraints so that internal points correspond to feasible external points, i.e., $f^{-1} : internal\_space \rightarrow constrained\_external\_space$. This greatly simplifies the design and implementation of the reproductive operators used to explore the internal space. For example, if the external space is the unit circle, i.e., all points (x,y) such that $x^2 + y^2 \leq 1$, representing points internally using *polar* coordinates captures the constrained space naturally, whereas the use of *cartesian* coordinates does not.

Unfortunately, many interesting applications have external spaces defined by complex, nonlinear constraints for which constraint-preserving maps are difficult to define. One solution that is often used is to embed such spaces into a larger space with simpler constraints (e.g., embedding complex shapes into bounding rectangles). Since fitness is defined on external spaces, the fitness function must now be extended to the larger space. This can be done in many ways, from simply defining the fitness points in the extended space to have maximum negative fitness, to various penalty function techniques similar to those in regular use for solving constrained-optimization problems.

Alternatively, one can modify the generation of the initial population and the reproductive operators to respect external constraints so that the only points in internal space ever generated are those that satisfy the external constraints. The argument in support of this approach is that it is likely to be more efficient to add constraint knowledge to an EA than to have an EA discover the constraints via negative fitness feedback. Alternatively, one might allow points to be generated that violate external constraints, and then "repair" them in some fashion. Which of these approaches is best is application dependent. Currently, the primary source of guidance is from empirical studies and not from formal theories.

A final property to be considered is whether $f^{-1} : internal\_space \rightarrow external\_space$ is many-to-one or one-to-one. The biological world is replete with examples of redundant genetic encodings, but no firm consensus as to exactly what role they play. The most prevalent view is that these "neutral networks" of genotypes that all map onto single phenotypes allow for more complex adaptations than those achievable by one-to-one mappings. From an EA designer's point of view, there is no clear understanding of when it is helpful from a performance viewpoint to adopt a many-to-one representation. The results are highly application dependent and are derived from empirical studies (see, for example, Wu and Lindsey (1995)).

6.6.2   Defining Effective Reproduction Operators

At a high level of abstraction, one can think of mutation as a perturbation operator, and recombination as exchanging compatible subcomponents. Given a set of alternative internal representations of an external space, the focus should be on choosing one that facilitates the design of reproductive operators that have these properties.

6.6.2.1 Effective Mutation Operators

If we think of mutation as a perturbation operator, our goal is to define mutation in such a way that a mutation of an internally represented object results in a small change in the corresponding external object. This is achieved most easily if f preserves neighborhoods, i.e., if nearby points in external space correspond to nearby points in internal space. The distance metric for the external space is generally specified by the application domain. An advantage of choosing a *phenotypic* internal representation is that the same distance metric applies, and hence application-dependent notions of perturbations can be used directly in the design of mutation operators. So, for example, in solving real-valued parameter optimization problems, choosing real-valued vectors as the internal representation facilitates the implementation of a mutation operator based on the intuitive notion of a Gaussian perturbation.

Choosing a *genotypic* internal representation requires more thought, as it is generally more difficult to define neighborhood-preserving maps, since the "natural" distance metrics of internal genotypic representations can be quite different from the external ones. For example, if one chooses to use an internal binary string representation for solving real-valued parameter optimization problems, then Hamming distance is the natural internal metric. Mutation operators like bit-flip mutation make small changes in Hamming space that may or may not correspond to small changes in parameter space, depending on the way in which parameter space is mapped into Hamming space. Standard (simple) binary encodings do not fare too well in this respect. However, switching to Gray coding can improve the situation considerably (Rowe et al., 2004).

Alternatively, one can view a mutation operator as defining a distance metric on the internal space. From this perspective, one defines a mutation operator on the internal representation space in such a way as to make the metric it induces compatible with the application-defined external metric. For example, one can redefine bit-string mutation operators that induce metrics that are more compatible with Euclidean distance metrics (Grajdeanu and De Jong, 2004).

6.6.2.2 Effective Recombination Operators

If we think of recombination as a way of exchanging subcomponents (building blocks), it is helpful to choose an internal representation that in some sense reflects or preserves the meaningful application-dependent subcomponents in order to facilitate the design of recombination operators. This can be difficult to do for many application domains for several reasons. First, complex objects such as computer programs, graph structures and robot behaviors are often easier to describe in a holistic manner than in terms of their subcomponents (not unlike the difference between the ASCII text of an English sentence and its representation as a parse tree). Recombination operators that exchange components of parse trees are more likely to produce useful offspring than those that exchange arbitrary pieces of ASCII text.

Frequently, finding useful subcomponents is part of the problem being posed by an application domain. In such cases one is given (or has a good sense of) the lowest-level building blocks (primitive elements) and the goal is to discover how best to group (link) these elements into higher-level subcomponents. This means that the representation and the reproductive operators must facilitate the discovery and preservation of important linkages. Here again, we understand how this can be accomplished in particular cases such as representing executable code as Lisp parse trees or representing graph structures as adjacency lists. However, an overarching theory remains out of reach.

6.7 Landscape Analysis

The final piece of the puzzle in defining effective EAs is the fitness landscape used to bias the evolutionary search. Intuitively, we want fitness landscapes that are "evolution friendly" in the sense that they facilitate the evolutionary discovery of individuals with high fitness. In order for this to be true, the landscape must have several desirable properties. First, landscapes must provide hints as to where individuals with high fitness might be found. This sounds intuitively obvious, but care must be taken since there are many applications in which the simplest, most natural notions of fitness do not have this property. Boolean satisfiability problems are a good example of such a situation, in which the goal is to find truth assignments to a set of Boolean variables that will make a complicated Boolean expression involving those variables true. For any particular assignment, either you win or you lose, and for difficult problems there are very few winning combinations. If we use winning/losing as our fitness landscape, we have presented our EA with a binary-valued fitness landscape the value of which is zero almost everywhere. By providing no hints as to where winning combinations might be found, EAs (and all other search techniques) can do no better than random search. Suppose, however, that the fitness landscape could be redefined to appear more like a bed sheet draped over this spiky landscape. Then, losing combinations provide hints (in the form of gradients) as to where one might find winning combinations (see, for example, Spears (1990)).

A more subtle difficulty arises when a fitness landscape provides insufficient or misleading information. For example, if the landscape consists of a large number of independently distributed local optima, following local optima information will not improve the chances of finding a global optimum. This situation is made worse if the landscape is deceptive, in the sense that the hints it provides draw an EA away from the best solutions rather than toward them. If something is known about the nature of such landscapes, EAs can be designed to deal with them (see, for example, Goldberg (2002)).

Even when a landscape is evolution friendly, it still remains the job of the EA designer to choose an internal representation and reproductive operators to take advantage of the information provided. Theoretical guidance for this comes in the form of Price's theorem that was introduced and discussed in section 6.5. Recall that Price's theorem had two terms: one corresponding to improvements in fitness due to selection, and a second term corresponding to improvements in fitness due to reproductive variation. If we think of this from a landscape viewpoint, it means exploiting the information provided by the current population via parent selection, and leveraging that information via reproductive variation. If we assume that the fitness of an individual will be the same regardless of its internal representation, then the EA designer has the opportunity to improve EA performance by choosing an internal representation and reproductive operators that improve the contributions of the second term of Price's theorem.

A nice example of how this can be done is given in Manderick et al. (1991), in which improvements in parent-child fitness correlation were directly linked to improvements in overall EA performance. This, of course, does not describe how to achieve high correlation. It just helps to quantify progress toward that goal. But we now have a collection of hints as to how to proceed. First, we try our best to define an evolution-friendly fitness landscape, and then we choose an internal representation that preserves that friendliness and facilitates the definition of mutation and recombination operators with high fitness correlations. These ideas are explored in considerable detail in Jones (1995).

6.8 Models of Canonical EAs

In addition to component-oriented analyses of EA, considerable theoretical work has also been done for specific instances of EAs, primarily the canonical EAs discussed in chapter 3. In keeping with the earlier sections of this chapter, the focus here is on application-independent analyses and application-dependent analyses are deferred to a later section in this chapter. Of the three canonical EAs, GAs have been the most extensively analyzed in domain-independent frameworks. This analysis is summarized in the following subsections.

6.8.1 Infinite Population Models for Simple GAs

Recall that a canonical GA uses an internal fixed-length *binary string* representation for individuals. Hence, choosing a string length of L implies an underlying genospace consisting of $r = 2^L$ unique genotypes and population vectors of the form:

$$P(t) = \ <c_1(t), c_2(t), ..., c_r(t)>$$

Recall also that simple GAs choose parents via fitness-proportional selection. If f_i represents the fitness of genotype i, then for infinite population models, the probability of selecting genotype i at time t is given by:

$$select_i(t) = \frac{c_i(t) * f_i}{\sum_{j=1}^{r} c_j(t) * f_j}$$

Recall that asexual reproduction in a simple GA is implemented as cloning, followed by a bit-flip mutation operator that is applied to each cloned gene position with a fixed probability of p_{mut}. Hence, in a simple GA, $reproduce_{ij}$ is independent of time and can be calculated simply by knowing the Hamming distance d between genotypes i and j, namely:

$$reproduce_{ij} = bitflip_{ij} = (1 - p_{mut})^{L-d} * (p_{mut})^d$$

in which none of the $L - d$ gene values shared by both i and j are mutated, and *all* of the differing gene values are mutated.

Combining this with fitness-proportional selection gives us the population update rules for a mutation-only GA:

$$c_i(t+1) \;=\; ((1 - p_{mut})^{L-d} * (p_{mut})^d) * \left(\frac{c_i(t)*f_i}{\sum_{j=1}^{r} c_j(t)*f_j} \right)$$

However, in simple GAs, offspring are also produced using sexual reproduction involving two parents. If we focus initially on a GA using only sexual reproduction (and no mutation), our population update rules take the form:

$$c_i(t+1) \;=\; \sum_{j=1}^{r} \sum_{k=1}^{r} reproduce_{ijk}(t) \;*\; select_{jk}(t)$$

where $reproduce_{ijk}(t)$ is the probability that sexual reproduction will produce an offspring with genotype i from parental genotypes j and k, and $select_{jk}(t)$ is the probability of selecting the first parent of genotype j and the second of type k. Since, in a simple GA, sexual reproduction is implemented as a time-invariant 1-point crossover operator and parents are selected independently using fitness-proportional selection, the population update rules simplify to:

$$c_i(t+1) \;=\; \sum_{j=1}^{r} \sum_{k=1}^{r} onepoint_{ijk} \;*\; select_j(t) * select_k(t)$$

where $onepoint_{ijk}$ is the probability that 1-point crossover will produce an offspring with genotype i from parental genotypes j and k.

To calculate $onepoint_{ijk}$, we need to focus on the gene locations at which the various genotypes differ. In particular, if a is the index of the *first* gene that differs between genotypes j and i, then the crossover point must occur before a. Similarly, if b is the index of the *last* gene that differs between genotype k and i, then the crossover point must occur after b. This can be easily seen in the following example. Suppose the selected genotypes are:

```
                   -------
genotype j:    0 0 0 1 0 0

                ==>            genotype i:    0 0 0 1 1 1

                   -----
genotype k:    0 1 1 1 1 1
```

then $a = 5$ and $b = 3$, resulting in exactly $(a - b) = 2$ choices for the crossover point that will produce an offspring of type i from j and k. Since the 1-point crossover operator selects one of the $L - 1$ crossover points uniformly at random, the probabilities needed are simply:

$$onepoint_{ijk} = \tfrac{a-b}{L-1} \text{ if } a > b, \text{ and}$$
$$onepoint_{ijk} = 0 \text{ otherwise.}$$

So, we now have population update rules for a GA using only mutation, and a second set of update rules for a GA using only 1-point crossover. In a simple GA, however, these two reproductive operators interact in the following manner. A fraction p_{xover} of the offspring population is produced by first using 1-point crossover to generate a candidate offspring, and then applying bit-flip mutation to the result. The remaining offspring are produced using cloning and mutation alone. Thus, the combined population update rules are of the form:

$$c_i(t+1) = (p_{xover} * (\sum_{j=1}^{r} \sum_{k=1}^{r} \sum_{l=1}^{r} bitflip_{ij} * onepoint_{jkl} * select_k(t) * \\ select_l(t))) + ((1 - p_{xover}) * (\sum_{j=1}^{r} bitflip_{ij} * select_j))$$

With this formulation we now have an exact infinite population model for how the population of a simple GA changes over time. This allows us to answer a variety of dynamical systems questions about the model itself, such as whether it has any fixed points, and if so, how many there are and what their properties are. For example, one can show that:

- An infinite-population GA consisting of a randomly generated initial population and population dynamics that involve only fitness-proportional selection and reproductive cloning will converge to a population fixed point of the form:

$$P(fixed\_point) = < 0, 0, ..., 0, 1, 0, ..., 0 >$$

namely, a homogeneous population consisting entirely of copies of the genotype in the initial population with maximal fitness. Mathematically, this corresponds to the observation that all evolutionary trajectories in the $(r-1)$-dimensional simplex terminate at one of the vertices.

- Adding an n-point crossover operator results in an infinite population GA that continues to converge to a homogeneous population, but not necessarily the one containing the genotype from the initial population with maximal fitness.

- Adding a constant-rate mutation operator results in an infinite population GA that no longer converges to homogeneous populations. While this infinite population GA appears to always converge to a fixed point, it remains an open question as to whether there are fitness landscapes on which this GA does not converge at all.

- While fitness landscapes exist that result in an infinite number of fixed points, the overriding majority of landscapes produce a finite number of fixed points.

- Each such fixed point is the center of a basin of attraction in the $(r-1)$-dimensional simplex. A randomly generated initial (infinite) population will lie in one of these basins of attraction. An infinite-population GA converges to the fixed point associated with that basin of attraction.

These issues have been explored extensively in the literature. The interested reader is encouraged to see Vose (1995), Wright and Vose (1995), or Vose (1999) for more details.

6.8.2   Expected Value Models of Simple GAs

Recall that the infinite population model of simple GAs was given by update rules of the form:

$$c_i(t+1) = (p_{xover} * (\sum_{j=1}^{r} \sum_{k=1}^{r} \sum_{l=1}^{r} bitflip_{ij} * onepoint_{jkl} * select_k(t) * \\ select_l(t))) + ((1 - p_{xover}) * (\sum_{j=1}^{r} bitflip_{ij} * select_j))$$

For the finite population case, the expected value model is identical:

$$E[c_i(t+1)] = (p_{xover} * (\sum_{j=1}^{r} \sum_{k=1}^{r} \sum_{l=1}^{r} bitflip_{ij} * onepoint_{jkl} * select_k(t) *$$
$$select_l(t))) + ((1 - p_{xover}) * (\sum_{j=1}^{r} bitflip_{ij} * select_j))$$

since the selection and reproduction terms are the same for both finite and infinite EAs. This formulation is an exact expected-value model of how the population of a simple GA changes over time, and is the basis for the historically important GA schema theory.

6.8.2.1   GA Schema Theory

The schema theory developed initially by Holland (1975) to analyze simple GAs is another example of how these models of population dynamics can be used to better understand EAs. One of the things that Holland was interested in was characterizing how a GA explores an unknown fitness landscape over time. If we view each individual created by a GA as taking a sample of the fitness landscape, the idea is to characterize how a GA uses this accumulating information to create new individuals with high fitness. Since simple GAs use a fixed-length binary representation for individuals, one can use a "schema" or "hyperplane" notation to describe subsets of genotypes such as 1***...*** , the set of all genotypes whose first gene has a value, or 0***...**0, the set of all genotypes that begin and end with a zero.

If we adopt this schema notation, it is easy to see that, if we enumerate all the schemata defined over a particular set of k binary-valued genes, we have specified a uniform partition of the genospace consisting of 2^k hyperplane subspaces h_i. For example, the following set of second-order schemata:

```
h1:   00****...***
h2:   01****...***
h3:   10****...***
h4:   11****...***
```

uniformly partitions the (binary) genotype space into 4 hyperplane subspaces. As we increase k (the order of the schemata), we exponentially increase the number of hyperplanes that make up the corresponding uniform partition.

Using this schema framework, one can now describe how a GA population is distributed among a particular set of hyperplane subspaces over time:

Schema Theorem 1: If $m_i(t)$ represents the number of individuals in a GA population at time t that are elements of partition hyperplane h_i, then:

$$E[m_i(t+1)] \geq m_i(t) * \frac{\bar{f}_i(t)}{\bar{f}(t)} * (1 - \epsilon_i)$$

where $\bar{f}_i(t)$ is the average fitness of the $m_i(t)$ individuals in hyperplane h_i, $\bar{f}(t)$ is the average fitness of the individuals in the population, and $(1 - \epsilon_i)$ is the probability that the reproductive operators preserve membership in h_i (i.e, offspring of parents in h_i are also members of h_i).

To understand this result, note that if a GA uses no reproductive operators, i.e., offspring are just parental clones, then any change in $m_i(t)$ is due to parental selection alone. In this case schema theorem 1 simplifies to:

$$E[m_i(t+1)] \;=\; m_i(t) \;*\; \frac{\bar{f}_i(t)}{\bar{f}(t)}$$

To see that this is true, recall that simple GAs select parents using fitness-proportional selection, i.e., the probability of a particular individual j in $P(t)$ being selected as a parent is defined to be:

$$select_j(t) \;=\; \frac{f_j}{\sum_{k=1}^{m} f_k(t)}$$

If we sample this probability distribution m times to produce the next generation, the expected number of offspring from a particular individual j in $P(t)$ is given by:

$$E[o_j(t+1)] \;=\; m*select_j(t) \;=\; \frac{f_j}{\frac{1}{m}\sum_{k=1}^{m} f_k(t)} \;=\; \frac{f_j}{\bar{f}(t)}$$

This is easily extended to the expected number of offspring produced by parents from hyperplane h_i by just adding up the individual expectations:

$$E[O_i(t+1)] \;=\; \sum_{j=1}^{m_i(t)} E[o_j(t+1)] \;=\; \sum_{j=1}^{m_i(t)} \frac{f_j}{\bar{f}(t)} \;=\; m_i(t)*\frac{\bar{f}_i(t)}{\bar{f}(t)}$$

So, in the absence of any reproductive variation, over time the individuals in a GA population migrate (at a fitness-proportional rate) from hyperplane partition elements with observed *below-average* fitness to partition elements with observed *above-average* fitness.

With this understood, we can now model the effects of reproductive variation in terms of the probability that offspring will be members of the same hyperplane h_i as their parents. Obviously, that probability is 1 when only cloning occurs, but $(1-\epsilon_i)$ when there is reproductive variation, where ϵ_i is the probability that an offspring is a member of a different hyperplane than h_i. However, in order to calculate ϵ_i, we need to be more specific about the internal representation and the reproductive operators being used. Holland was able to prove:

> **Schema Theorem 2:** Assume a simple GA using a bit string representation of length L with bit-flip mutation and 1-point crossover. Then, for any partition of the genotype space defined by order K schemata, the probability ϵ_i that offspring of parents in partition element h_i are not themselves members of h_i is bounded above by:
>
> $$\epsilon_i \;\leq\; 1 - ((1-p_{mut})^K) + (p_{xover} * \tfrac{dl_i}{L-1}))$$
>
> where K is the order of the partition element h_i, p_{mut} is the probability of mutation flipping a bit, p_{xover} is the probability that the crossover operator is used to produce an offspring, and dl_i is the "defining length" of schema associated with h_i.

This theorem is best understood with an example. Suppose the schemata defining a particular hyperplance partition are of the form xy****...***, that is, second order schemata. Then, the gene values x and y will only be inherited if mutation does not flip either gene value *and* if the gene values are not split up by crossover. Since the probability of mutation *not* changing both x and y is clearly $(1-p_m)^2$, the probability that a change will occur is

$(1-(1-p_m)^2)$. The only way 1-point crossover can possibly change things is if the crossover point falls in between the x and y genes. In this particular example, the probability of that happening is $1/(L-1)$.

If, on the other hand, the schemata defining a particular partition are of the form x****...**y, the effects of mutation would be the same as before. However, the probability of picking a crossover point between x and y is now 1! Of course, it is possible that the second parent selected for crossover is a member of the same partition element as the first parent. In this case, regardless of where the crossover point occurs, the offspring will also be a member of that partition element. So, $dl_i/(L-1)$ is only an upper bound on the probability of a change due to crossover.

Taken together, schema theorems 1 and 2 create the following intuitive picture of how canonical GAs with populations of sufficient size evolve over time: hyperplanes defined by low order schemata with short definition lengths gain (and lose) population members at a rate that is approximately proportional to their average fitness.

To make these ideas even more concrete, suppose that the fitness landscape is defined to be $f(x) = x_2$ over the interval [0.0, 4.0]. If we assume a canonical GA with a standard internal binary representation that discretizes this interval down to a resolution of 10^{-6}, then the required length L of the internal bitstrings is $log_2(4*10^6) = 22$. If we focus on the hyperplane partition given by the first-order schemata:

```
h1:    0***...***    <-->    [0.0,2.0]
h2:    1***...***    <-->    [2.0,4.0]
```

the first hyperplane, h_1, corresponds (roughly) to the interval [0.0,2.0] and the second one, h_2 to [2.0,4.0]. With such a simple fitness function, it is easy to estimate the average fitness of each hyperplane as:

$$\bar{f}_1 \approx \frac{\int_0^2 x^2 dx}{2} = \frac{8}{6} = 1.333$$
$$\bar{f}_2 \approx \frac{\int_2^4 x^2 dx}{2} = \frac{56}{6} = 9.333$$

as well as the average fitness of the entire interval:

$$\bar{f} \approx \frac{\int_0^4 x^2 dx}{4} = \frac{64}{12} = 5.333$$

If we randomly generate the initial GA population uniformly over the 22-bit string space, we would expect approximately one half to be members of h_1 and the other half in h_2. If the GA population size m is of sufficient size, then the average fitness of the population members in h_i, $\bar{f}_i(0)$, will be close to the average fitness $\bar{f}_i$ of the underlying hyperplane h_i.

Since the schema in this example are of order 1, schema theorems 1 and 2 predict that there will be a rapid shift of population individuals from h_1 to h_2, since the fitness of h_1 is well *below* average and the fitness of h_2 is well *above* average.

In fact, the schema theorems make an even stronger prediction. Since crossover can have no effect on schemata of order 1, the only observed reproductive variation will be due to the bit-flip mutation operator, and hence:

$$\epsilon_i \leq (1 - (1 - p_m)) = p_m$$

If we set the probability of mutation, p_m, to its default setting of $1/L$, then $p_m = 0.0455$ and hence the term $(1 - \epsilon_i)$ in schema theorem 1 is approximately 0.96. So, the stronger prediction in this case is that the initial rate of increase of population members in h_2 will be approximately:

$$\frac{\bar{f_2}}{\bar{f}} * 0.955 = \frac{9.333}{5.333} * 0.955 = 1.67$$

We can check the accuracy of this prediction by running an actual GA multiple times. For example, using a population size of 50, a set of 5 independent runs produced:

run	$m_2(1)$	$m_2(2)$	*rate of increase*
1	23	40	1.74
2	19	39	2.05
3	25	42	1.68
4	30	44	1.46
5	26	43	1.65
		Average:	1.71

where $m_2(1)$ is the number of individuals in h_2 at generation 1, and $m_2(2)$ is the number at generation 2. So, already with a population size of 50, the predicted population shift to h_2 is quite close to what we observe in practice.

It is tempting to apply this same logic to make a prediction about the rate of increase from generation 2 to generation 3. But notice that, already in generation 2, the dynamically observed averages $\bar{f_1}(2)$, $\bar{f_2}(2)$, and $\bar{f}(2)$ are no longer likely to be reasonable approximations of the static averages $\bar{f_1}$, $\bar{f_2}$, and $\bar{f}$, since they no longer represent unbiased sample averages. In each succeeding generation this divergence increases.

Notice that the schema theorems are not about any particular schemata partition, but are true for any such partition. So, using our previous example, if we pick the partition:

```
h1:    ***...***0
h2:    ***...***1
```

the first hyperplane, h_1, corresponds to all of the points in [0.0,4.0] whose binary representation is "even", and h_2 contains all the "odd" points. Since both represent a uniform subsample of [0.0,4.0], it is easy to estimate the average fitness of each hyperplane as:

$$\bar{f_1} \approx \bar{f_2} \approx \bar{f}$$

If, as before, we randomly generate our initial GA population uniformly over the 22-bit string space, we would expect approximately one half to be members of h_1 and the other half in h_2. Since both schemata have equal fitness, the schema theorems predict no significant change in the number of odd and even binary strings in moving from generation 1 to generation 2.

Using the same sample GA runs as before, but focusing now on the last gene position, we see:

run	$m_2(1)$	$m_2(2)$	rate of increase
1	22	22	1.0
2	24	27	1.125
3	25	28	1.12
4	22	24	1.09
5	26	23	0.885
		Average:	1.04

So, already with a population size of 50, the predicted lack of a population shift is quite close to what we observe in practice.

Now suppose we focus on order 2 hyperplane partitions, beginning with:

```
h1:   00***...***    <-->    [0.0,1.0]
h2:   01***...***    <-->    [1.0,2.0]
h3:   10***...***    <-->    [2.0,3.0]
h4:   11***...***    <-->    [3.0,4.0]
```

Each hyperplane, h_i, now corresponds (roughly) to the intervals [0.0,1.0], [1.0,2.0], [2.0,3.0], and [3.0,4.0]. With such a simple fitness function, it is easy to estimate the average fitness of each hyperplane as:

$$\bar{f}_1 \approx \frac{\int_0^1 x^2 dx}{1} = \frac{1}{3} = 0.333$$

$$\bar{f}_2 \approx \frac{\int_1^2 x^2 dx}{1} = \frac{7}{3} = 2.333$$

$$\bar{f}_3 \approx \frac{\int_2^3 x^2 dx}{1} = \frac{19}{3} = 6.333$$

$$\bar{f}_4 \approx \frac{\int_3^4 x^2 dx}{1} = \frac{37}{3} = 12.333$$

Since hyperplane partition element h_4 has a significant selective advantage over the other partition elements, we focus on it. The schema theorems predict in this case that the initial rate of increase of population members in h_4 will be approximately:

$$\frac{\bar{f}_4}{\bar{f}} * 0.863 = \frac{12.333}{5.333} * 0.863 = 1.996$$

where 0.863 is the $(1 - \epsilon)$ term for this particular second order schema. We can check the accuracy of this prediction by using the same set of 5 GA runs as before, and we observe:

run	$m_4(1)$	$m_4(2)$	rate of increase
1	10	23	2.30
2	14	30	2.14
3	15	25	1.66
4	16	31	1.93
5	13	24	1.85
		Average:	1.97

which again matches the predicted values quite closely.

To complete the example, we switch our focus to another second order partition, namely:

```
0***...***0
0***...***1
1***...***0
1***...***1
```

Since the odd and even components again correspond to uniform samples of the subintervals $[0.0, 2.0]$ and $[2.0, 4.0]$, we have the same values as we saw earlier with the first order example:

$$\bar{f}_1 \approx \frac{\int_0^2 x^2 dx}{2} = \frac{8}{6} = 1.333$$

$$\bar{f}_2 \approx \frac{\int_0^2 x^2 dx}{2} = \frac{8}{6} = 1.333$$

$$\bar{f}_3 \approx \frac{\int_2^4 x^2 dx}{2} = \frac{56}{3} = 9.333$$

$$\bar{f}_4 \approx \frac{\int_2^4 x^2 dx}{2} = \frac{56}{3} = 9.333$$

If we focus again on h_4, the predicted rate of increase will be approximately:

$$\frac{\bar{f}_4}{\bar{f}} * 0.613 = \frac{9.333}{5.333} * 0.613 = 1.07$$

where 0.613 is the $(1 - \epsilon)$ term for this particular second order schema. This is a significantly lower predicted growth rate than we saw before, and is due to the disruptive effects of crossover on schemata with long (and in this case, maximal) defining lengths.

If we check the accuracy of this prediction by using the same set of 5 GA runs as before, we observe much higher actual growth rates than predicted:

run	$m_4(1)$	$m_4(2)$	*rate of increase*
1	10	20	2.00
2	09	23	2.55
3	14	23	1.64
4	14	21	1.50
5	08	15	1.87
		Average:	1.91

This is still consistent with the schema theorems since they only give lower bound estimates of growth rates and do not take into account the fact that the simultaneous disruptive effects happening in the other 3 partition elements can (and do) result in offspring residing in h_4. These contributions can be taken into account, resulting in the so-called "exact" schema theorems (see for example, Goldberg (1989) or Vose (1999)).

So, what sort of predictions can the schema theorems make about *future* generations beyond generation 2? Since any finite-population GA can only provide estimates of the underlying hyperplane averages, it is not possible to make precise *quantitative* predictions about rates of increase in hyperplane sampling. However, it is possible to make some insightful *qualitative* predictions.

Corollary 1: If the observed fitness of a particular hyperplane partition remains consistently above average, the simple GA will fairly quickly shift most of its population members to that subspace.

To see this, refer back to the earlier hyperplane partition:

```
h1:    00***...***
h2:    01***...***
h3:    10***...***
h4:    11***...***
```

With the simple $f(x) = x^2$ fitness landscape, h_4 will satisfy corollary 1. If we go back and look at our 5 sample GA runs, on average at least 95% of the population resides in h_4 by generation 10.

By contrast, hyperplanes unable to maintain above-average fitness will not be able to produce such steady gains. To see this, refer back to the earlier hyperplane partition:

```
h1:    0***...***0
h2:    0***...***1
h3:    1***...***0
h4:    1***...***1
```

involving schemata with maximal defining lengths. In this case, most of the population has shifted out of h_1 and h_2 by generation 10. However, even after 4000 generations, convergence to h_3 or h_4 has not yet occurred since h_3 and h_4 maintain roughly equal observed fitness averages.

If we combine these observations with the fact that all of this is happening simultaneously in every such hyperplane partition, we get the following corollary, sometimes referred to as implicit parallelism:

> **Corollary 2:** A simple GA will quickly distribute its population members to hyperplane partition elements that are able to maintain high average fitness.

Our example shows this nicely once we observe that every schema with all leading 1s satisfies corollary 2. If we look at our sample runs, we observe rapid convergence on average to the following partition elements:

partition element	phenotypic interval	generations to convergence
1****...***	[2.0,4.0]	8
11***...***	[3.0,4.0]	15
111**...***	[3.5,4.0]	35

This gives a pleasing and intuitive view of a landscape on which a simple GA dynamically shifts its attention to the hyperplane partition containing the individual with maximal fitness, namely 1111...111, and gives rise to a more general "Building Block" hypothesis that characterizes a simple GA as using the rapidly emerging low-order schemata with high average fitness as building blocks to form stepping stones to more highly fit individuals.

At the same time, schema analysis provides insight into when that will not happen, namely with "deceptive" landscapes that place such "optimal" building blocks in partition elements with low average fitness. In such cases we have:

Corollary 3: Even if a partition element contains an individual of maximum fitness, if that hyperplane's observed average fitness is persistently below average, the simple GA will distribute its population members to other hyperplane partition elements that are able to maintain high average fitness, thus significantly decreasing over time the likelihood that that particular "optimal" individual will be encountered.

These issues have been explored extensively in the literature. The interested reader is encouraged to see, for example, Holland (1975) or Goldberg (1989) for more details.

6.8.2.2 Summary

Both the infinite population and the finite population models of EAs in general and GAs in particular have shortcomings, in that they are unable to make strong quantitative predictions about the properties of future generations of implementable EAs. If we hope to improve our predictive ability, we will need to strengthen (and likely complicate) our theoretical models. In the next few sections several historically important ways of doing so are summarized.

6.8.3 Markov Models

Because of the stochastic nature of EAs, a natural way to strengthen the population dynamics models is to embed them in a more complex probabilistic framework. For example, suppose we focus on the space of all conceivable populations that a particular EA might produce. As we saw earlier with infinite population models of EAs that use a fixed-length genotype, this space of all possible populations is elegantly captured mathematically as an $(r-1)$-dimensional simplex where r is the number of distinct genotypes. Imagine now a probability distribution $PD(t)$ defined over this simplex that expresses the probability that our EA of interest exhibits a particular population configuration at generation t. Of interest, then, is how $PD(t)$ changes over time as evolution proceeds. That is, we seek probability distribution update rules of the form:

$$PD(t+1) = evolve(PD(t))$$

While such rules are difficult to obtain in general, there are a number of specific cases in which useful results can be obtained, primarily by using results from the well-developed area of Markov chain analysis. Markov models characterize a system by assuming that one can define the set of possible states it might be in at any given time, together with a probability distribution over that set of states that expresses the likelihood of the system being in that state. To complete the model, a probability update rule must be given to indicate how this probability distribution changes over time. This is generally expressed in the form of a state transition matrix Q, in which each entry q_{ij} specifies the probability of a transition from state i to j in one time step. To obtain some degree of mathematical tractability, it is additionally required that the system is "memoryless", in the sense that the Q matrix does not change over time.

Having constructed such a model, one can now specify an initial probability distribution $PD(0)$ and obtain the update rule:

$$PD(t) = Q^t * PD(0)$$

In particular, if we allow t to approach infinity, we have a characterization of the steady-state behavior of the system in terms of the Markov chain Q^t. In general, of course, for systems of any complexity the number of possible states can be quite large and explicit enumeration is not feasible. Rather, the properties of the Q matrix are used to mathematically characterize the steady-state behavior of the chain.

6.8.3.1   Markov Models of Finite Population EAs

It should be clear by now that the simple EAs we have been discussing are quite amenable to being represented by Markov models (see, for example, Eiben et al. (1990)). In particular, if we assume that the state of an EA corresponds to its population contents, then it is possible (at least in principle) to construct a Q matrix in which q_{ij} represents the probability of going from population i to population j in one generation. If we additionally assume that the selection and reproductive mechanisms are time-invariant, then Q is time-independent and Markov chain analysis tools can be applied.

As a simple example of this, consider a non-overlapping-generation EA that uses only a stochastic-uniform parent-selection procedure and cloning to produce the next generation. Such finite population EAs exhibit the well-known property of "genetic drift", namely that, in spite of the fact that the selection pressure is uniform, genotypes are steadily lost from the population over time, resulting in convergence to a population fixed point (an absorbing state) consisting of a homogeneous population of one of the initial population genotypes. The rate at which genotypes are lost is related directly to the population size m. As m increases, the loss rate decreases. Given an initial population makeup, the expected time to convergence can be derived directly from the Markov model (see, for example, De Jong (1975) or Goldberg and Segrest (1987)).

Suppose that we now add to this EA a mutation operator that is applied at a fixed nonzero rate. This implies that, at any given time, all population states have some nonzero probability of being reached. Hence, there are no population fixed points (absorbing states). All entries in the Q matrix for such EAs are nonzero, making the Markov chain "ergodic". It is a well-known theorem that ergodic Markov chains converge to steady-state distributions that are independent of the initial conditions.

If we then decide to anneal the mutation rate over time to zero, we again obtain convergence to a homogeneous fixed point, but not necessarily one consisting of a genotype from the initial population (see, for example, Davis and Principe (1993)).

The key element in all this is our ability to characterize the elements of Q, namely:

$$q_{ij} = prob(pop_j = evolve(pop_i))$$

This requires that, for a particular EA, we calculate for each population state s_i the probability that in one generation it will transition to population state s_j. While this seems a rather daunting task, it can and has been done for a number of simple EAs. We briefly illustrate this for simple GAs.

6.8.3.2 Markov Models of Simple GAs

If we assume that the GA uses a simple fixed-length binary string representation, then the total number of genotypes is given by $r = 2^L$ where L is the string length. If we assume that the GA maintains a constant population of size m, then, as we saw earlier, a population state is uniquely characterized by an unnormalized genotype frequency vector:

$$s_i = < c_{i1}, c_{i2}, ..., c_{ir} >$$

in which the c_{ij} must sum to m. If we ask how many such states S there are, it is relatively straightforward to show that:

$$S(m, r = 2^L) = \left(\begin{array}{c} m + r - 1 \\ r - 1 \end{array} \right)$$

To get a sense of how large this state space can get, note that for a simple GA with a population size of $m = 10$ and bit strings of length $L = 4$, $S = 3,268,760$!

What remains, then, is to characterize the transition probabilities q_{ij} for the $S \times S$ matrix Q. In order to do this we have to characterize the effects of selection and reproduction on a population. This has been done successfully in the literature for a number of simple GAs. Perhaps the earliest and best known is that of Nix and Vose (1992) for a generational GA using fitness-proportional selection along with standard bit flipping mutation and 1-point crossover. As we saw earlier, the key is to focus on the effects of the reproductive operators via an $r \times r$ matrix R that calculates the probability that a parent with genotype k will produce an offspring with genotype l. For a particular population state s_i, its genotype vector specifies the frequency of each genotype. If, in addition, we know the fitness of each genotype, we can easily calculate the probability of a particular genotype from s_i being selected as a parent via fitness-proportional selection. Combining that selection probability vector with the reproductive matrix R gives us a probability distribution over the genotype vector describing the offspring population, which in a generational GA is the population at time $t + 1$.

The final step, then, is to calculate the probability that a particular offspring population state s_j will be produced from s_i. Since the order in which the m offspring are produced is immaterial, this comes down to an exercise in counting how many distinct ways a population of type j can be produced from a population of type i. The result is generally something of the form:

$$q_{ij} = m! * \prod_{k=1}^{r} \frac{(prob_{ik})^{c_{jk}}}{c_{jk}!}$$

where $prob_{ik}$ is the probability that a population state s_i will produce genotypes of type k. The interested reader can see (Vose, 1999) for a more detailed description of such an approach. For our purposes, the focus is on what one can do with such models. In particular, we would like to know if we can now make stronger predictions about EA population dynamics than we could before. The answer is a qualified "yes", in that one can now show:

- As the population size m increases, the population trajectories begin to approximate those of the corresponding infinite population model more closely.

Figure 6.54: Visualization of Q^t for t=1,4,10.

- The transient behavior of a finite population GA is determined by its initial population makeup and the fixed points of the corresponding infinite population model.

- With a constant nonzero mutation rate, a finite population GA will at some point escape from any local basin of attraction, only to be drawn into another one.

- A finite population GA spends most of its time in basins of attraction associated with the fixed points of the corresponding infinite population model.

While these are interesting general observations about GA behavior, they do not provide specific details as to the location, size, and number of such basins of attraction. To get more detailed insights into this transient behavior, an interesting approach worth exploring is to consider the possibility of computationally iterating the Markov model itself as a means of making more specific predictions about GA population dynamics. This approach is similar in spirit to Whitley (1992).

The difficulty is that, as we saw earlier, the size S of the underlying state space grows combinatorially with population size and the length of the genotype. Hence, computable models can only be feasibly constructed for very small EAs (e.g., $m = 10$ and $L = 4$ for binary GAs). Hence, the concern is whether properties observed by iterating these small GA models are in fact also present in larger models.

This approach was explored in some detail in De Jong et al. (1994). One of the immediate advantages was the ability to visualize the individual entries of Q^t as illustrated in figure 6.54. Since each entry, q_{ij}^t, represents a probability, its magnitude was represented visually in terms of a gray scale from black (a probability of 0.0) to white (a probability of 1.0). What was surprising was that already by generation $t = 10$, vertical bands of accumulating probability mass associated with the limiting distribution were visually quite evident.

Another advantage of this model iteration approach is that it allows one to *quantitatively* characterize transient GA behavior. Since with practical applications we seldom run a GA to steady state, what we observe is the GA's transient behavior. Iterating these Markov models allows one to make precise quantitative statements about things like: 1) the probability of observing in the population at time t a particular genotype k, or 2) the expected waiting time until a particular genotype k (e.g., one with maximal fitness) appears for the first time in the population, and more importantly, how changes in selection pressure and reproductive operators affect such transient properties. The interested reader should see De Jong et al. (1994) for more details.

6.8.3.3 Summary

As we have seen, Markov models can make stronger predictions about EA population dynamics, but at a price of considerable additional mathematical and computational complexity. A common strategy for dealing with combinatorially explosive state-space models is to explore ways of "lumping" similar states together in order to reduce state-space growth while still maintaining the ability to construct the corresponding Q matrices. This possibility was explored to some extent in Spears and De Jong (1996) for Markov models of simple GAs, and exhibited some modest success.

An alternative strategy that has been proposed is to adopt some of the statistical mechanics techniques developed by physicists when faced with similar issues. We explore this briefly in the next section.

6.8.4 Statistical Mechanics Models

The basic idea behind statistical mechanics is to model large, complex systems in terms of their statistical properties, thus avoiding the sort of combinatorial explosion of detail that we saw with the Markov models in the previous section. So, a statistical mechanics approach to modeling population dynamics involves characterizing populations by their statistical properties, and then providing the update rules that define how these statistical properties change during evolution.

One such approach developed by Prügel-Bennett and Shapiro (1994) focuses on characterizing evolving populations in terms of their fitness distributions, and seeks update rules that describe how these fitness distributions change over time:

$$FD(t+1) = evolve(FD(t))$$

For example, suppose the fitness values of the members of our initial population were normally distributed with mean μ and variance σ. Intuitively, after applying selection and cloning, the fitness distribution of the offspring population is no longer normal, but skewed in the direction of higher fitness with a much higher mean fitness. Now suppose we add in some reproductive variation operators that have the (approximate) effect of renormalizing the fitness distribution of the offspring population. If this is a non-overlapping-generation EA, this is the fitness distribution for the next generation with a higher mean and (most likely) smaller variance.

If this process is repeated in each generation, our statistical mechanics model would consist of update rules of the form:

$$\mu(t+1) = f_1(\mu(t), \sigma(t))$$
$$\sigma(t+1) = f_2(\mu(t), \sigma(t))$$

Of course, in practice things are never this simple! Figures 6.55 and 6.56 illustrate this by plotting how the population fitness distributions change over time for two different fitness

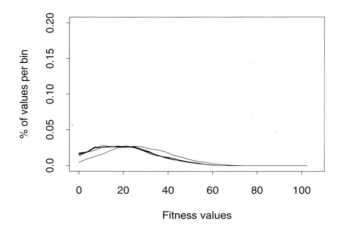

Figure 6.55: Evolving population fitness distributions for a simple quadratic landscape.

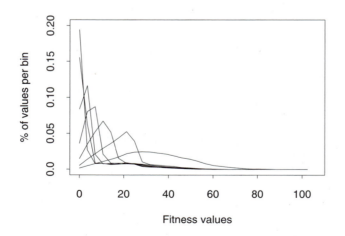

Figure 6.56: Evolving population fitness distributions for a complex, multi-peaked landscape.

landscapes. Both are posed as minimization problems, so the distributions are shifting to the left over time.

Observations of this sort make it quite clear that one needs a way to describe non-normal distributions. The preferred approach in statistical mechanics is to use, in addition to the mean and variance, the higher order cumulants k_i (skewedness, excess, etc.). So our statistical mechanics model now takes the form:

$$k_1(t+1) = f_1(k_1(t), k_2(t), k_3(t), ...)$$
$$k_2(t+1) = f_2(k_1(t), k_2(t), k_3(t), ...)$$
$$k_3(t+1) = f_3(k_1(t), k_2(t), k_3(t), ...)$$
$$...$$

The difficulty, of course, is in deciding how many cumulants are required, and more importantly, in having the ability to derive the update rules f_i. In general, these rules depend heavily on the structure of the particular fitness landscape, and as such have only been derived for a few simple functions (see, for example, Shapiro and Prügel-Bennett (1996) or Prügel-Bennett and Shapiro (1997)). So, the jury is still out as to the scalability of this approach.

6.8.5 Summary

We have now explored a number of different ways to model EA population dynamics, and as we have seen, each approach has certain strengths and weaknesses. While these analyses provide us with an application-independent understanding, they leave unanswered important application-dependent questions. This aspect is explored in the next section.

6.9 Application-Oriented Theories

Without question, the most dominant EC application area is its use in solving difficult optimization problems and, as a result, this is also the area for which there is the most domain-dependent theory. There are a few scattered theoretical results in other application areas such as machine learning and automatic programming, but these are highly specialized and beyond the scope of this book. Consequently, in this section the focus is on optimization-oriented theory.

6.9.1 Optimization-Oriented Theories

The first question that comes to mind with optimization applications is the question of convergence. Since EAs are population-based algorithms, it is important to define clearly what convergence means. In the earlier sections of this chapter we have seen two kinds of convergence related to population dynamics. The first kind is associated with population trajectories that terminate at a fixed point in the simplex. As we saw, this kind of convergence only happened with EAs in which there was no mutation at all or EAs in which mutation is active for only an initial period of time. If the mutation rate is continuously active, every point in the simplex is reachable. In this case, EAs were seen to converge to a steady-state probability distribution over the entire simplex.

A related question involves how one extracts the "answer" to an optimization problem from an EA. One possibility is to define the answer as the best individual in the final population. If we track that best individual in the population over time from generation to generation, we would like to know the extent to which it converges to the global optimum. However, as we have seen, it is quite possible that the best individuals can disappear from the population when using EAs that have non-overlapping generations. This means that trajectories of the best-of-generation are not monotonically improving over time, making convergence analysis difficult. A better definition of the "answer" is the best individual found over the entire evolutionary run, regardless of whether it is in the final population. If we track those individuals over time, their "best-so-far" trajectories are monotonically improving over time, making them easier to visualize and characterize in terms of convergence to a global optimum.

For population trajectories that terminate in a fixed point, there will obviously be no further improvement in their best-so-far trajectories. So, they have converged as well. For population trajectories that do not terminate in a fixed point, but rather converge to a steady-state distribution over the entire simplex, the best-so-far curves converge in a probabilistic sense in that the likelihood of any future improvement decreases over time.

With these notions of convergence in mind, the focus is now on characterizing the ability of an EA to converge to a global optimum.

6.9.1.1   Convergence and Rates of Convergence

Surprisingly, proofs of convergence to a global optimum are trivial for most of the EAs used in practice and, as such, are not particularly informative. These proofs are a direct result of the fact that most EAs are run with a nonzero mutation rate. As we noted above, in such cases every point in the simplex is reachable, so it is just a matter of time before an optimal point is encountered. This proof also holds for random and exhaustive search, and hence does not provide much insight into the properties of evolutionary search.

So, for most EAs, characterizations of the rates of convergence are much more useful. However, as is true with most theoretical work on optimization algorithms, it is difficult to prove convergence rate theorems without making assumptions about the characteristics of the particular problem and the precise details of the optimization algorithm. Theorems of this sort provide useful insights but tend to be less general than one would wish. Invariably, these analyses are accompanied by a set of experimental studies to validate the results for those cases in which the assumptions are met, and to get a sense of the extent to which the theoretical results hold when various assumptions are violated.

6.9.1.2   ESs and Real-Valued Parameter Optimization Problems

As discussed in chapter 3, Evolution Strategies (ESs) were invented to solve difficult real-valued parameter optimization problems. Recall that these ESs use real-valued vectors as their internal representation of the space to be searched. The simplest ES to analyze formally is the (1+1)-ES, in which a single parent produces a single offspring using a Gaussian mutation operator. The offspring replaces the parent only if its fitness is greater than the parent's. In the terminology of this book, the parent population size m is 1, the offspring population size n is 1, the generations are overlapping, and survival selection is truncation. In more general search terminology, a (1+1)-ES is a random hill-climber. The Gaussian mutation operator $G(0, \sigma)$ determines the expected step size (i.e., the distance between parent and offspring). Extremely large step sizes will produce a more global search strategy, but will not be particularly effective when close to an optimum. Very small step sizes are helpful when close to the optimum, but ineffective when far away. Ideally, one would like to vary the step size as a function of the distance from the optimum. Since the location of the optimum is unknown, some other indicator must be used to adapt the step size. The obvious candidate for a simple (1+1)-ES is its success rate, the expected number of offspring that need to be generated before one replaces the parent. The intuition is that very small step sizes are too exploitive (conservative), in that they generate lots of successes but do not make much progress toward the optimum. Conversely, step sizes that are too large seldom produce a success and thus make little progress as well. What remains, then, is a characterization of an "ideal" success rate, and a mechanism for adapting the step size dynamically to achieve this rate.

This was first done in Rechenberg (1965) using two simple fitness landscapes (one linear and one quadratic). The somewhat surprising result was that in both cases the optimal success rate was approximately 20%, resulting in the now-famous 1/5 step size adaptation rule:

> If the current step size is producing a success rate of more than 20%, increase the step size; else if the current success rate is below 20%, decrease the step size.

Left unspecified by the analysis was the frequency and the amount of the step size changes. Checking the success rate every $i * k$ mutations (where i is a small integer and k is the size of the parameter vector) and changing the step size by 10–15% seems to be quite effective in practice.

As originally defined, there was a single mutation step size applied to all of the parameters in a parameter vector. This can cause problems if there is considerable variance in fitness sensitivity among parameters. So an obvious extension is to maintain and adapt mutation step sizes for each of the k parameters. Additional problems are caused when there are strong nonlinear interactions among the parameters. This can be discovered dynamically and adapted to by also maintaining a covariance matrix.

This sort of analysis becomes much more difficult as we increase the complexity of the ES by increasing the offspring population size $((1 + \lambda)$-ES), by increasing the size of the parent population $((\mu + \lambda)$-ES), by switching to a non-overlapping-generation model $((\mu, \lambda)$-ES, by adding a recombination operator, and so on. The effects that such changes have on optimization performance have been extensively analyzed by the ES community and are accessible in a number of excellent books including Schwefel (1995), Bäck (1996), and Beyer (2001).

6.9.1.3 Simple EAs and Discrete Optimization Problems

Consider now an analogous (1+1)-EA that is designed to solve discrete optimization problems by maintaining an internal binary string representation, producing offspring via a bit-flip mutation operator. The number of bits flipped correspond to step size in Hamming space. However, as discussed in section 6.6, there is often no direct correspondence between Hamming distance and the distance metric of the external application-defined space. As a consequence, adapting the step size in Hamming space with something analogous to the 1/5 rule is generally an ineffective way to improve the rate of convergence to an optimum. Rather, one focuses on how changes to this simple EA affect the convergence rate. For discrete problems, this convergence rate is generally measured in terms of the "first hitting time": the number of offspring that must be generated in order to obtain a copy of an optimal point.

Clearly, the optimal number of bits to be flipped (on average) when producing an offspring can vary from one fitness landscape to the next. Experimentally, a default value of $1/L$, where L is the length of the binary string, has been shown to be quite robust. If we assume that default value, we can ask if there is anything else that can be done to improve convergence rates. For example, we can increase the offspring population size (($1 + \lambda$)-EA), we can increase the parent population size (($\mu + \lambda$)-EA), we can switch to non-overlapping generations, we can add a crossover operator, and so on.

For discrete optimization problems, it is important not only to have the answers to these questions for a particular binary string length L, but to understand the effects that increasing string length has on the results. The tools for doing so are derived from the standard analysis of algorithm techniques that characterize how the running time of an algorithm changes as the size of the input problem increases (see, for example, Corman et al. (2001)). Not unlike the case for real-valued optimization problems, these analyses are difficult to obtain even for simple discrete fitness landscapes such as OneMax and LeadingOnes. Progress is being made slowly. One interesting result is that for ($1+\lambda$)-EAs, dynamically varying the offspring population size λ based on success rates appears to improve convergence rates in a fashion similar to the 1/5 rule for real-valued problems (Jansen et al., 2005).

6.9.1.4   Optimizing with Genetic Algorithms

Recall that the canonical GA is a non-overlappping-generation EA that uses a binary string representation, fitness-proportional parent selection, 1-point crossover, and bit-flip mutation. Even though it is often referred to as a "simple" GA, optimization-oriented proofs are quite difficult. As a result, many of the results are proved for even simpler GAs. One simplification is to turn off mutation and focus on GAs that use only crossover. As we saw in section 6.4, the population trajectories of crossover-only EAs with any form of fitness-biased selection converge to a fixed point that corresponds to one of the vertices of the simplex, i.e., a homogeneous population. Which particular vertex it converges to is a function of the size and content of initial population, the selection pressure, and the recombination rate. If there is no recombination, then convergence is to one of the members of the initial population, but not necessarily the one with highest fitness because of drift effects. If selection is neutral (deterministic-uniform), then crossover drives the population to a Robbins equilibrium.

So, if we want to prove optimization-oriented convergence theorems about GAs with positive selection pressure and crossover only, the focus is on whether and how fast the population converges to a vertex of the simplex corresponding to a global optimum. To do so requires a population of sufficient size to provide enough raw material (building blocks) to allow crossover to generate a global optimum and to minimize the effects of drift. Selection pressure must be sufficiently weak to allow crossover time to construct optimal points. In this context, convergence theorems have been constructed for simple landscapes like OneMax (see, for example, Ceroni et al. (2001)), but are still lacking for more complex fitness landscapes.

If we put mutation back in, things get more complicated. As we saw earlier, EAs with mutation have a nonzero probability of visiting any point in the simplex. So, finding an optimal point is not the issue, but rather how long it will take. As we saw in the previous subsection, first hitting time analyses are difficult for even EAs that have only mutation active. Analytically, the most appropriate tool is Markov chain analysis. But as we saw in section 6.8.3, the corresponding Markov chains are hard to solve in closed form without further simplifying assumptions. Rather, the "proofs" we have about first hitting times are obtained by computationally iterating Markov models (see, for example, Spears and De Jong (1996)).

6.10 Summary

The goal of this chapter was to use the unified EC framework to organize and survey the important theoretical developments in the field. This was accomplished by first analyzing EAs from a dynamical systems perspective, and then from an applications perspective.

Because the basic elements of an EA interact in complex, nonlinear ways, the dynamical systems analysis began with simple selection-only EA and explored the insights provided by both finite and infinite population models. This analysis was repeated for simple reproduction-only EAs in order to obtain a clear understanding of the interacting effects of crossover and mutation. Once the effects of selection and reproduction were understood in isolation, we looked at their combined effects on the dynamics of simple EAs. From this perspective we were able to analyze the impact of choices of internal representations and fitness landscapes on EA dynamics.

In order to use an EA to solve a problem, a decision needs to be made regarding what it means for a population-based dynamical system to provide an "answer". Once that decision is made, our understanding of an EA as a dynamical system is key to our understanding of its problem-solving capabilities. The most natural (and most prevalent) EA application domain is optimization. In this domain, the most important characteristics of optimization techniques are convergence and rates of convergence. In this context we saw that our understanding of EA dynamics provided the basis for theorems regarding EA convergence and rates of convergence.

Along the way, our survey also revealed the fact that there are many gaps in our understanding of EAs, both from a dynamical systems perspective and from an applications perspective. Hopefully, this will serve as a catalyst for further progress in EC theory.

Chapter 7

Advanced EC Topics

The primary focus of the preceding chapters was to characterize and analyze in a unified manner the dynamical behavior and problem-solving properties of simple EAs, namely single-population EAs with random mating, simple linear representations, and operating on time-invariant landscapes. In one sense, it is quite surprising to see the wide range of complex behaviors exhibited by these simple EAs and their effectiveness as problem-solving procedures. On the other hand, it is not surprising that their limitations have become more evident as they are applied to new and more difficult problem domains. This presents a continuing challenge to the EC community regarding how to improve EA performance. True to its roots, many such efforts are biologically inspired and take the form of relaxing or generalizing some of the assumptions made in simple EAs. In this chapter we briefly survey some of the important directions these developments are taking.

7.1 Self-adapting EAs

A theme that has been arising with increasing frequency in the EC community is desire to include internal mechanisms within EAs to control parameters associated with population size, internal representation, mutation, recombination, and selection. This trend is due in part to the absence of strong predictive theories that specify such things *a priori*. It is also a reflection of the fact that EAs are being applied to more complex and time-varying fitness landscapes.

On a positive note, the EC community has already empirically illustrated the viability of various self-adaptive mechanisms, most notable of which is the early work in the ES community on an adaptive mutation operator (Rechenberg, 1965). In the GA community there was also early work on adaptive reproductive operators (Schaffer and Morishima, 1987; Davis, 1989), as well as adaptive representations like Argot (Shaefer, 1987), messy GAs (Goldberg et al., 1991), dynamic parameter encoding schemes (Schraudolph and Belew, 1992), and Delta coding (Whitley et al., 1991).

Since EAs are themselves adaptive search procedures, the terminology used to describe changes made to improve their adaptability can be confusing and contradictory at times (see, for example, Spears (1995) or Eiben et al. (1999)). There are no ideal choices for some of these terms, but the ideas behind them are quite clear. There are three general opportunities for adaptation: at EA design time, in between EA runs, and during an EA run. Each of these issues is briefly discussed in the following subsections.

7.1.1   Adaptation at EA Design Time

At the EA design level, we generally tinker with various design decisions (such as the selection mechanism, the reproductive operators, population size, etc.) in an attempt to adapt our design to a particular problem domain. Once those design decisions are made, the EA is run and, depending on the outcome of one or more runs, may result in redesign. Since EA design space is quite large, exploring it manually can be quite tedious and time consuming, providing a strong incentive to automate the design adaptation process. On the other hand, evaluating the effectiveness of a particular EA design typically involves multiple EA runs and can be computationally quite expensive. So, a natural reaction is to consider the use an EA to search EA design space, i.e., a meta-EA.

That, of course, raises the question of the design of the meta-EA! To avoid an infinite regress, design space exploration at this level is generally a manual process. One of the earliest examples of this meta-EA approach was Grefenstette (1986) in which various GA design parameters were optimized for a test suite of optimization problems.

One of the important observations that has come from these meta-EA studies is that most EAs are relatively insensitive to specific values of design parameters. Rather, there is a range of values within which acceptable performance is obtained. This robustness allows many applications to run in "turnkey" mode with a set of default values.

7.1.2   Adaptation over Multiple EA Runs

Since the complexity of the fitness landscape of many difficult application problems is not well-understood *a priori*, it is not unusual for an EC practitioner to make a series of EA runs in which the observations and feedback from initial runs is used to modify the EA design used in subsequent runs. This can be tedious and time consuming, and raises interesting questions involving the extent to which this process can be automated by embedding an EA in an outer loop controlling a sequence of multiple EA runs.

A key issue is the determination of the kind of information that can be extracted from individual runs and used to improve performance on subsequent runs. One possibility is to use information acquired about the fitness landscape to bias the direction of search in subsequent runs. A good example of this approach is described in Beasley et al. (1993) in which difficult multimodal fitness landscapes are explored by sequentially deforming the landscape to remove peaks found on earlier runs.

Alternatively, a strategy of having repeated EA restarts using initial populations that are a combination of individuals from previous runs and randomly generated ones has also been shown to be quite effective. Perhaps the most striking example of this approach is CHC, a turnkey optimization package that does not require the user to set *any* EA parameters (Eshelman, 1990).

A third possibility is to use performance feedback from earlier EA runs to modify the parameter values of an EA on subsequent runs. A good example of this approach is the nested version of an ES in which the outer ES adapts the parameters of the inner ES (Rechenberg, 1994).

7.1.3 Adaptation during an EA Run

On the other hand, there is a need for EAs that have a more dynamic sense of self-adaptation, by allowing design decisions to vary over time during a run based on feedback obtained during that run. The classic early example of this is the Gaussian mutation operator that adapts its step size over time (Rechenberg, 1965). As noted in chapter 6, fitness-proportional selection adapts parent selection pressure over time. In addition to identifying which part of an EA is being adapted dynamically, it is helpful to specify *how* the changes are being made. The more engineering-oriented control theory approach is to define a feedback mechanism that controls when and how much change is desired. The "1/5" rule for adapting the step size of a Gaussian mutation operator is an example of this approach, as is Davis' mechanism for dynamically changing the probabilities used to select among a set of reproductive operators (Davis, 1989). Alternatively, we can let evolution do the work by extending the internal representation of individuals to include "control genes" that are modified and selected for as evolution proceeds (see, for example, Schwefel (1995) or Spears (1995)).

7.1.4 Summary

An exhaustive survey of these various approaches to designing self-adaptive EAs is beyond the scope of this book. An excellent survey can be found in Eiben et al. (1999). It is clear that there are significant advantages to improving our EAs in this respect. But it is also clear that much more work needs to be done to improve our understanding of self-adaptive EAs.

7.2 Dynamic Landscapes

One of the fairly strong assumptions of the EAs we have studied in the preceding chapters is that the fitness landscape does not change during an evolutionary run. However, the world in which we live is far from static and presents us with an ever-changing set of challenges. We optimize the design of a mechanical structure based on strength and cost, only to discover that the price of raw materials has changed significantly. Our robot vision system is doing just fine until new lighting is installed. An automated stock trader's performance suddenly degrades as a side effect of a foreign country's monetary crisis.

In each case, human intervention is required to restate the problem and redesign the system on the basis of the changed environment. If we are using EC techniques to solve the statically posed versions of these problems, a natural question is whether we can use these techniques to design systems capable of self-tuning over time. That possibility is explored in this section.

7.2.1   Standard EAs on Dynamic Landscapes

There is considerable evidence that many of our EAs do not perform particularly well in a changing environment. This is due, largely, to the fact that we have "overfit" many of our EAs to various classes of static optimization problems, with the focus on getting the representation and the operators to produce rapid convergence to (near) optimal points. However, this rapid telescoping down from a diverse initial population to a highly fit homogeneous one can be a significant detriment if the fitness landscape suddenly changes. In such cases this lack of diversity results in rather weak capabilities to respond and adapt to change.

It is rather easy to illustrate these issues with very simple experimental setups. Figure 7.1 depicts a two-state landscape in which each of the two states, A and B, are simple piecewise linear functions over the interval $[0, 4]$, and have a global maximum of 10.0 at $x = 3.5$ and $x = 0.5$ respectively.

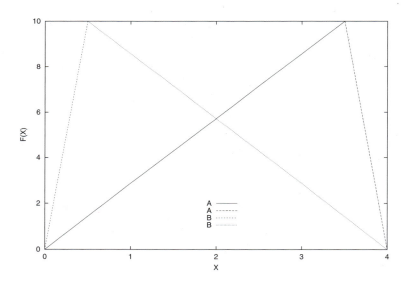

Figure 7.1: A simple two-state landscape.

Alone, neither landscape poses a particularly difficult challenge for any EA, but abruptly switching from one to the other during an evolutionary run presents some difficulties. An interesting exercise is to try your favorite EA on something as simple as this. Figure 7.2 illustrates the sort of behavior you are likely to see by running two simple EAs with standard settings for 1000 trials (births). About halfway through the landscape abruptly switches from state A to state B.

A $(1 + 10)$-ES starts approximately in the middle of the interval $[0, 4]$ and quickly climbs to the top of A's peak, located at 3.5. The disadvantage of maintaining only one parent is seen after about 500 trials, when the landscape abruptly changes from A to B and the parent's fitness drops from 10 to less than 2. It does manage to recover and find the new

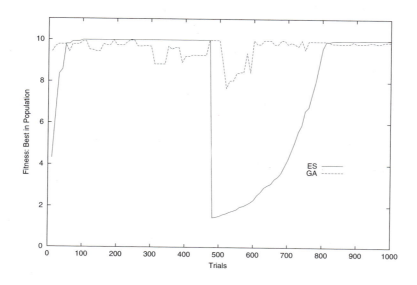

Figure 7.2: EA response to a single abrupt change.

peak at 0.5; however, it moves more slowly than before primarily because the self-adapting mutation operator had evolved to a very small step size.

By contrast, a GA (generational with a population of size 10, using fitness-proportional selection) maintains a fair amount of diversity. The fact that it is non-elitist means that the fitness of the best individual in the population can actually decrease from one generation to the next, yielding additional diversity. Consequently, an abrupt change has less effect on it.

Clearly there are parameter changes we could make to both algorithms that would improve their performance on such abrupt landscape changes. The point here is simply that tuning EAs for dynamic landscapes is likely to decrease performance on static problems and vice versa.

7.2.2 Modified EAs for Dynamic Landscapes

In one of the earliest published studies, Goldberg and Smith looked at biologically motivated diploid representations (two strands of genetic material) as a kind of memory function to improve the response of GAs to an environment that oscillated between two quite different landscapes (Goldberg and Smith, 1987). Cobb and Grefenstette adopted a different strategy that introduced the notions of triggered hypermutation and random migration (Cobb and Grefenstette, 1993). Angeline looked at the ability of EP-style evolutionary algorithms to track moving optima (Angeline, 1997), and Bäck did a similar study for Evolutionary Strategies (ESs) (Bäck, 1998).

More recently, several experimental testbeds have been developed in order to provide a more systematic framework in which to study EA performance on dynamic landscapes (see, for example, Morrison and De Jong (1999)). This has led to an increased interest in this area, as reflected by the number of workshops and conference papers, and entire PhD theses on the subject such as Branke (2002) or Morrison (2004). As a result, a clearer understanding of how to design EAs for dynamic landscapes is beginning to emerge. This understanding is summarized in the following subsections.

7.2.3   Categorizing Dynamic Landscapes

One of the difficulties that must be addressed is that the term "nonstationary landscapes" leaves us with a rather large and unstructured set of possibilities. Clearly, if landscapes are free to change in arbitrarily random ways, there is likely to be a "no free lunch" theorem lurking in the background. Fortunately, real world problems do not exhibit random changes in their landscapes. Rather, they exhibit patterns of change that can be discovered and exploited. There are several such representative categories that appear to be important.

The first category involves drifting landscapes whose topology does not change much over time. This is reflective of situations such as the control of a large chemical production process in which aging equipment, minor changes in the quality of raw materials, and other factors, result in gradual movement of the optimal control point over a high dimensional parameter space. The goal is to develop an algorithm capable of tracking this moving optimum.

A second category of interest corresponds to landscapes that are undergoing significant morphological changes over time, in which interesting peaks of high fitness shrink and new regions of high fitness emerge from previously uninteresting regions. This is reflective of competitive marketplaces in which opportunities for significant profit come and go as the levels of competition change. The goal here is to develop algorithms capable of responding to such changes and maintaining high levels of fitness (profit) over time.

A third category involves landscapes that exhibit cyclic patterns, spending most of their time repeatedly visiting a relatively small number of states. This is reflective of cyclical events such as seasonal climate changes, political election cycles, etc. The goal here is to develop algorithms capable of detecting and exploiting such cycles.

A final type of change to be considered is one that is abrupt and discontinuous, reflective of cataclysmic events such as the effects of a power station failure on a power distribution grid or the effects of a multi-vehicle accident on traffic flow.

There are, of course, many other ways in which landscapes can be nonstationary. However, these four categories are motivated by real world problems with similar characteristics, they cover a wide range of dynamic changes, and they present distinct challenges to traditional EAs.

7.2.4   The Importance of the Rate of Change

Additional insight into the difficulties associated with dynamic landscapes can be obtained by changing the landscape dynamics of figure 7.2 slightly so that it oscillates between A and B roughly every 300 trials. Figure 7.3 illustrates how the same two EAs handle these dynamics. The period between landscape changes is sufficiently long so that both EAs have time to recover. In the case of the ES we see a very regular oscillating pattern that corresponds to the landscape dynamics. In the case of the GA, notice how each change

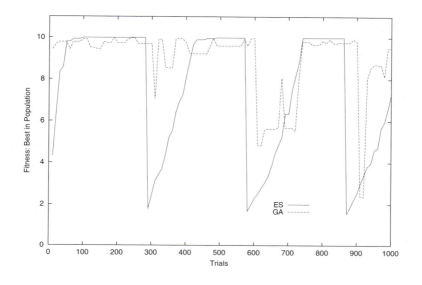

Figure 7.3: EA response to oscillating change.

produces a more pronounced effect and a longer recovery time. This is because after each recovery there is less diversity than before, making the population more sensitive to change.

This raises an important point. In addition to the type of nonstationarity, the rate of change of the environment relative to the evolutionary clock is also an important factor. One can imagine rates of change ranging from very rapid (within a generation) to very slow (many generations between changes). These effects are illustrated in figure 7.4, in which the frequency of oscillation of the simple landscape is increased to approximately every 100 trials.

As we increase the rate of change, we see signs that both EAs are struggling to keep up. Frequently, slower and suboptimal recovery is observed. As we increase the rate of change, these trends become even more evident.

In a similar manner, this simple landscape can be easily modified to test the ability of an EA to track a drifting peak (e.g., between A and B), or to test its ability to handle peaks whose heights are changing (by raising/lowering A and B). In each case we see the need for modifying and tuning our EAs in quite different ways than we do for static optimization. We focus now on this issue.

7.2.5   The Importance of Diversity

The dominant theme that emerges from these studies is the critical role that diversity plays in adapting to changing landscapes. However, the dynamics of the landscape determine whether an EA needs to maintain some diversity or is better off generating diversity on demand.

The need for maintaining diversity is most evident for landscapes exhibiting high rates

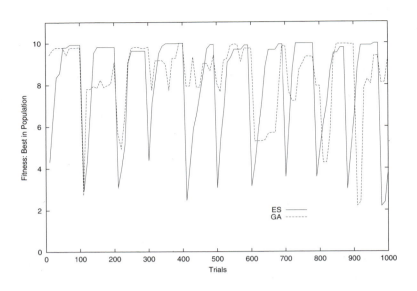

Figure 7.4: EA response to more rapid oscillating change.

of change. Increased diversity can be accomplished in a number of ways. The first and most obvious strategy is to weaken selection pressure. The difficulty with this approach is getting the right amount of selection pressure without *a priori* knowledge about the dynamics of the environment. Too much pressure (typical of many static optimizers) results in poor recovery performance. Too little pressure produces overall mediocre performance.

An alternative is to use some form of crowding (De Jong, 1975) or niching (Goldberg, 1989). Both approaches allow for strong initial selection, but restrict considerably the ability for individuals to take over the population.

An interesting alternative is to use some form of restricted mating and selection. Island models and diffusion models restrict selection and mating to local subpopulations, thus maintaining more diversity. Alternatively, the use of "tag bits" for mating restrictions permits more dynamically defined "species" (Spears, 1994).

So far, we have focused on maintaining diversity. A different strategy appears to be more useful when the environment undergoes occasional abrupt changes. In such cases the cost of maintaining diversity can be quite high. Instead, one can focus on providing diversity "on demand". The difficulty here is in recognizing when the need arises without *a priori* knowledge about the landscape dynamics. One approach is to monitor and detect significant environmental changes, and then trigger something like a hypermutation operator (Cobb and Grefenstette, 1993) to produce the needed diversity. Alternatively, self-tuning operators such as the "1/5" rule for adapting mutation step size (Bäck and Schwefel, 1993) appear to be useful.

7.2.6 Summary

Using a simple set of examples, this section surveyed and explored the issues involved in applying EAs to problems involving nonstationary landscapes. We have seen that there is a fairly consistent tension between designing and tuning EAs for static optimization problems versus dynamic ones. Improving performance on one invariably decreases performance on the other.

An important insight into understanding these issues is an appreciation of the key role that population diversity plays. Depending on the particular landscape dynamics, an EA may need to maintain fairly high levels of diversity or produce useful diversity when needed. This allows us to think, in a more focused manner, about the kinds of mechanisms one might use to improve the performance of EA-based systems that need to operate in changing worlds.

One of the difficult open questions is how to measure performance on dynamic landscapes in more precise and meaningful ways. Most of our insights to date tend to be more visual than systematic and statistical. Having both standard measures and standard test problems is necessary for future progress.

7.3 Exploiting Parallelism

One of the frequently stated virtues of evolutionary algorithms (EAs) is their "natural" parallelism. The increasing availability of parallel computing in both coarsely and finely grained architectures provides a tantalizing opportunity to exploit this power as we scale up EAs to solve larger and more complex classes of problems. In order to do so, there are a number of issues to be addressed. At a high level, these issues can be summarized as follows:

- Of the many variations of existing EAs, are some more effectively parallelized than others?

- Of the many variations of parallel architectures, are some better suited for parallel EAs than others?

- Are there parallel EAs that are *both* faster *and* better problem solvers than standard EAs?

We can begin to answer these questions by looking at an example of standard EA pseudo-code:

```
Randomly produce an initial population of individuals and evaluate them.
DO until some stopping criterion is met
    Select parents
    Produce children
    Evaluate the fitness of the children
    Select members of the next generation
end DO
Return a result.
```

If this EA is running on a single machine and fitness evaluation is expensive, then a "master-slave" configuration, in which slave processors are used to compute the fitness of individuals in parallel, is a straightfoward and natural way to speed up the running time if the cost of communication between processors is not prohibitive.

If we want to parallelize this EA further, the population itself must be distributed over multiple processors. This takes some additional care and thought if we only want to obtain speedup without changing the execution semantics of the EA. In particular, commonly used selection algorithms like fitness-proportional selection or truncation selection require global population information. So, to maintain their semantics, some sort of global synchronization is required, reducing much of the speedup achieved by decentralization. The only standard selection algorithms that do not require global information are uniform (neutral) selection and tournament selection.

This is the best we can do in terms of speeding up an EA through parallelization without changing the execution semantics of the EA. Additional speedup is possible if changes in execution semantics are permitted. Parallel EA architectures of this type fall into two general categories: coarse-grained architectures and fine-grained ones.

7.3.1   Coarse-Grained Parallel EAs

The most natural EA model for coarse-grained parallelism is an "island" model in which there are a number of centralized EAs running in parallel on different machines. If there is no interaction between the islands, then this is equivalent to speeding up the task of making a series of independent runs by running them in parallel on different machines. The interesting case is when there is interaction among the islands in the form of "migration" of individuals between islands. This raises a whole set of questions regarding island-model properties, such as:

- How many islands should there be?

- How are islands interconnected?

- Which individuals migrate?

- How often do migrations occur?

- Should each island be running an identical EA?

These questions and others have been the focus of many research papers and theses (see, for example, Cohoon et al. (1987), Whitley et al. (1999), Cantú-Paz (2001), or Skolicki and De Jong (2004)). The collective sense is that these island models can significantly improve the problem-solving capabilities of EAs, but a deeper understanding is required in order to design them effectively for particular applications.

7.3.2   Fine-Grained Models

Another fruitful direction to explore is the mapping of EAs onto fine-grained parallel architectures. In particular, there has been considerable interest in cellular architectures consisting of a large array of simple processors with high-speed interconnections with their neighbors. The most natural mapping is to have a single individual in each cell and a simple (1+1)-EA running in each cell in parallel that has access to a number of neighboring cells. That neighborhood defines the population from which each EA produces an offspring and conditionally replaces the existing population member in that cell with the offspring. Since the neighborhoods of the cells overlap, there is a cellular-automata-like diffusion of individuals over the entire array. This raises a whole set of questions regarding the properties of these models, including:

- What should the topology of the cellular array be?

- What should the size and shape of the neighborhoods be?

- How should parents be selected from a neighborhood?

- What reproductive operators should be used?

- What survival selection method should be used?

These questions and others have been the focus of many research papers and theses (see, for example, Collins and Jefferson (1991), Baluja (1993), or Sarma (1998)). The overall impression is that these fine-grained diffusion models can significantly improve the problem-solving capabilities of EAs, but a deeper understanding is required in order to design them in an effective way for specific applications.

7.3.3   Summary

Because of the natural parallelism within an EA, there continues to be considerable interest in the implementation of EAs for both fine- and coarse-grained parallel architectures. The results to date have been quite promising, but raise as many questions as they answer. The increasing availability of low-cost parallel hardware configurations make this a fruitful area for further research.

7.4   Evolving Executable Objects

As we saw in chapter 3, an important motivation for the development of the EP paradigm in the 1960s was the desire to evolve intelligent agent behaviors rather than hand-code them. This interest in "automatic programming" has continued to serve as a difficult and challenging subfield in the EC community. This section summarizes the current state of the art and some of the open issues.

7.4.1   Representation of Behaviors

Much of the interest in evolving executable objects comes from agent-oriented domains in which one would prefer to have agents learn and/or modify their behavior with little human intervention. If we think of an agent as having a set of input sensors and output effectors, the goal becomes one of learning appropriate input-output mappings. This mapping might be a simple stimulus-response (S-R) system or something more complex with internal states. As one might expect, representing and evolving the latter system is considerably more difficult than S-R systems.

Perhaps the simplest and most intuitive way to represent agent behaviors is with finite-state machines. This was the approach taken by Fogel et al. (1966) in their early EP work and continues to be of interest today (see, for example, Spears and Gordon (2000)). From an EC perspective, the primary issue to be addressed is how to represent finite-state machines internally in a form that allows for the design of effective reproductive operators. Adopting an internal phenotypic representation permits the creation of useful offspring via mutation operators that perturb the finite-state machines directly, but makes it quite difficult to define useful forms of recombination. By contrast, adopting an internal representation based on adjacency lists or connectivity matrices facilitates the use of recombination. How best to represent and evolve finite-state machines continues to be an interesting open question.

Alternatively, we might choose to represent behavioral mapping with an artificial neural network (ANN). The simplest way to do this is to assume that the structure of an ANN has been specified, and all that remains is to learn an appropriate set of weights. If the ANN is a feed-forward network (an S-R system), there are standard hill-climbing techniques (e.g., backprop) for doing so. However, these techniques are quite sensitive to the initial set of weights and are difficult to extend to networks with feedback loops. Consequently, a number of hybrid EA-ANN systems have been developed to make weight learning more robust (Yao, 1999).

A more interesting and more difficult goal is to evolve both the structure *and* the weights of an ANN. Historically, there have been a variety of approaches for doing so that fall into two general categories: those that use direct internal representations and those that use generative representations. The direct representation approach is a phenotypic one in which the ANNs are manipulated directly (see, for example, Potter (1997) or Stanley (2004)). The generative representations are a genotypic approach in which the plans for constructing an ANN are evolved rather than the ANN itself (see, for example, Harp et al. (1989), de Garis (1990), or Whitley et al. (1995)). Which approach is more effective from an EC perspective is an interesting open question.

Another natural representation for behaviors is as a set of situation-action rules. In the simplest case, these rule sets define S-R behaviors. More complex behavior is obtained by having the left-hand sides of rules (situations) include information from both sensor information and internal states, and to allow actions to include mechanisms for changing internal states as well as the activation of external effectors. Holland's classifier system architecture is a classic example of this approach (Holland, 1975) and has inspired considerable research in this area (see, for example, Booker (1982) or Wilson and Goldberg (1989), or Wilson (1994)).

Holland-style classifier systems evolved situation-action rules over time, using an EA in which the individuals in the population represented single rules. So, at any point in time, the population as a whole represented the current behavioral mapping of an agent. An alternative approach explored by De Jong and his students at the University of Pittsburgh was to have individuals in the population represent *entire* rule sets (Smith, 1983; De Jong, 1987), and consequently was dubbed "the Pitt approach". This approach required generalizing the standard fixed-length representation and reproductive operators, since rule sets can be of varying length. Pitt approaches have been used successfully to evolve a wide variety of behaviors ranging from poker playing (Smith, 1983) to agent team behaviors (Bassett and De Jong, 2000).

Grefenstette's Samuel system (Grefenstette et al., 1990) combined features from both classifier systems and Pitt systems and continues to be developed and applied to difficult problems in evolutionary robotics (Grefenstette, 1996; Daley et al., 1999).

The next step up in complexity for representing behavior is to explore the use of more traditional programming languages. The difficulty, of course, is that most programming languages have extremely complex syntax and semantics, making the design of useful reproductive operators difficult and language specific. One notable exception to this is the Lisp language, developed by the AI community to serve a variety of purposes, one of which was to facilitate the design of programs to write programs. Not surprisingly, there has been and continues to be a wide range of interest in evolving Lisp code. The early attempts at doing so came out of the GA community (see, for example, Fujiki and Dickinson (1987) or Koza (1989)), and consequently became known as Genetic Programming (GP) (Koza, 1992). Since then the GP community has grown significantly, both in size and diversity, to the point that there are are variety of books and specialty conferences in this area (see, for example, Banzhaf et al. (1998) or Langdon and Poli (2001)). The initial focus on using GAs to evolve Lisp code has broadened to include more traditional "linear" languages as well as the use of other types of EAs. At this point in time, this EC subfield is perhaps better described as "evolutionary programming", except that this term is already in use!

7.4.2 Summary

Each of the approaches to representing and evolving executable objects has certain advantages and disadvantages that make them suitable for different kinds of applications. Unfortunately, matching up particular applications with appropriate techniques is still more of an art than a science.

Although the focus in this section has been on the evolution of executable objects for the purpose of representing agent behaviors, many of the same techniques can and are being used more broadly as generative representations for other applications such as engineering design (see section 7.7.3).

7.5 Multi-objective EAs

Standard EAs are well-suited for optimization problems defined by a single objective function. However, many interesting and difficult engineering and manufacturing problems require the simultaneous optimization of more than one objective function. One easy solution is to combine the multiple objectives into a single objective function (e.g, a weighted sum). However, in many cases there may not be any reasonable way to combine the multiple objectives, and frequently no desire to do so. Rather, the designer prefers to see how one objective can be traded off against another, allowing him to choose a particular tradeoff point based on other considerations not captured in the objective functions.

If we represent each point in design space as a vector of fitness values, of interest are those points that are not dominated by any other points, in the sense that any attempt to improve the fitness associated with one objective results in a decrease in the fitness associated with one or more of the other objectives. This set of points is called the Pareto optimal front and represents the tradeoff curve required by the designer. Except for rather simplistic cases, Pareto optimal points cannot be determined analytically. Rather, they define challenging search problems and present a rather unique challenge to the EC community: how to use EAs to find Pareto optimal fronts efficiently, since standard EAs are designed to return a single point rather than a set of points as the answer to an optimization problem (Shaffer and Grefenstette, 1985).

One way to proceed would be to design an EA that is capable of finding a *single* Pareto optimal point, and then use it repeatedly to find additional points. Even this requires some thought since it is not entirely clear how to calculate a fitness value for individual points. Intuitively, points closer to the Pareto front dominate more points than those that are farther away. So, one possibility is to estimate the number of points dominated by a member of the population by calculating how many other members of the current population it dominates (Horn et al., 1994). Alternatively, one might estimate the dominance of a point by the size of the geometric area below it. Both approaches provide reasonable fitness gradients that can be used to generate individual points on or near the Pareto front.

By running one of these EAs repeatedly, one might hope to find enough distinct points on the Pareto front to be able to characterize it for the designer. However, repeated independent runs seems like a rather inefficient strategy. Since EAs are population-based techniques, it should be possible to design one that returns multiple points during a single run. One way of doing this is to introduce some form of niching in order to force the population to remain diversified (Horn et al., 1994). Another way is to maintain a separate data structure that contains the best points so far, and not insist that the points returned be members of the final population (Deb, 1999).

If that were not a difficult enough task, one would also prefer sets of points that are reasonably distributed across the Pareto front in order to provide the designer with uniformly accurate characterizations. All these requirements continue to challenge the EC community, and have resulted in a variety of books and specialty conferences (see, for example, Deb (2001) or Coello et al. (2002)). There is still much work to be done.

7.6   Hybrid EAs

Within a particular community, there is always the temptation to keep things simple and to solve problems with the techniques that we are most comfortable with. However, in real life, successful applications are invariably achieved from a systems-engineering perspective, namely, by thoughtfully choosing a set of problem-solving tools that are well-matched to particular aspects of an application and tools that integrate well into a larger framework. The information in this book provides an understanding of the strengths and weaknesses of EA-based problem solvers, and provides some insight into how EAs can be used as a component in a hybrid system. Armed with this knowledge, designing a system that combines the strengths of multiple techniques is often the difference between a passable result and an outstanding one.

One helpful perspective is to think of an EA as providing a global coarse-grained search component that can be coupled with a fine-grained local search technique to provide levels of performance that neither can attain alone. Another approach is to combine a very domain-specific technique (like decision tree learning) with a more domain-independent EA that is providing the context (the feature sets) in which learning is to take place in order to obtain a more robust learning system.

Within the EC community these ideas are most often discussed in the context of "memetic" algorithms (Moscato and Norman, 1992).

7.7 Biologically Inspired Extensions

Although inspired by nature, the majority of EAs in existence today bear little resemblance to an actual biological system. This is not too surprising, since the goal of most of the work in EC has not been to build models of biological systems, but to use biological abstractions and principles to build effective computational problem-solving systems. The EAs that have been studied in great detail in the preceding chapters are all quite similar in their simplifying assumptions (e.g, single population, single species, random mating, etc.). As such, an important direction of research is to explore the extent to which our standard EAs can be improved by removing some of these simplifying assumptions.

Of course, if our goal is to build models of actual biological systems, any additional biological realism is an improvement. However, if our goal is to improve evolutionary *computation*, then we need to understand how additional biological realism improves our computational problem-solving capabilities.

There are many possible directions that biologically inspired improvements might take. In this section a few of the more promising ones are summarized.

7.7.1 Non-random Mating and Speciation

One of the well-understood characteristics of single-population, random mating EAs is that, even with modest amounts of selection pressure, the population loses diversity rapidly. Computationally, this is a virtue if the goal is to converge rapidly to an optimum in a single local basin of attraction. But it raises problems when the goal is to simultaneously explore multiple basins of attraction, or to respond robustly to dynamic changes in the fitness landscape.

Early attempts to deal with this problem were based intuitively on the biological notion of "overgrazing" in which too many individuals in an environmental niche resulted in a depletion of resources and a corresponding reduction in offspring. Computationally, this intuition was implemented in a variety of ways including crowding (De Jong, 1975) and niching (Goldberg, 1989). The effect is to restrict considerably the loss of diversity in a population. However, the difficulty with these approaches is that they require some *a priori* notion of genotypic or phenotypic distance metrics, and in the case of niching, some reasonable estimate of the number of basins of attraction.

An alternative approach is to maintain diversity via non-random mating. This issue in this case is selecting the basis for doing so. One possibility is to introduce a topology on the population and introduce a distance bias on mate selection (Sarma, 1998). Another possibility is to implement multi-population "island models" in which mating can only occur among individuals on the same island (Whitley et al., 1999). A third possibility is to explicitly model the notion of species within a population and only allow mating within species. In some contexts the number and type of species is known *a priori*. However, for many applications it is desirable for speciation to evolve over time. One of the more elegant ways of implementing this computationally is to define a set of species tags that are assigned initially at random. Mating can only occur between individuals with similar tags, and offspring inherit these tags. Over time, selection and reproduction eliminate many of the tags, resulting in a set of clearly defined "emergent" species (Spears, 1994).

Each of these approaches has been shown to improve the problem-solving abilities of standard EAs. At the same time, they introduce additional algorithmic complexity and require additional design decisions on the part of the EC practitioner. In each case there is a need for a deeper understanding of when and how these extensions should be used.

7.7.2 Coevolutionary Systems

One of the simplifying assumptions implicit in most EAs is that the fitness of an individual is defined and computed in a fashion that is independent of the current state of the system. Typically this is done by invoking an external "oracle" to provide a fitness assessment of an individual. In part, this assumption is a reflection of the heavy emphasis on using EAs to solve static "black box" optimization problems for which the notion of an oracle is quite natural. However, there are many problems for which the notion of an explicitly defined fitness function is difficult (and some times impossible) to obtain. A classic example of this is the problem of evolving a world-class game-playing program (for checkers, chess, Go, etc.). The best and most accurate measure of fitness is how well you do against your opponents. But playing against a static set of externally defined opponents is not likely to produce a world-class program, just one capable of beating that particular set of opponents. Once that is accomplished, no further progress is made unless the set of opponents is improving over time as well (see, for example, Rosin and Belew (1995)).

A second example are situations in which fitness is defined by how well individuals complement each other in collectively trying to solve a problem (e.g., team surveillance, design teams, diagnostic tests, etc.). While important, individual skills must be evaluated in the context of the collective whole. The primary goal is that the makeup of the collective whole be capable of evolving over time (see, for example, Potter (1997)).

A third example are situations in which the evaluation of an individual is logically possible, but computationally infeasible (e.g., exhaustive testing of software on all possible inputs). In such cases it is important to find computationally feasible approximations that provide adequate fitness feedback. While it is possible in some cases to define fitness approximations *a priori*, the more difficult situations are those in which the approximations must evolve over time as well. Hillis' work on evolving sorting networks is a classic example of this (Hillis, 1990).

7.7.2.1   CoEC Architectures

So, how do we turn a standard EA into a coevolutionary one? The simplest way is to introduce the notion of *contextual* fitness evaluation. By this we mean that the fitness of an individual is a function of the other individuals in the population. For example, the population might consist of individuals representing chess-playing programs. The fitness of individual programs is determined by a series of competitive matches with other members of the population (see, for example, Angeline and Pollack (1993)). Alternatively, the population might consist of individuals representing basic agent behaviors. The fitness of an individual behavior is determined by its performance on a task when combined with other behavioral elements in the population (see, for example, Holland (1986)).

Biologists, however, are likely to view such single-population architectures as standard evolutionary systems. To be coevolutionary, a system should have more than one species (restricted mating populations) with the property that the fitness of individuals in one population is dependent on the individuals in the other population. For example, in Hillis (1990) there was one population of evolving sorting networks and one population of evolving test sets. In Potter and De Jong (2000) there was one population for each of the evolvable subcomponents of a complex system.

With multiple populations, the fitness of an individual in one population is determined by its interaction with one or more individuals selected from the other populations. Ideally, the best assessment of fitness would come from interactions with *every* member of the other populations. Since this can be quite computationally expensive as the size and number of populations increases, in practice only a few selected interactions are used to assess fitness. How best to select these interactions is an interesting open question for which we have some initial understanding (Wiegand, 2004).

7.7.2.2   CoEC Dynamics

Although a captivating and intriguing idea, getting a CoEC system to "work" can be quite challenging. There are two primary reasons for these difficulties. The first is that CoEC designers generally use some sort of external metric for evaluating the progress or success of their system (e.g., how competitive an evolved game-playing program is against expert human players). However, since this external metric is not part of the internal fitness metric of the CoEC system, there is no *a priori* reason to believe that success on an internal metric will imply success on an external metric.

The second (more subtle) reason for CoEC difficulties is that, from a dynamical systems point of view, the dynamics of a coevolutionary system can be quite complex. For example, one can have:

- Mediocre stable states in which none of the populations are able to improve,

- Oscillatory states in which the populations cycle endlessly,

- Degenerate states in which one or more populations provide no useful fitness interactions, or

- Steady improvements in fitness in all of the populations.

The last of these states, the notion of steady improvement, is what most CoEC practitioners have in mind, but is usually difficult to achieve (see, for example, Ficici and Pollack (1998)). Theoretical help is beginning to emerge. One promising approach currently being explored is the use of evolutionary game theory (Ficici and Pollack, 2000; Wiegand, 2004). Additional insights are being provided by studying the characteristics of the coevolutionary fitness landscapes (Popovici and De Jong, 2004).

7.7.3   Generative Representations and Morphogenesis

Historically, much of the EA work has involved the evolution of fairly simple structures that could be represented in phenotypic form or be mapped easily onto simple genotypic representations. However, as we attempt to evolve increasingly more complex structures, it becomes increasingly difficult to represent them internally in a form that facilitates the construction of mutation and recombination operators that are capable of producing structurally sound and interesting new individuals (see, for example, Bentley (1999)). If we look to nature for inspiration, we do not see many evolutionary operators at the phenotype level (e.g., recombining parental arms and legs!). Rather, changes occur at the genotype level and the effects of those changes are instantiated via growth and maturation. If we hope to evolve such complexity, we may need to adopt an analogous strategy of evolving the plans for complex objects rather than the objects themselves. To assess fitness of a plan (genotype), it must be used to construct one or more of the desired objects (phenotypes) via a well-defined growth process (morphogenesis).

One way of achieving this is to develop domain-specific genotypes and morphogenesis processes. For example, there has been a variety of such approaches to evolving neural networks (see, for example, Harp et al. (1989), Whitley et al. (1995), or Stanley (2004)). Alternatively, one might use a more general "generative" representation at the genotype level that is capable of being "executed" by a general purpose interpreter, the output of which is the desired phenotype (Hornby, 2003). A well-known example of this are "L-systems", a parallel rule system interpreter which has been used to model the growth process in many biological systems (Lindenmayer, 1968). The input to an L-system interpreter is a set of if-then rules to be used during the growth process and an initial state (the seed). In this way, significant increases in complexity can be obtained by evolving the rule sets rather than the objects themselves (Hornby, 2003).

Another candidate for generative representations are cellular automata (CA) systems (Wolfram, 1994). In this case, the patterns generated by the execution of a cellular automata can be interpreted as the desired phenotype. The input to a CA is a set of update rules and an initial state. By evolving CA input sets, more complex objects can be evolved than when using direct representations (see, for example, Kita and Totoda (2000) or Kicinger et al. (2004)).

While these examples show the potential of using generative representations, designing such systems is not easy. In particular, designing reproductive operators that manipulate generative representations in useful ways can be difficult. Considerable research is still needed before these systems support turnkey applications.

7.7.4 Inclusion of Lamarckian Properties

Jean-Baptiste Lamarck was a 19th century naturalist whose name is now associated with the theory that offspring can inherit acquired traits from their parents (such as the acquired physique of a weight lifter). Although we know today that this is not true for most biological systems, that does not prevent us from exploring the usefulness of the idea for EC systems. The idea generally comes up when there is a learning component associated with the evaluation of the fitness of individuals. For example, suppose the goal is to evolve agents capable of performing various tasks in a complex world. When placed in the world for fitness evaluation, it is possible to design the agents to acquire information about the world (e.g., via reinforcement learning), and pass that information along to their offspring.

Although not biologically correct, this is certainly the way that cultural evolution works, reducing significantly the need for future generations to rediscover things already known to past generations. Not surprisingly, these ideas have shown up in the EC community in various forms including "cultural algorithms" (Ostrowski et al., 2002) and "memetic algorithms" (Moscato and Norman, 1992). Although they can add complexity to the underlying EC system, these ideas have been shown to be quite effective for some difficult optimization problems (e.g., see Turner (1998)).

7.7.5 Agent-Oriented Models

In most EC applications, individuals in the population are just passive objects being manipulated by a top-level evolutionary algorithm. Suppose we allow these individuals to be more active "agents" in some sense. Clearly, in order to do so, the agents must have some world in which they can operate. The interest in and ability to construct interesting simulations of agent-oriented worlds has grown dramatically since the ground-breaking Swarm Project (Langton et al., 1995). A computational modeler can now choose from a variety of multi-agent simulators including Ascape (Parker, 2001), Repast (Collier, 2001), and Mason (Luke et al., 2005). That poses the interesting question of the relationship between agent-based modeling and EC.

The most straightforward answer is that agent-based models provide a powerful set of tools for constructing environments in which to evolve complex agent behaviors. Rather than evaluating the fitness of agents using a simple fitness function, fitness can be evaluated from behavioral trajectories obtained from these simulated worlds. This approach is already standard practice in the evolutionary robotics community (Nolfi and Floreano, 2000). However, in addition to providing more complex ways to assess fitness, agent-based models provide an environment for evolving agents with learning capabilities as well as the ability to evolve team-oriented behaviors (see, for example, Bassett and De Jong (2000) or Panait and Luke (2005)). This, in turn, raises a new set of questions regarding how best to represent such behaviors to facilitate their evolution.

Once we have interesting simulated worlds, we can begin to contemplate giving our evolutionary agents even more autonomy, such as the freedom to mate and reproduce in the simulated world rather than under control of an EA as in the ECHO system defined by Holland (1992) or the evolutionary bots in Watson et al. (1999). If this is beginning to sound like a segue into the field of Artificial Life, it is! But, other than noting that most ALife systems now include an evolutionary component, further discussion is beyond the scope of this book.

7.7.6   Summary

This section has focused on some of the more promising biologically inspired extensions to standard EAs. In most cases these extensions do not contribute much in the way of increasing the *biological fidelity* of EAs. Rather, they are motivated by the desire to increase the ability of an EA to solve difficult computational problems. That does not mean, however, that there is nothing of interest here for someone interested in understanding real evolutionary systems. Even though an EA may model an evolutionary system at a high level of abstraction, the underlying dynamics are representative of many complex adaptive systems. As such, understanding how these dynamics play out in simple, artificial systems provides useful insights into more complex, real-life systems.

7.8   Summary

The goal of this chapter was to provide an overview of the important directions in which the EC field is growing and expanding. In doing so, one cannot help but sense the richness, vibrancy, and diversity of the EC community today. Although based initially on rather simple evolutionary algorithms, the community has grown in many different directions with respect to both new and innovative algorithms and challenging application areas.

At the same time new growth means new challenges. Most of the topics discussed in this chapter ended with a comment of the form "a deeper understanding is needed here". So, roll up your sleeves and get to work!

Chapter 8

The Road Ahead

As a well-known American philosopher, Yogi Berra, once said: making predictions is hard, especially about the future! I could not agree more. Having been fortunate enough to be part of the EC community since its early days, I have been asked many times over the years to present my views on the current state of the field and where it is headed. When I look back on those occasions now, it reminds me how cloudy crystal balls can be.

As part of the discussion of the advanced EC topics in Chapter 7, I pointed out many specific places in which there is a need for additional work. So, I will conclude here by briefly outlining a few broad themes that I think represent important future directions.

8.1 Modeling General Evolutionary Systems

There is a growing trend by scientists to incorporate computer modeling into the very core of what they do. We see this in physics, chemistry, biology, psychology, and anthropology, to name a few. Even the fairly conservative funding agency, NIH, is beginning to take *in silicio* science seriously, perhaps encouraged to do so by Wolfram (2002) and others. I see this as a tremendous opportunity for the EC community. We have a long and distinguished history of using EAs to solve difficult engineering problems, but relatively little work in modeling evolutionary systems.

As has been pointed out repeatedly throughout this book, there is good reason for this state of affairs. Invariably, biological fidelity and computational effectiveness pose conflicting EA design objectives. But I see a core of overlapping interest that motivated the way chapter 6 was organized; namely, by first focusing on EAs as dynamical systems, and then using those insights to understand EAs as problem solvers. It is the dynamical systems perspective that we share with evolutionary systems modelers, and to which we have much to contribute.

But there is a broader issue here as well. Our EA models also have the potential for providing significant insights into complex adaptive systems. A colleague, Eric Bonabeau, has put together a wonderful set of examples that illustrate how poorly humans make predictions about the dynamics of even the simplest adaptive systems, and how even simple computation models can be used to provide the necessary understanding. In today's world, high-level decision makers are struggling to develop policies for a wide range of complex, adaptive systems including improving internet security, handling epidemiological threats, and dealing with global warming. It is hard for me to imagine how intelligent decisions can be made without the kinds of insights our community can provide.

8.2   More Unification

This book, from start to finish, reflects my belief that to make further progress, the EC community must continue to work at developing an overarching framework that provides a consistent view of the field. Having such a framework is critical for a number of reasons. First, it provides a means by which "outsiders" can obtain a high-level understanding of EC. This is not only important for defining what we are about, but also to open the door for interdisciplinary collaboration. Second, it provides a means for comparing and contrasting various EC techniques. The good news is that EC is a dynamic and growing field. The bad news is that it is easy for "demes" to form that act as barriers to seeing relationships with analogous work in other demes. Third, it provides for a more principled way to apply EC to new application areas. Rather than starting with a particular EA favorite and forcing it to fit an application, a unified perspective facilitates top-down design in which the properties of the application control the design of a suitable EA. Finally, a unified view of EC serves to clarify where the gaps in our understanding lie and what the open research issues are.

However, a critical assessment of this book will reveal that the goal of a unified EC framework has not yet been achieved. Rather, it provides a first step in that direction by providing a unified framework for simple EAs. Much more work needs to be done to begin to include in a more systematic fashion the areas discussed in chapter 7.

8.3   Summary

Putting this book together has been a long journey for me, in part because it is an attempt to do something that had not been done before. But, more importantly, it was made difficult because of the dynamic character of the EC community. Each conference I attended and each paper I read lead to additions and revisions to the text in order to incorporate new developments. However, at some point I had to stop and get this frozen snapshot published. As such, there are many things that have not been included in this edition, and already a long list of items for the next edition. Enjoy!

Appendix A

Source Code Overview

Rather than include the source code for the EC systems described in this book, I have adopted the strategy of providing a textual overview together with the appropriate URLs for access to the source code itself. The source code is organized in a way that reflects how I teach courses on Evolutionary Computation and how this book is organized; namely by starting out simple and then adding complexity. I find that easiest to achieve by presenting a series of EC programs, each of which is an independent computational entity, but is derived from the previous version.

I also feel strongly about having educational software of this type be as platform independent as possible. In my mind the best way to achieve this is by using Java as the programming language and by minimizing the use of graphical user interfaces. This means that the software, while not optimized for speed or user friendliness, compiles and runs with no difficulty on any platform that provides a standard Java programming environment.

Each time I use this software in one of my courses, I tinker with it, fixing some bugs and adding new features. So, there are really two versions of this software, a frozen version that corresponds to the software used to generate the examples in this book, and the most recent evolving version. The static version is available from the MIT Press website (http://mitpress.mit.edu/evolutionary-computation/DeJong). The evolving version is available from the George Mason Evolutionary Computation Laboratory website (www.cs.gmu.edu/~eclab).

A.1   EC1: A Very Simple EC System

EC1 is the system that was used to generate the examples in chapter 1, in which the goal was to expose the basic structure and components of an evolutionary computation system by taking a simple evolutionary algorithm (EA) and illustrating how it can be applied to a simple class of problems. As such, the Java code in this directory was designed with strong adherence to the KISS principle: Keep It Simple, Stupid!

At the same time, the object-oriented features of Java have been used to expose the generality of the architecture, in that other EAs and other problems can be easily added to EC1. In fact, EC1 is the basis for the more complex code examples described in later chapters.

For both portability and simplicity reasons, the initial code examples are command-line oriented rather than having a GUI. This poses a bit of a problem, in that most EC systems are designed with a number of user-controlled configuration settings. In EC1 this is done in the following way: whenever possible, reasonable default values have been chosen that can be overridden by the user in a configuration text file. The simple syntax of an EC1 configuration file is dictated by the Properties class provided by Java and takes the form:

```
property_name=property_values
```

where the actual property names and values are program specific. For example, a typical EC1 configuration file might be:

```
Landscape=RVP Parabola 2 -4.0 6.0 soft - 50.0
PopSize=10
Mutation=gaussian 2.0
SimLimit=1000
RandSeed=123456789
Report=full
```

A full discussion of the meaning of EC1 parameters is provided later in this document. For now, it is sufficient to understand how configuration files are used. At the command line, EC1 can be invoked in two ways:

```
java EC1 config_file_name
    or
java EC1
```

In the first case, EC1 will read in any parameter settings specified in the user-specified configuration file. In the latter case EC1 will look for a file named ec1.cfg in the current directory and read parameter settings from it.

A.1.1   EC1 Code Structure

The file EC1.java contains the top-level main code for EC1. It looks for a configuration file as described above, reads a subset of the Landscape properties information from it, and activates an appropriate "EA application".

The EA_application class is the base class for matching up a particular EA with a particular class of problems (landscapes), and for setting up the basic simulation parameters. In EC1 this is quite simple, since it implements exactly one problem class (real-valued parameter optimization) and exactly one EA (EV), but sets the stage for adding other problem classes and EAs. The file RvpEA_application.java contains the code for extending (specializing) the EA_application class to real-valued parameter problems.

The file EA.java defines the base class for all EAs, which is then specialized in RvpEA.java to the class RvpEA defining EAs for solving real-valued parameter optimization problems, and specialized again in RvpEV.java to implement the simple EV algorithm.

The base class for the population maintained by an EA is defined in Population.java. The base class for individuals contained in a population is defined in Individual.java, and the base class for an individual's genome is defined in Genome.java. In EC1 there is only one type of genome supported, namely a vector of real-valued genes.

The base class for problems is defined in Landscape.java, which is then specialized in RvpLscape.java to the class RvpLscape (real-valued parameter landscapes), and specialized again in Parabola.java to parabolic landscapes. The code in Parabola.java can be used as a template to easily add other more interesting landscapes.

Finally, EC_rand.java and Pad.java provide some convenient utility code.

A.1.2 EC1 Parameters

The EC1 configuration file discussed earlier is used to modify the behavior of EC1 from one run to the next. EC1 uses the Java-provided Properties class to read in the information in a configuration file. The Properties class provided the ability to read in lines of the form:

```
property_name=property_values
```

When retrieving information from a file, the Properties class does a keyword search on the property name, so properties can be specified in any order in the file, one line per property.

The properties implemented by EC1 are:

```
Landscape=<type of landscape> <name of landscape> ...
PopSize=<population size>
Mutation=<type of mutation> ...
SimLimit=<simulation limit specified by # of births>
RandSeed=<random number seed>
Report=<type of report>
```

So, for example, a typical configuration file might be:

```
Landscape=RVP Parabola 2 -4.0 6.0 soft - 50.0
PopSize=10
Mutation=gaussian 2.0
SimLimit=1000
RandSeed=123456789
Report=full
```

which specifies the general class of landscape to be RVP (real-valued parameter); the particular landscape of type Parabola; the particular parabola is 2-dimensional with initial lower/upper parameter bounds of -4.0 and 6.0; the initial bounds are soft (not hard), meaning that an EA is allowed to explore outside them; and the parabola is inverted (-) with a maximum value of 50.0.

In addition, a population size of 10 is to be used, and the mutation operator to be used is Gaussian with an average step size of 2.0. The simulation is to be run for 1000 births (100 generations), the pseudo-random number generator is to be initialized with the seed value 123456789, and a full report of the simulation is to be generated.

In EC1 there are no other landscape types implemented. So, the only variation in configuration files comes from specifying different numerical values, by choosing between a simple delta mutation operator and a Gaussian one (discussed in chapter 1), and/or by choosing a different report type.

A full report (the default) prints out the kind of information seen in chapter 1: after every generation global and local population statistics are printed along with a dump of the contents of the current population. Various parts of this voluminous output can be suppressed by selecting one of the alternative report types:

```
Report=local prints only local population statistics each generation
Report=global prints only global population statistics each generation
Report=bsf prints only best-so-far statistics each generation
Report=pop_stats prints only local population statistics in a format
                           easily read by a plotting program.
```

Another example configuration file is:

```
SimLimit=1000
Mutation=delta 5.0
Landscape=RVP Parabola 3 -10.0 10.0 hard
Report=bsf
```

In this case PopSize and RandSeed are unspecified and default to 10 and 12345, respectively.

Of course, the best way to sort this all out is to read the code, which is what you are expected to do!

A.2   EC2: A More Interesting EC System

The Java code in this directory is a generalization of the EC1 code in the directions discussed in hapter 3, namely, the introduction of the code for canonical versions of the three historically important evolutionary algorithms (EAs): Evolutionary Strategies (ESs), Evolutionary Programming (EP), and Genetic Algorithms (GAs).

The design goal for EC2 was to use the object-oriented features of Java to build a simple but flexible system that allowed one to try out the canonical EAs and get a sense of how they differ from each other, and to provide some limited capabilities for changing some of the internal components of an EA to see how EA behavior is affected.

In keeping with the KISS philosophy of EC1, EC2 is also implemented as a command-line system rather than a GUI, and uses the same configuration file paradigm as EC1 to add user-selectable options to EC2. In particular, a configuration file can now contain:

```
EA=xx
```

where xx can be one of: ev, es, ep, or ga, allowing a user to choose which EA to apply to a particular problem. This is implemented by generalizing the class EA and adding new specializations: ES_EA, EP_EA, and GA_EA.

For simplicity in chapter 3 and in the EC2 code, there is still only one class of problems (fitness landscapes): namely, real-valued parameter optimization problems. However, canonical EAs differ in how they represent such problems internally and which reproductive operators they use. Such choices are parameterized in EC2 and take the form:

```
Representation=xxx
Mutation=yyy ...
Crossover=zzz ...
```

where xxx can be real or binary; where yyy can be none, delta, gaussian, or bitflip; and where zzz can be none, one_point, or two_point.

So, an example EC2 configuration file might be:

```
EA=es
PopSize=1 5
Representation=real
Mutation=gaussian 1.0
Crossover=none
Landscape=RVP Parabola 1 -5.0 5.0 hard
SimLimit=1000
RandSeed=12345
Report=full
```

that represents a fairly traditional (1+5)-ES with a real-valued representation, Gaussian mutation, and no crossover. Alternately, a fairly traditional GA can be specified as:

```
EA=ga
PopSize=50
Representation=binary
Mutation=bitflip
Crossover=one_point
Landscape=RVP Parabola 1 -5.0 5.0 hard
SimLimit=1000
RandSeed=12345
Report=full
```

As with EC1 the complete details are best understood by reading the EC2 code. In comparing the EC2 code with EC1, what you should see in addition to the EA extensions is that the Genome class is now the base class for binary and real representations and their associated operators, and the classes Population and Individual have been generalized and specialized to handle both real and binary representations.

A.3 EC3: A More Flexible EC System

The Java code in this directory is a generalization of the EC2 code as discussed in chapter 4: namely, parameterizing the choices for each of the basic EA components to allow tinkering with the components of the canonical EAs, and to be able to assemble entirely new EAs by mixing and matching the basic components.

In keeping with the KISS philosophy of EC1 and EC2, EC3 is also implemented as a command-line system rather than a GUI, and uses a configuration file paradigm to specify user-selectable options to EC3. In particular, a configuration file can now contain:

```
EA=xx
```

where xx can be one of: EV, EP, ES, GA or UN, allowing a user to choose which EA to apply to a particular problem. If no EA=xx is present, the system defaults to UN (unspecified). Whenever the EA is UN, all the basic components must be specified. For the other EA types, the basic components can be specified but standard defaults are provided. The required components are:

```
1. A parent selection method specified as ParentSelection=xxx
where xxx can be:
    uniform_stochastic (EV default)
    uniform_deterministic (EP and ES defaults)
    fitness_proportional (GA default)
    binary_tournament

2. An indication of the type of generational model to be used
specified as GenerationType=xxx where xxx can be:
    overlapping (EV, EP, and ES defaults)
    nonoverlapping (GA default)

3. A survival selection method specified as SurvivalSelection=xxx
where the values that xxx can be depend on the GenerationType.
For overlapping generations xxx can be:
    truncation (EP and ES defaults)
    binary_tournament (EV default)

For nonoverlapping generations with offspring population sizes
larger that their parent population size, xxx can be:
    truncation    (ES default)
    binary_tournament
    fitness_proportional
    uniform_stochastic

4. A representation type specified as Representation=xxx where xxx
can be:
    real  (EV, EP, and ES defaults)
    binary (GA default)
```

The specification for reproductive operators is now expanded to:

```
Mutation=<type> <freq> <step> <adapt>
```

```
where <type> can be:
   none, delta, or gaussian (real representations)
   none or bitflip (binary representations)
```

```
where <freq> can be:
   one (mutate one gene on average)
   all (mutate all genes on average)
```

where <step> is the real-valued step size for delta and gaussian mutation, and where <adapt> is the real-valued mutation adaptation parameter.

Crossover is currently representation independent and specified via:

```
Crossover=<type> <freq>
```

where <type> can be none, one_point, two_point or uniform
and <freq> is the real-valued parameter for uniform crossover.

So, an EC3 configuration file might be:

```
EA=ES
PopSize=1 10
Representation=real
Mutation=gaussian all 1.0 0.1
GenerationType=nonoverlapping
Landscape=RVP Parabola 2 -4.0 6.0 hard
SimLimit=1000
RandSeed=12345
Report=full
```

which represents a fairly traditional (1,5)-ES with a real-valued representation and Gaussian mutation. Alternately, a rather unconventional EA can be specified as:

```
EA=UN
PopSize=20 3
ParentSelection=uniform_deterministic
GenerationType=overlapping
SurvivalSelection=binary_tournament
Representation=binary
Mutation=bitflip
Crossover=uniform 0.2
Landscape=RVP Parabola 2 -4.0 6.0 hard
SimLimit=1000
RandSeed=12345
Report=bsf
```

For simplicity in chapter 4 and in the EC3 code, there is still only one class of problems (fitness landscapes), namely, real-valued parameter optimization problems. These will be generalized in EC4.

As with EC1 and EC2 the complete details are best understood by reading the EC3 code. The major differences between EC2 and EC3 are to be found in the EA class extensions.

A.4   EC4: An EC Research System

The changes to EC3 that resulted in EC4 were motivated by chapter 6 (EC Theory). In that chapter, we encountered many situations in which the formal analysis of a particular EC property was mathematically intractable unless significant simplifying assumptions were made. Rather than doing so, EC4 was used to get an empirical sense of the phenomena. In order to accomplish this, the EC3 code was augmented to provide the ability to collect statistics on convergence times, fixed points, diversity measurements, etc. These changes are documented in the source code.

Bibliography

Altenberg, L. (1994). The schema theorem and Price's theorem. In M. Vose and D. Whitley (Eds.), *Foundations of Genetic Algorithms 3*, pp. 23–49. Morgan Kaufmann.

Angeline, P. (1997). Tracking extrema in dynamic environments. In *Sixth International Conference on Evolutionary Programming*, pp. 335–345. Springer Verlag.

Angeline, P. and J. Pollack (1993). Competitive environments evolve better solutions for complex tasks. In S. Forrest (Ed.), *Proceedings of the Fifth International Conference on Genetic Algorithms and their Applications*, pp. 264–270. Morgan Kaufmann.

Bäck, T. (1994). Order statistics for convergence velocity analysis of simplified evolutionary algorithms. In L. Whitley and M. Vose (Eds.), *Proceedings of the Third Workshop on Foundations of Genetic Algorithms*, pp. 91–102. Morgan Kaufmann.

Bäck, T. (1996). *Evolutionary Algorithms in Theory and Practice*. New York: Oxford University Press.

Bäck, T. (1998). On the behavior of evolutionary algorithms in dynamic fitness landscapes. In *IEEE International Conference on Evolutionary Computation*, pp. 446–451. IEEE Press.

Bäck, T. and H.-P. Schwefel (1993). An overview of evolutionary algorithms for parameter optimization. *Evolutionary Computation 1*(1), 1–24.

Baker, J. (1987). Reducing bias and inefficiency in the selection algorithm. In J. J. Grefenstette (Ed.), *Proceedings of the Second International Conference on Genetic Algorithms and Their Applications*, pp. 14–21. Lawrence Erlbaum Associates.

Baluja, S. (1993). Structure and performance of fine-grained parallelism in genetic search. In *Proceedings of the Fifth International Conference on Genetic Algorithms*, pp. 155–162. Morgan Kaufmann.

Baluja, S. and R. Caruana (1995). Removing the genetics from the standard genetic algorithm. In A. Prieditis and S. Russel (Eds.), *The Int. Conf. on Machine Learning 1995*, pp. 38–46. Morgan Kaufmann.

Banzhaf, W., P. Nordin, R. E. Keller, and F. D. Francone (1998). *Genetic Programming – An Introduction; On the Automatic Evolution of Computer Programs and its Applications.* San Mateo, CA: Morgan Kaufmann.

Bassett, J. and K. De Jong (2000). Evolving behaviors for cooperating agents. In Z. Ras and S. Ohsuga (Eds.), *Proceedings of ISMIS-2000*, pp. 157–165. Springer-Verlag.

Beasley, D., D. Bull, and R. Martin (1993). A sequential niche technique for multimodal function optimization. *Evolutionary Computation 1*(2), 101–126.

Bentley, P. (1999). *Evolutionary Design by Computers.* San Mateo, CA: Morgan Kaufmann.

Bentley, P. and D. Corne (2001). *Creative Evolutionary Systems.* San Mateo, CA: Morgan Kaufmann.

Beyer, H. (1995). Toward a theory of evolution strategies: On the benefits of sex. *Evolutionary Computation 3*(1), 81–111.

Beyer, H. (2001). *The Theory of Evolution Strategies.* Berlin: Springer-Verlag.

Bierwirth, C. and D. Mattfeld (1998). Production scheduling and rescheduling with genetic algorithms. *Evolutionary Computation 7*(1), 1–18.

Booker, L. (1982). *Intelligent Behavior as an Adaptation to the Task Environment.* Ph. D. thesis, The University of Michigan.

Box, G. (1957). Evolutionary operation: a method for increasing industrial productivity. *Applied Statistics 6*(2), 81–101.

Branke, J. (2002). *Evolutionary Optimization in Dynamic Environments.* Boston: Kluwer.

Cantú-Paz, E. (2001). Migration policies, selection pressure, and parallel evolutionary algorithms. *Journal of Heuristics 7*(4), 311–334.

Ceroni, A., M. Pelikan, and D. E. Goldberg (2001). Convergence-time models for the simple genetic algorithm with finite population. IlliGAL Report No. 2001028, Illinois Genetic Algorithms Laboratory, University of Illinois at Urbana-Champaign, Urbana, IL.

Cobb, H. and J. Grefenstette (1993). Genetic algorithms for tracking changing environments. In *Fifth International Conference on Genetic Algorithms*, pp. 523–530. Morgan Kaufmann.

Coello, C., D. Veldhuizen, and G. Lamont (2002). *Evolutionary Algorithms for Solving Multi-objective Problems.* Boston: Kluwer.

Cohoon, J., S. Hegde, W. Martin, and D. Richards (1987). Punctuated equilibria: A parallel genetic algorithm. In J. Grefenstette (Ed.), *Proceedings of the Second International Conference on Genetic Algorithms*, pp. 148–154. Lawrence Erlbaum Associates.

Collier, N. (2001). Repast: An agent based modelling toolkit for java. http://repast.sourceforge.net.

Collins, R. and D. Jefferson (1991). Selection in massively parallel genetic algorithms. In *Proceedings of the Fourth International Conference on Genetic Algorithms*, pp. 249–256. Morgan Kaufmann.

Corman, T., C. Leiserson, and R. Rivest (2001). *Introduction to Algorithms*. New York: McGraw Hill.

Cramer, N. (1985). A representation for the adaptive generation of simple sequential programs. In J. J. Grefenstette (Ed.), *Proceedings of an International Conference on Genetic Algorithms and Their Applications*, pp. 183–187. Lawrence Erlbaum Associates.

Culberson, J. (1994). Mutation-crossover isomorphisms and the construction of discriminating functions. *Evolutionary Computation 2*(3), 279–311.

Daley, R., A. Schultz, and J. Grefenstette (1999). Co-evolution of robot behaviors. In *Proceedings of ISAM '99*. SPIE.

Davis, L. (1989). Adapting operator probabilities in genetic algorithms. In *Third International Conference on Genetic Algorithms*, pp. 61–69. Morgan Kaufmann.

Davis, L. (1991). *The Handbook of Genetic Algorithms*. New York: Van Nostrand Reinhold.

Davis, T. and J. Principe (1993). A Markov chain framework for a simple GA. *Evolutionary Computation 1*(3), 269–288.

Dawkins, R. (1986). *The Blind Watchmaker*. New York: W.W. Norton.

de Garis, H. (1990). Building artificial nervous systems using genetically programmed neural network modules. In B. Porter and R. Mooney (Eds.), *Proceedings of the Seventh International Conference on Machine Learning*, pp. 132–139.

De Jong, K. (1975). *Analysis of Behavior of a Class of Genetic Adaptive Systems*. Ph. D. thesis, University of Michigan, Ann Arbor, MI.

De Jong, K. (1985). Genetic algorithms: A 10 year perspective. In J. J. Grefenstette (Ed.), *Proceedings of an International Conference on Genetic Algorithms and Their Applications*, pp. 169–177. Lawrence Erlbaum Associates.

De Jong, K. (1987). On using genetic algorithms to search program spaces. In J. J. Grefenstette (Ed.), *Proceedings of the Second International Conference on Genetic Algorithms and Their Applications*, pp. 210–216. Lawrence Erlbaum Associates.

De Jong, K. (1988). Learning with genetic algorithms: An overview. *Machine Learning 3*(3), 121–138.

De Jong, K. (1999). Evolving in a changing world. In Z. Ras and A. Skowron (Eds.), *Proceedings of ISMIS'99*, pp. 512–519. Springer-Verlag.

De Jong, K. and W. Spears (1992). A formal analysis of the role of multi-point crossover in genetic algorithms. *Annals of Mathematics and Artificial Intelligence 5*(1), 1–26.

De Jong, K. and W. Spears (1993). On the state of evolutionary computation. In S. Forrest (Ed.), *Proceedings of the Fifth International Conference on Genetic Algorithms and their Applications*, pp. 618–623. Morgan Kaufmann.

De Jong, K., W. Spears, and D. Gordon (1994). Using Markov chains to analyze GAFOs. In L. Whitley and M. Vose (Eds.), *Proceedings of the Third Workshop on Foundations of Genetic Algorithms*, pp. 115–138. Morgan Kaufmann.

Deb, K. (1999). Multi-objective genetic algorithms: Problem difficulties and construction of test problems. *Evolutionary Computation 7*(3), 205–230.

Deb, K. (2001). *Multi-objective Optimization Using Evolutionary Algorithms*. New York: John Wiley and Sons.

Eiben, A., E. Aarts, and K. van Hee (1990). Global convergence of genetic algorithms: A Markov chain analysis. In H.-P. Schwefel and R. Männer (Eds.), *Parallel Problem Solving from Nature (PPSN I)*, pp. 4–12. Springer.

Eiben, A., R. Hinterding, and Z. Michalewicz (1999). Parameter control in evolutionary algorithms. *IEEE Transactions on Evolutionary Computation 3*(2), 124–141.

Eiben, A., P. Raué, and Z. Ruttkay (1994). Genetic algorithms with multi-parent recombination. In Y. Davidor, H.-P. Schwefel, and R. Männer (Eds.), *Parallel Problem Solving from Nature (PPSN III)*, pp. 78–87. Springer.

Eshelman, L. (1990). The CHC adaptive search algorithm. In G. Rawlins (Ed.), *Foundations of Genetic Algorithms 1*, pp. 265–283. Morgan Kaufmann.

Ficici, S. and J. Pollack (1998). Challenges in coevolutionary learning: Arms–race dynamics, open–endedness, and mediocre stable states. In C. Adami, R. Belew, H. Kitano, and C. Taylor (Eds.), *Proceedings of the Sixth International Conference on Artificial Life*, pp. 238–247. MIT Press.

Ficici, S. and J. Pollack (2000). Game–theoretic investigation of selection methods used in evolutionary algorithms. In D. Whitley (Ed.), *Proceedings of CEC 2000*, pp. 880–887. IEEE Press.

Fogel, D. (1995). *Evolutionary Computation: Toward a New Philosophy of Machine Intelligence*. Piscataway, NJ: IEEE Press.

Fogel, D. (1998). *Evolutionary Computation: The Fossil Record*. Piscataway, NJ: IEEE Press.

Fogel, L., A. Owens, and M. Walsh (1966). *Artificial Intelligence through Simulated Evolution*. New York: John Wiley & Sons.

Fonseca, C. and P. Fleming (1995). An overview of evolutionary algorithms in multiobjective optimization. *Evolutionary Computation 3*(1), 1–16.

Frank, S. A. (1995). George Price's contributions to evolutionary genetics. *Journal of Theoretical Biology 175*, 373–388.

Friedberg, R. (1959). A learning machine: Part 1. *IBM Research Journal 3*(7), 282–287.

Friedman, G. (1956). Select feedback computers for engineering synthesis and nervous system analogy. Master's thesis, UCLA.

Fujiki, C. and J. Dickinson (1987). Using the genetic algorithm to generate Lisp source code to solve the prisoner's dilemma. In J. J. Grefenstette (Ed.), *Proceedings of the Second International Conference on Genetic Algorithms*, pp. 236–240. Lawrence Erlbaum Associates.

Geiringer, H. (1944). On the probability theory of linkage in Mendelian heredity. *Annals of Mathematical Statistics 15*, 25–57.

Goldberg, D. (1989). *Genetic Algorithms in Search, Optimization, and Machine Learning*. New York: Addison-Wesley.

Goldberg, D. (2002). *The Design of Innovation: Lessons from and for Competent Genetic Algorithms*. Boston: Kluwer.

Goldberg, D. and K. Deb (1990). A comparative analysis of selection schemes used in genetic algorithms. In G. Rawlins (Ed.), *Proceedings of the First Workshop on Foundations of Genetic Algorithms*, pp. 69–92. Morgan Kaufmann.

Goldberg, D., K. Deb, and B. Korb (1991). Don't worry, be messy. In R. K. Belew and L. B. Booker (Eds.), *Proceedings of the Fourth International Conference on Genetic Algorithms*, pp. 24–30. Morgan Kaufmann.

Goldberg, D. and P. Segrest (1987). Finite Markov chain analysis of genetic algorithms. In J. Grefenstette (Ed.), *Proceedings of the Second International Conference on Genetic Algorithms and their Applications*, pp. 1–8. Lawrence Erlbaum Publishing.

Goldberg, D. and R. Smith (1987). Nonstationary function optimization using genetic dominance and diploidy. In *Second International Conference on Genetic Algorithms*, pp. 59–68. Morgan Kaufmann.

Grajdeanu, A. and K. De Jong (2004). Improving the locality properties of binary representations. In H.-G. B. et al (Ed.), *Proceedings of GECCO-2005*, pp. 1186–1196. Springer-Verlag.

Grefenstette, J. (1986). Optimization of control parameters for genetic algorithms. *IEEE Transactions on Systems, Man, and Cybernetics 16*(1), 122–128.

Grefenstette, J. (1989). A system for learning control strategies with genetic algorithms. In J. Schaffer (Ed.), *Proceedings of the Third International Conference on Genetic Algorithms*, pp. 183–190. Morgan Kaufmann.

Grefenstette, J. (1994). Predictive models using fitness distributions of genetic operators. In D. Whitley and M. Vose (Eds.), *Foundations of Genetic Algorithms 3*, pp. 139–162. Morgan Kaufmann.

Grefenstette, J. (1996). Genetic learning for adaptation in autonomous robots. In F. P. M. Jamshidi and P. Dauchez (Eds.), *Proc. Sixth Intl. Symposium on Robotics and Manufacturing*, pp. 265–270. ASME Press.

Grefenstette, J., C. Ramsey, and A. Schultz (1990). Learning sequential decision rules using simulation models and competition. *Machine Learning 5*(4), 355–381.

Harp, S., T. Samad, and A. Guha (1989). Towards the genetic synthesis of neural networks. In J. Schaffer (Ed.), *Proceedings of the Third International Conference on Genetic Algorithms and their Applications*, pp. 360–369. Morgan Kaufmann.

Hillis, D. (1990). Co-evolving parasites improve simulated evolution as an optimization procedure. In C. Langton, C. Taylor, J. Farmer, and S. Rasmussen (Eds.), *Artificial Life II*, pp. 313–324. Addison-Wesley.

Hofbauer, J. and K. Sigmund (1998). *Evolutionary Games and Population Dynamics*. Cambridge University Press.

Holland, J. (1962). Outline for a logical theory of adaptive systems. *JACM 9*, 297–314.

Holland, J. (1967). Nonlinear environments permitting efficient adaptation. In *Computer and Information Sciences II*. Academic Press.

Holland, J. (1975). *Adaptation in Natural and Artificial Systems*. Ann Arbor, MI: University of Michigan Press.

Holland, J. (1986). Escaping brittleness: The possibilities of general purpose learning algorithms applied to parallel rule-based systems. In R. Mishalski, J. Carbonell, and T. Mitchell (Eds.), *Machine Learning II*, pp. 593–623. San Mateo, CA: Morgan Kaufmann.

Holland, J. (1992). *Adaptation in Natural and Artificial Systems, 2nd Edition*. Cambridge, MA: MIT Press.

Horn, J., N. Nafpliotis, and D. Goldberg (1994). A niched Pareto genetic algorithm for multiobjective optimization. In *Proceedings of the First IEEE Conference on Evolutionary Computation*, pp. 82–87. IEEE Press.

Hornby, G. (2003). *Generative Representations for Evolutionary Design Automation*. Ph. D. thesis, Brandeis University.

Jansen, T. and K. De Jong (2002). An analysis of the role of offspring population size in EAs. In W. B. L. et al. (Ed.), *Proceedings of the Genetic and Evolutionary Computation Conference (GECCO 2002)*, pp. 238–246. Morgan Kaufman.

Jansen, T., K. De Jong, and I. Wegener (2005). On the choice of offspring population size in evolutionary algorithms. *Evolutionary Computation 13*(4), 413–440.

Jones, T. (1995). *Evolutionary algorithms, fitness landscapes, and search.* Ph. D. thesis, University of New Mexico.

Kicinger, R., T. Arciszewski, and K. De Jong (2004). Morphogenesis and structural design: Cellular automata representations of steel sturctures in tall buildings. In *Proceedings of the Congress on Evolutionary Computation*, pp. 411–418. IEEE Press.

Kinnear, K. (1994). *Advances in Genetic Programming.* Cambridge, MA: MIT Press.

Kita, E. and T. Totoda (2000). Structural design using cellular automata. *Structural and Multidisiplinary Optimization 19*, 64–73.

Koza, J. (1989). Hierarchical genetic algorithms operating on populations of computer programs. In *Proceedings of the 11th International Joint Conference on Artificial Intelligence*. Morgan Kaufmann.

Koza, J. (1992). *Genetic Programming.* Cambridge, MA: MIT Press.

Koza, J. (1994). *Genetic Programming II.* Cambridge, MA: MIT Press.

Koza, J., F. Bennett III, F. Bennett, and D. Andre (1999). *Genetic Programming III: Automatic Programming and Automatic Circuit Synthesis.* San Mateo, CA: Morgan Kaufmann.

Langdon, W. and R. Poli (2001). *Foundations of Genetic Programming.* Berlin: Springer.

Langton, C., M. Nelson, and R. Burkhart (1995). The Swarm simulation system: A tool for studying complex systems. Technical report, Sante Fe Institute, Sante Fe, NM.

Lindenmayer, A. (1968). Mathematical models for cellular interaction in development. *Journal of Theoretical Biology 18*, 280–315.

Luke, S., C. Cioffi-Revilla, L. Panait, K. Sullivan, and G. Balan (2005). Mason: A multi-agent simulation environment. *Simulation 81*, 517–527.

Manderick, B., M. de Weger, and P. Spiessens (1991). The genetic algorithm and the structure of the fitness landscape. In R. K. Belew and L. B. Booker (Eds.), *The Fourth International Conference on Genetic Algorithms and Their Applications*, pp. 143–150. Morgan Kaufmann.

Maynard-Smith, J. (1982). *Evolution and the Theory of Games.* Cambridge University Press.

Michalewicz, Z. (1994). *Genetic Algorithms + Data Structures = Evolution Programs.* New York: Springer-Verlag.

Michalewicz, Z. and M. Schoenauer (1996). Evolutionary algorithms for constrained parameter optimization problems. *Evolutionary Computation 4*(1), 1–32.

Mitchell, M. (1998). *An Introduction to Genetic Algorithms*. Cambridge, MA: MIT Press.

Morrison, R. (2004). *Designing Evolutionary Algorithms for Dynamic Environments*. Berlin: Springer-Verlag.

Morrison, R. and K. De Jong (1999). A test problem generator for non-stationary environments. In Z. Michalewicz, M. Schoenauer, X. Yao, and A. Zalzala (Eds.), *Proceedings of the 1999 Congress on Evolutionary Computation*, pp. 2047–2053. IEEE Press.

Morrison, R. and K. De Jong (2002). Measurement of population diversity. In P. Collet, C. Fonlupt, J. Hao, E. Lutton, and M. Schoenauer (Eds.), *Artificial Evolution, LCNS 2310*, pp. 31–41. Springer-Verlag.

Moscato, P. and M. Norman (1992). A memetic approach for the traveling salesman problem. In M. V. et al. (Ed.), *Paralle Computing and Transputer Applications*, pp. 187–194. IOS Press.

Mühlenbein, H. (1997). The equation for the response to selection and its use for prediction. *Evolutionary Computation 5*(3), 303–346.

Mühlenbein, H. and D. Schlierkamp-Voosen (1993). Predictive models for the breeder genetic algorithm. *Evolutionary Computation 1*(1), 39–80.

Nix, A. and M. Vose (1992). Modeling genetic algorithms with Markov chains. *Annals of Mathematics and Artificial Intelligence 5*, 79–88.

Nolfi, S. and D. Floreano (2000). *Evolutionary Robotics: The Biology, Intelligence, and Technology of Self-Organizing Machines*. Cambridge, MA: MIT Press.

Ostrowski, D. A., T. Tassier, M. P. Everson, and R. G. Reynolds (2002). Using cultural algorithms to evolve strategies in agent-based models. In D. B. Fogel, M. A. El-Sharkawi, X. Yao, G. Greenwood, H. Iba, P. Marrow, and M. Shackleton (Eds.), *Proceedings of the 2002 Congress on Evolutionary Computation CEC2002*, pp. 741–746. IEEE Press.

Panait, L. and S. Luke (2005). Cooperative multi-agent learning: The state of the art. *Autonomous Agents and Multi-Agent Systems (to appear)*.

Parker, M. (2001). What is Ascape and why should you care? *Journal of Artificial Societies and Social Simulation 4*(1).

Popovici, E. and K. De Jong (2004). Understanding competitive co-evolutionary dynamics via fitness landscapes. In S. Luke (Ed.), *AAAI Fall Symposium on Artificial Multiagent Learning*. AAAI Press.

Potter, M. (1997). *The Design and Analysis of a Computational Model of Cooperative CoEvolution*. Ph. D. thesis, George Mason University, Fairfax, Virginia.

Potter, M. and K. De Jong (2000). Cooperative coevolution: An architecture for evolving coadapted subcomponents. *Evolutionary Computation 8*(1), 1–29.

Potter, M. A., J. K. Bassett, and K. A. De Jong (2003). Visualizing evolvability with Price's equation. In *Proceedings of the 2003 Congress on Evolutionary Computation*, pp. 2785–2790. IEEE.

Price, G. (1970). Selection and covariance. *Nature 227*, 520–521.

Prügel-Bennett, A. and J. Shapiro (1994). An analysis of genetic algorithms using statistical mechanics. *Physical Review Letters 72*(9), 1305–1309.

Prügel-Bennett, A. and J. Shapiro (1997). The dynamics of a genetic algorithm for simple random ising systems. *Physica D 104*, 75–114.

Radcliffe, N. (1991). Forma analysis and random respectful recombination. In R. Belew and L. Booker (Eds.), *Proceedings of the Fourth International Conference on Genetic Algorithms*, pp. 271–278. Morgan Kaufmann.

Ramsey, C., K. De Jong, J. Grefenstette, A. Wu, and D. Burke (1998). Genome length as an evolutionary self-adaptation. In A. Eiben, M. Schoenauer, T. Bäck, and H.-P. Schwefel (Eds.), *Proceedings of the 5th International Conference on Parallel Problem Solving from Nature*, pp. 345–353.

Ray, T. (1994). An evolutionary approach to synthetic biology: Zen and the art of creating life. *Artificial Life 1*(1/2), 195–226.

Rechenberg, I. (1965). Cybernatic solution path of an experimental problem. In *Library Translation 1122*. Farnborough: Royal Aircraft Establishment.

Rechenberg, I. (1994). *Evolutionsstrategie '94*. Stuttgart: Frommann-Holzboog.

Reeves, C. and T. Yamada (1998). Genetic algorithms, path relinking and the flowshop sequencing problem. *Evolutionary Computation 6*(1), 45–60.

Ros, J. (1992). Learning Boolean functions with genetic algorithms: A PAC analysis. In L. Whitley (Ed.), *Proceedings of the Second Workshop on Foundations of Genetic Algorithms*, pp. 257–276. Morgan Kaufmann.

Rosin, C. and R. Belew (1995). Methods for competitive co-evolution: Finding opponents worth beating. In L. Eshelman (Ed.), *Proceedings of the Sixth International Conference on Genetic Algorithms and their Applications*, pp. 373–380. Morgan Kaufmann.

Rowe, J., D. Whitley, L. Barbulescu, and J. P. Watson (2004). Properties of Gray and binary representations. *Evolutionary Computation 12*(1), 47–76.

Samuel, A. L. (1959). Some studies in machine learning using the game of checkers. *IBM Journal of Research and Development 3*(3), 210–229.

Sarma, J. (1998). *An Analysis of Decentralized and Spatially Distributed Genetic Algorithms*. Ph. D. thesis, George Mason University.

Schaffer, D. and A. Morishima (1987). An adaptive crossover mechanism for genetic algorithms. In J. Grefenstette (Ed.), *Proceedings of the Second International Conference on Genetic Algorithms*, pp. 36–40. Morgan Kaufmann.

Schraudolph, N. and R. Belew (1992). Dynamic parameter encoding for genetic algorithms. *Machine Learning 9*(1), 9–22.

Schwefel, H.-P. (1975). *Evolutionsstrategie und numerishe Optimierung*. Ph. D. thesis, Technical University of Berlin, Berlin, Germany.

Schwefel, H.-P. (1981). *Numerical Optimization of Computer Models*. New York: John Wiley & Sons.

Schwefel, H.-P. (1995). *Evolution and Optimum Seeking*. New York: John Wiley & Sons.

Shaefer, C. (1987). The ARGOT strategy: adaptive representation genetic optimizer technique. In J. Grefenstette (Ed.), *Proceedings of the Second International Conference on Genetic Algorithms*, pp. 50–58. Lawrence Erlbaum.

Shaffer, J. and J. Grefenstette (1985). Multiple objective optimization with vector evaluated genetic algorithms. In J. J. Grefenstette (Ed.), *Proceedings of an International Conference on Genetic Algorithms and Their Applications*, pp. 93–100. Lawrence Erlbaum Associates.

Shapiro, J. and A. Prügel-Bennett (1996). Genetic algorithm dynamics in a two-well potential. In M. Vose and D. Whitley (Eds.), *Foundations of Genetic Algorithms 4*, pp. 101–116. Morgan Kaufmann.

Skolicki, Z. and K. De Jong (2004). Improving evolutionary algorithms with multi-representation island models. In X. Y. et al. (Ed.), *Proceedings of PPSN VIII*, pp. 420–429. Springer-Verlag.

Smith, S. (1983). Flexible learning of problem solving heuristics through adaptive search. In A. Bundy (Ed.), *Proceedings of the Eighth International Joint Conference on Artificial Intelligence*, pp. 422–425. Morgan Kaufmann.

Spears, W. (1990). Using neural networks and genetic algorithms as heuristics for NP-complete problems. Master's thesis, George Mason University, Fairfax, VA.

Spears, W. (1992). Crossover or mutation? In D. Whitley (Ed.), *Foundations of Genetic Algorithms*, Volume 2, pp. 221–237. Morgan Kaufmann.

Spears, W. (1994). Simple subpopulation schemes. In A. Sebald and D. Fogel (Eds.), *Proceedings of the Third Conference on Evolutionary Programming*, pp. 297–307. World Scientific Publ.

Spears, W. (1995). Adapting crossover in evolutionary algorithms. In J. McDonnell, R. Reynolds, and D. Fogel (Eds.), *Proceedings of the Fourth Conference on Evolutionary Programming*, pp. 367–384. MIT Press.

Spears, W. (2000). *Evolutionary Algorithms: The Role of Mutation and Recombination.* Berlin: Springer.

Spears, W. and K. De Jong (1991). On the virtues of parameterized uniform crossover. In R. K. Belew and L. B. Booker (Eds.), *International Conference on Genetic Algorithms*, Volume 4, pp. 230–236. Morgan Kaufmann.

Spears, W. and K. De Jong (1996). Analyzing GAs using Markov models with semantically ordered and lumped states. In R. Belew and M. Vose (Eds.), *Proceedings of the Fourth Workshop on Foundations of Genetic Algorithms*, pp. 85–100. Morgan Kaufmann.

Spears, W. and D. Gordon (2000). Evolving finite-state machine strategies for protecting resources. In Z. Ras and S. Ohsuga (Eds.), *Proceedings of ISMIS 2000, LNCS 1932*, pp. 166–175. Springer.

Stanley, K. (2004). *Efficient Evolution Of Neural Networks Through Complexification.* Ph. D. thesis, University of Texas at Austin.

Syswerda, G. (1989). Uniform crossover in genetic algorithms. In *International Conference on Genetic Algorithms*, Volume 3, pp. 2–9. Morgan Kaufmann.

Turner, M. (1998). *Performance-based Self-adaptive Evolutionary Behavior.* Ph. D. thesis, George Washington University.

Vose, M. (1992). Modeling simple genetic algorithms. In L. Whitley (Ed.), *Proceedings of the Second Workshop on Foundations of Genetic Algorithms*, pp. 63–74. Morgan Kaufmann.

Vose, M. (1995). Modeling simple genetic algorithms. *Evolutionary Computation 3*(4), 453–472.

Vose, M. (1999). *The Simple Genetic Algorithm.* Cambridge, MA: MIT Press.

Watson, R., S. Ficici, and J. Pollack (1999). Embodied evolution: Embodying an evolutionary algorithm in a population of robots. In Z. Michalewicz, M. Schoenauer, X. Yao, and A. Zalzala (Eds.), *Proceedings of the 1999 Congress on Evolutionary Computation*, pp. 335–342. IEEE Press.

Whitley, D. (1989a). The Genitor algorithm and selection pressure: Why rank-based allocation of reproductive trials is best. In J. Schaffer (Ed.), *Proceedings of the Third International Conference on Genetic Algorithms*, pp. 116–121. Morgan Kaufmann.

Whitley, D. (1989b). Scheduling problems and traveling salesmen: The genetic edge recombination operator. In J. Schaffer (Ed.), *Proceedings of the Third International Conference on Genetic Algorithms*, pp. 133–140. Morgan Kaufmann.

Whitley, D. (1992). An executable model of a simple genetic algorithm. In D. Whitley (Ed.), *Proceedings of Second Workshop on the Foundations of Genetic Algorithms*, pp. 45–62. Morgan Kaufmann.

Whitley, D. (2000). Local search and high precision Gray codes: Convergence results and neighborhoods. In W. Martin and W. Spears (Eds.), *Proceedings of the Sixth Workshop on Foundations of Genetic Algorithms*, pp. 295–312. Morgan Kaufmann.

Whitley, D., F. Gruau, and L. Pyeatt (1995). Cellular encoding applied to neurocontrol. In L. Eshelman (Ed.), *Proceedings of Sixth International Conference on Genetic Algorithms*, pp. 440–467. Morgan Kaufmann.

Whitley, D., K. Mathias, and P. Fitzhorn (1991). Delta coding: an iterative search strategy for genetic algorithms. In R. K. Belew and L. B. Booker (Eds.), *Proceeding of the Fourth International Conference on Genetic Algorithms*, pp. 77–84. Morgan Kaufmann.

Whitley, D., S. Rana, and R. Hechendorn (1999). The island model genetic algorithm: On separability, population size and convergence. *Journal of Computing and Information Technology 2*(1), 33–47.

Wiegand, R. (2004). *An Analysis of Cooperative Coevolutionary Algorithms*. Ph. D. thesis, George Mason University.

Wilson, S. (1994). ZCS: A zeroth level classifier system. *Evolutionary Computation 2*(1), 1–18.

Wilson, S. and D. Goldberg (1989). A critical review of classifier syetems. In *Third International Conference on Genetic Algorithms*, pp. 244–255. Morgan Kaufmann.

Wolfram, S. (1994). *Cellular Automata and Complexity*. Reading, MA: Addison-Wesley.

Wolfram, S. (2002). *A New Kind of Science*. Champaign, IL: Wolfram Media.

Wright, A. and M. Vose (1995). Finiteness of the fixed point set for the simple genetic algorithm. *Evolutionary Computation 3*(3), 299–310.

Wright, S. (1932). The roles of mutation, inbreeding, crossbreeding, and selection in evolution. In *Proc. of the 6th International Congress on Genetics*, Volume 1, pp. 356–366.

Wu, A. and R. Lindsey (1995). Empirical studies of the genetic algorithm with noncoding segments. *Evolutionary Computation 3*(2), 121–148.

Yao, X. (1999). Evolving artificial neural networks. *Proc. of the IEEE 87*(9), 1423–1447.

Zitzler, E., K. Deb, and L. Thiele (2000). Comparison of multiobjective evolutionary algorithms: Empirical results. *Evolutionary Computation 8*(2), 173–196.

Zitzler, E. and L. Thiele (1998). Multiobjective optimization using evolutionary algorithms – a comparative case study. In A. Eiben, T. Bäck, M. Schoenauer, and H.-P. Schwefel (Eds.), *Proceedings of the Fifth International Conference on Parallel Problem Solving from Nature*, pp. 292–301. Springer-Verlag.

Index